Language Curriculum Design

Crystal-clear and comprehensive yet concise, this text describes the steps involved in the curriculum design process, elaborates and justifies these steps and provides opportunities for practising and applying them. The description of the steps is done at a general level so that they can be applied in a wide range of particular circumstances. The process comes to life through plentiful examples of actual applications of the steps. Each chapter includes:

- Descriptions of examples from the authors' experience and from published research
- Tasks that encourage readers to relate the steps to their own experience
- Case studies and suggestions for further reading that put readers in touch with others' experience

Curriculum, or course, design is largely a "how-to-do-it" activity that involves the integration of knowledge from many of the areas in the field of Applied Linguistics, such as language acquisition research, teaching methodology, assessment, language description and materials production. Combining sound research/theory with state-of-the-art practice, *Language Curriculum Design* is widely applicable for ESL/EFL language education courses around the world.

I.S.P. Nation is Professor in Applied Linguistics at Victoria University of Wellington, New Zealand. In addition to books, his extensive list of publications on teaching and learning vocabulary, language teaching methodology, and curriculum design, includes journal articles, book chapters and book reviews. He has taught in Indonesia, Thailand, the United States, Finland and Japan.

John Macalister is Senior Lecturer at Victoria University of Wellington, New Zealand. He specialises in the fields of language teaching methodology and curriculum design and draws on experience in teacher education and curriculum design in Thailand, Cambodia, Kiribati, Vanuatu and Namibia.

ESL & Applied Linguistics Professional Series

Eli Hinkel, Series Editor

Hinkel · *Teaching Academic ESL Writing: Practical Techniques in Vocabulary and Grammar*

Hinkel/Fotos, Eds. · *New Perspectives on Grammar Teaching in Second Language Classrooms*

Hinkel · *Second Language Writers' Text: Linguistic and Rhetorical Features*

Visit **www.routledge.com/education** for additional information on titles in the ESL and Applied Linguistics Professional Series

Language Curriculum Design

I.S.P. Nation and John Macalister

Routledge
Taylor & Francis Group

NEW YORK AND LONDON

First published 2010
by Routledge
711 Third Avenue, New York, NY 10017

Simultaneously published in the UK
by Routledge
2 Park Square, Milton Park, Abingdon, Oxon OX14 4RN

*Routledge is an imprint of the Taylor & Francis Group,
an informa business*

© 2010 Taylor & Francis

Typeset in Bembo by Swales & Willis Ltd., Exeter, Devon

Printed and bound in the United States of America by
Edwards Brothers Malloy on sustainably sourced paper.

Library of Congress Cataloging-in-Publication Data
Nation, I.S.P.
Language curriculum design / I.S.P. Nation and John Macalister.
p. cm.—(ESL & applied linguistics professional series)
Includes bibliographical references and index.
1. English language—Study and teaching–Foreign speakers.
2. English teachers–Training of.   I. Macalister, John, 1956–
II. Title.
PE1128.A2N38 2009
428.0071—dc22
                                                2009010312

ISBN10: 0–415–80605–4 (hbk)
ISBN10: 0–415–80606–2 (pbk)
ISBN10: 0–203–87073–5 (ebk)

ISBN13: 978–0–415–80605–3 (hbk)
ISBN13: 978–0–415–80606–0 (pbk)
ISBN13: 978–0–203–87073–0 (ebk)

Brief Contents

Contents

Preface

There is nothing more difficult to plan, more doubtful of success, nor more danger-ous to manage than the creation of a new system. For the initiator has the enmity of all who would profit by the preservation of the old system and merely lukewarm defenders in those who would gain from the new one.

(Machiavelli (1513) *The Prince*)

Curriculum, or course, design is largely a "how-to-do-it" activity and so a large part of this book involves description of the steps involved in the curriculum design process and the elaboration and justification of these steps. The book also provides opportunities for practising and applying the steps.

Chapter 1 provides an overview of Chapters 2 to 8 which are the major steps in the curriculum design process. Chapter 9 describes several ways in which these steps can be covered. Chapters 10 to 14 take up important issues in curriculum design, namely involving learners in curriculum design, choosing and modifying course books, innovation theory, retraining teachers and helping teachers and learners make use of a course.

Although curriculum design is a "how-to-do-it" activity, the description of the steps needs to be done at a general level in order that they can be applied in a wide range of particular circumstances. Such a description will only come to life if there are plenty of examples of actual applications of the steps. In this book this is done in the following ways in each chapter.

1 Examples from the writers' experience and from published research are described.
2 Tasks are provided which encourage the users of the book to relate the steps to their own experience.
3 Case studies are described and further reading is suggested that will put the users of this book in touch with others' experience.

Curriculum design involves the integration of knowledge from many of the areas in the field of Applied Linguistics, such as language acquisition research, teaching methodology, assessment, language description and materials production. In many ways, the study of curriculum design is central to the study of Applied Linguistics. Combining sound research/theory with state-of-the-art practice, *Language Curriculum Design* is widely applicable for ESL/EFL language education courses around the world.

Chapter 1

Language Curriculum Design
An Overview

Parts of the Curriculum Design Process

Curriculum design can be seen as a kind of writing activity and as such it can usefully be studied as a process. The typical sub-processes of the writing process (gathering ideas, ordering ideas, ideas to text, reviewing, editing) can be applied to curriculum design, but it makes it easier to draw on current curriculum design theory and practice if a different set of parts is used. The curriculum design model in Figure 1.1 consists of three outside circles and a subdivided inner circle. The outer circles (principles, environment, needs) involve practical and theoretical considerations that will have a major effect in guiding the actual process of course production. There is a wide range of factors to consider when designing a course. These include the learners' present knowledge and lacks, the resources available including time, the skill of the teachers, the curriculum designer's strengths and limitations, and principles of teaching and learning. If factors such as these are not considered then the course may be unsuited to the situation and learners for which it is used, and may be ineffective and inefficient as a means of encouraging learning. In the curriculum design process these factors are considered in three sub-processes, environment analysis, needs analysis and the application of principles. The result of environment analysis is a ranked list of factors and a consideration of the effects of these factors on the design. The result of needs analysis is a realistic list of language, ideas or skill items, as a result of considering the present proficiency, future needs and wants of the learners. The application of principles involves first of all deciding on the most important principles to apply and monitoring their application through the whole design process. The result of applying principles is a course where learning is given the greatest support.

Some curriculum designers distinguish curriculum from syllabus. In the model, both the outer circles and the inner circle make up the curriculum. The inner circle represents the syllabus.

The inner circle has goals as its centre. This is meant to reflect the importance of having clear general goals for a course. The content and sequencing part of the inner circle represents the items to learn in a course, and the order in which they occur, plus the ideas content if this is used as a vehicle for the items and not as a goal in itself. Language courses must give consideration to the language content of a course even if this is not presented in the course as a discrete item. Consideration of content makes sure that there is something useful for the learners to learn to advance their control of the language, that they are getting the best return for learning effort in terms of the usefulness of what they will meet in the course, and that they are covering all the things they need to cover for a balanced knowledge of the language.

The format and presentation part of the inner circle represents the format of the lessons or units of the course, including the techniques and types of activities that will be used to help learning. This is the part of the course that the learners are most aware of. It is important that it is guided by the best available principles of teaching and learning.

The monitoring and assessment part of the inner circle represents the need to give attention to observing learning, testing the results of learning, and providing feedback to the learners about their progress. It is often not a part of commercially designed courses. It provides information that can lead to changes at most of the other parts of the curriculum design process.

It is possible to imagine a large circle drawn completely around the whole model. This large outer circle represents evaluation. Evaluation can involve looking at every aspect of a course to judge if the course is adequate and where it needs improvement. It is generally a neglected aspect of curriculum design.

Chapters 2 to 8 of this book examine each of the parts of the curriculum design process in detail, drawing on relevant theory and research. It is possible to design courses without drawing on relevant research, theory and experience. In all but a few fortunate cases this results in common faults in curriculum design being made yet again.

The shape of the model in Figure 1.1 is designed to make it easy to remember. The three-part shape that occurs in each of the outer circles (the "Mercedes" symbol) also occurs in the large inner circle, and also occurs in the way the three outer circles connect to the inner circle.

In this first chapter of this book, we will look briefly at an overview of the parts of the curriculum design process that will be looked at in more detail in the following chapters of the book, with each of the early chapters focusing on a different part of the model.

Considering the Environment

Environment analysis involves considering the factors of the situation in which the course will be used and determining how the course should take account of them. One way of approaching environment analysis is to work from a list of questions which focus on the nature of the learners, the teachers and the teaching situation (see Chapter 2).

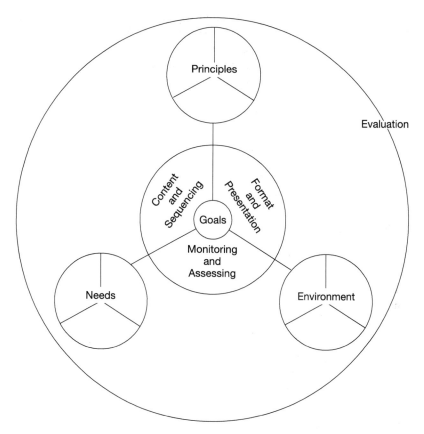

Figure 1.1 A model of the parts of the curriculum design process.

There is value in spending some time on these questions particularly if the answers are ranked according to something like the following instructions and criterion.

> Choose three factors which will have the strongest effect on the design of your course. Rank these three from the factor which will most determine what you should do to the one which has the least influence of the three.

To show the value of doing this, here are some of the top factors decided on by several teachers designing different courses for different learners.

1   One teacher decided that the learners' lack of interest in learning English should be the major factor influencing curriculum design. The learners were obliged to do an English course as part of their degree but

received no credit for it. This meant that the teacher's goal of making the course as interesting and motivating as possible guided the design of the course, particularly the format and presentation of lessons.

2   One teacher decided that the learners' plan to move on to academic study in university or technical institute courses should have the greatest effect on design of the English course. This had a far-reaching effect on the language items and the language skills focused on, and the type of learning activity.

3   One teacher decided that the externally designed and administered test at the end of the course should be the major factor. This meant that the course book always had to make it obvious to the learners that the work they were doing was directly related to the test.

Here is a short list of some of the other factors that teachers considered most important.

- The small amount of time available for the course
- The large size of the classes
- The wide range of proficiency in the class
- The immediate survival needs of the learners
- The lack of appropriate reading materials
- The teachers' lack of experience and training
- The learners' use of the first language in the classroom
- The need for the learners to be more autonomous

There are many examples of unsuccessful curriculum design where the background questions were not considered. Here are some examples.

1   The communicatively based course which was deserted by its Vietnamese learners because they were not getting the grammar teaching that they expected. They set up their own grammar-based course.

2   The course for Agricultural students which had a simplified version of *The Moonstone* by Wilkie Collins as its main reading text. Some of the learners produced their own translation of it which they copied and sold to other learners. They saw no value in coming to grips with its content through English.

3   The adult conversation course which began with the game "Simon Says". Half the students stopped attending after the first lesson. There is no conversation in "Simon Says".

Each important factor needs to be accompanied by one or more effects. For example, the factor "the large size of the class" could have the following effects on the curriculum design.

1   A large amount of group work.
2   Use of special large class techniques like oral reproduction, blackboard reproduction, the pyramid procedure involving the individual–pair–group–class sequence (Nation and Newton, 2009).
3   Independent work or individualised tasks.

The importance of environment analysis is that it makes sure that the course will really be suitable, practical and realistic.

Discovering Needs

Hutchinson and Waters (1987) make a useful division of learners' needs into necessities (what the learner has to know to function effectively), lacks (what the learner knows and does not know already) and wants (what the learners think they need). These are discovered by a variety of means: by testing, by questioning and interviewing, by recalling previous performance, by consulting employers, teachers and others involved, by collecting data such as textbooks and manuals that the learners will have to read and analysing them, and by investigating the situations where the learners will need to use the language. Ways of doing needs analysis can be evaluated by the same general criteria used to evaluate tests – reliability, validity and practicality.

Necessities, lacks and wants may all involve some kind of comparison or reference to lists of items which can act as the learning goals of the course. An exception to this is to base the course on what the learners request. In this case the lists are created by the learners. This is effective if the learners have very clear purposes for learning English which they are aware of. For example, a course for immigrants who have been in the country a few months could very effectively be based on a list of things that they suggest they want to be able to do in English. We will look more closely at this in the chapter on negotiated syllabuses.

Following Principles

Research on language teaching and learning should be used to guide decisions on curriculum design. There is considerable research on the nature of language and language acquisition which can guide the choice of what to teach and how to sequence it. There is also a lot of research on how to encourage learning in general and language learning in particular which can be used to guide the presentation of items to be learned. The principles derived from this research include principles on the importance of repetition and thoughtful processing of material, on the importance of taking account of individual differences and learning style, and on learner attitudes and motivation.

It is very important that curriculum design makes the connection between the research and theory of language learning and the practice of designing lessons and courses. There is a tendency for this connection not to be made, with the result that curriculum design and therefore learners do not benefit from developments in knowledge gained from research. A striking example of this is the failure of courses to take account of the findings regarding the interference that occurs when semantically and formally related items, such as opposites, near synonyms and lexical sets, are presented together (Higa, 1963; Tinkham, 1993). In spite of the clear findings of this research, which is supported by a large body of research less firmly in the area of language learning, course books continue to present names of the parts of the body, items in the kitchen, opposites such as *hot–cold, long–short, old–new*, numbers, days of the week and articles of clothing in the same lesson. As Tinkham (1993) and Higa (1963) show, this will have the effect of making learning more difficult than it should be.

Chapter 4 of this book describes a list of 20 principles that can be used to guide curriculum design. It is not an exhaustive list and is based to some degree on the personal prejudices of the writers. Curriculum designers may wish to create their own lists (see Brown, 1993; Ellis, 2005 and Jones, 1993 for examples of other short lists; see also Richards, 2001 and Tomlinson, 2003 for discussion of the application of principles in materials development). What is important is that curriculum design is treated as a normal part of the field of applied linguistics and thus draws on available knowledge to guide it.

Goals

The curriculum design model in Figure 1.1 has goals as its centre. This is because it is essential to decide why a course is being taught and what the learners need to get from it.

Goals can be expressed in general terms and be given more detail when considering the content of the course. Here are some examples of goals that have been set for language courses.

1   The aim of communicative teaching is to encourage students to exploit all the elements of the language that they know in order to make their meanings clear. Students cannot be expected to master every aspect of the language before they are allowed to use it for communicative purposes.

   (*Orbit*, Harrison and Menzies, 1986)

2   *Trio* aims to

   (a)   encourage students to communicate in a wide range of everyday situations.
   (b)   sustain interest and motivation . . .
   (c)   help students understand and formulate the grammatical rules of English.

(d) develop students' receptive skills beyond those of their productive skills.

(e) give students insights into daily life in Britain.

(f) develop specific skills, including skills required for examination purposes.

(g) contribute to the students' personal, social and educational development.

(Trio, Radley and Sharley, 1987)

3   Passages extends students' communicative competence by developing their ability to:

- expand the range of topics they can discuss and comprehend in English
- speak English fluently (express a wide range of ideas without unnecessary pauses or breakdowns in communication)
- speak English accurately (use an acceptable standard of pronunciation and grammar when communicating).

(Passages, Richards and Sandy, 1998)

4   Students continue to develop speaking and listening skills necessary for participating in classroom discussions with an introduction to oral presentation and critical listening skills.

(College Oral Communication, Roemer, 2006)

Having a clear statement of goals is important for determining the content of the course, for deciding on the focus in presentation, and in guiding assessment.

Content and Sequencing

The content of language courses consists of the language items, ideas, skills and strategies that meet the goals of the course. The viewpoint taken in this book is that even though the units of progression in a course might be tasks, topics or themes, it is important for the curriculum designer to keep some check on vocabulary, grammar and discourse to make sure that important items are being covered and repeated. If there is no check being made, it may happen that learners are not meeting items that are important for their later use of the language. It may also happen that items are not being met often enough to establish them.

One way to provide a systematic and well-researched basis for a course is to make use of frequency lists and other lists of language items or skills. These lists should be chosen and adapted as a result of the needs analysis in order to set the language learning content of the course. A list may be used as a way of checking or determining the content of a course, but this does not mean that the lessons have to consist of item by item teaching. A conversation course for example could be carefully planned to cover the important high-frequency vocabulary and structures, and still consist of a series of very free task-based conversation activities (Joe, Nation and Newton, 1996). Working from lists makes sure that what should be covered is covered and is not left to chance.

Typical lists include:

1   Frequency-based vocabulary lists. These consist of lists of words with indicators of their frequency of occurrence. Perhaps the best known is Michael West's (1953) *General Service List of English Words* which contains 2,000 high-frequency word families. This is a good source for courses at the beginner and intermediate level. Other lists include *The Cambridge English Lexicon* (Hindmarsh, 1980) and the First 1,000, Second 1,000, and Third 1,000 lists produced by the English Language Institute (Nation, 1984). The COBUILD dictionary (1995) indicates the frequency levels of higher-frequency vocabulary. At a more specialised and advanced level, the academic word list (Coxhead, 2000) contains 570 word families useful for study in the upper levels of English-medium secondary schools and at university.

2   Frequency lists of verb forms and verb groups. These contain items such as simple past, present continuous, verb + *to* + stem (where the stem is dominant) *going to* + stem, and *can* + stem (ability) along with information about their frequency of occurrence, mainly in written text. The most striking feature of these lists is the very high frequency of a small number of items, such as simple past, verb + *to* + stem, and the very low frequency of most of the items studied (many of which are given unjustified prominence in many course books and grading schemes for simplified readers). These lists can be found in George 1963a, 1963b, and 1972; see also Appendix 1 of this book. The more recent Biber *et al.* (1999) grammar contains frequency information. Comparison of beginners' books of published courses with these lists shows that the course books contain a mixture of high-frequency and low-frequency items and could be considerably improved with more informed selection.

3   Lists of functions and topics. These lists are not frequency-based and as a result selection of items must be based on perceived need which is less reliable than frequency evidence. The most useful of the available lists is Van Ek and Alexander (1980).

4   Lists of subskills and strategies. These include the subskills of listening, speaking, reading and writing, and language coping and learning strategies.

5   There are lists of tasks, topics and themes that curriculum designers can refer to (Munby, 1978; Van Ek and Alexander, 1980; Prabhu, 1987), but it is better for curriculum designers to develop their own lists

taking account of the background factors of their learners and their needs.

One important aspect of using lists is that they not only check or determine the items that should be in the course, but they can be used to exclude those that should not be there, that is, those that are not in the list. The result of analyses based on lists of language items is a set of items that represent sensible and achievable language goals for the course.

Needs analysis can play a major role in determining the content of courses, particularly for language items. As well as using needs analysis to set language goals, it is useful to decide the basis for the ideas content of the course.

An important decision at this stage involves choosing the form the syllabus will take. Dubin and Olshtain (1986) describe several syllabus forms including linear, modular, cyclical and matrix. Whatever form is chosen will have a marked effect on the opportunity for repetition of items to be learned.

Finding a Format and Presenting Material

The material in a course needs to be presented to learners in a form that will help learning. This presentation will involve the use of suitable teaching techniques and procedures, and these need to be put together in lessons. Some lessons might consist of an unpredictable series of activities, while others might be based on a set format, where the same sequence of activities occurs in all or most of the lessons.

There are several advantages to having a set format for lessons. Firstly, the lessons are easier to make because each one does not have to be planned separately. It also makes the course easier to monitor, to check if all that should be included is there and that accepted principles are being followed. Finally, it makes the lessons easier to learn from because the learners can predict what will occur and are soon familiar with the learning procedures required by different parts of the lesson.

The sources of the material used as a basis for the lessons will have decisive effects on the ease of making the lessons and of the possibility of future distribution or publication of the course. A shortcut here is simply to take suitable material from other courses, adapting it as required.

There is a substantial set of principles that need to be applied at this stage (see Chapter 4). These concern not only presentation but also selection aspects, such as sequencing and the amount of time given to fluency work.

The lesson format needs to be checked against the environment analysis of the course to make sure that the major environmental factors are being considered.

Because curriculum design is not a linear process, it may be necessary to alter the content or sequencing to suit the lesson format and to reorder the list of environmental factors. The lessons may still require adjustment as a result of consideration of other stages of the curriculum design. Perhaps the most difficult task at this stage is making sure that the learning goals of the course are met. That is, that the wanted language items are well-represented and well-presented in the course.

It can be argued that the first presentation of an item is not as important as the later repetitions of that item. This is often neglected in courses, but it is crucial to learning. It is through repeated meetings that items are enriched and established.

Monitoring and Assessing

The aims of curriculum design are to make a course that has useful goals, that achieves its goals, that satisfies its users, and that does all this in an efficient way. An important recurring part of the design process is to assess how well these aims are achieved.

Assessing generally involves the use of tests. An important distinction in testing is between proficiency tests which measure what a learner knows of the language, and achievement tests which measure what has been learned from a particular course. Proficiency tests may be used to measure a learner's level of language knowledge before entering a course and after a course is completed and has been assessed. Achievement tests are closely related to a course and the items in the tests are based on the content of the course and the learning goals of the course. Short-term achievement tests are tests that occur at the end of each lesson or at the end of a group of lessons. They provide the teacher and learners with information about how much has been learned. They can have a strong effect on motivation, on the speed of movement through the lessons, and on adapting and supplementing the course. Well-designed courses should include short-term achievement tests in the curriculum design.

Larger achievement tests can occur at the end of a course and perhaps halfway through the course. The information gained from such tests can be useful in evaluating the course.

Other kinds of tests include placement tests (to see if the course is suitable for a prospective learner or to see where in the course the learner should begin) and diagnostic tests (to see if learners have particular gaps in their knowledge).

But testing is only one way of gaining information about the progress of learners and the effectiveness of the course. Other ways include observing and monitoring using checklists and report forms, getting learners to keep diaries and learning logs, getting learners to collect samples of their work in folders, and getting learners to talk about their learning. Curriculum design can include planned opportunity for this kind of data gathering.

Evaluating a Course

Information gained from assessment is a useful source of data about the effectiveness of a course, but it is only one of the sources of information that can contribute to the evaluation of a course. Basically, evaluation tries to answer the question "Is this a good course?". The range of meanings that can be attached to "good" determines the range of sources of information for carrying out an evaluation.

A "good" course could be one that:

1   attracts a lot of students
2   makes a lot of money
3   satisfies the learners
4   satisfies the teachers
5   satisfies the sponsors
6   helps learners gain high scores in an external test
7   results in a lot of learning
8   applies state-of-the-art knowledge about language teaching and learning
9   is held in high regard by the local or international community
10   follows accepted principles of curriculum design.

An evaluation of a course can have many purposes, the main ones being to continue or discontinue the course, or to bring about improvements in the course. Responsible curriculum design includes ongoing evaluation of the course.

Summary of the Steps

1   Examine the environment.
2   Assess needs.
3   Decide on principles.
4   Set goals, and choose and sequence content.
5   Design the lesson format.
6   Include assessment procedures.
7   Evaluate the course.

The purpose of this chapter has been to briefly describe the major parts of the curriculum design model. In the following chapters, each of the parts will be looked at in more detail. In addition, topics including evaluating course books, innovation, and designing in-service courses will be covered. Curriculum design is in essence a practical activity. Because of this the tasks which follow each chapter provide an important part of learning about curriculum design.

Tasks

Task 1 Examining a published course

Look at a published course book and see what decisions were made for each of the parts of the model in Figure 1.1. Choose one feature for each part of the curriculum design model. For example, find one example of the effects of environment analysis.

Task 2 Using the parts of the model to overview the planning of a course

Quickly decide what kind of course you wish to design. For each of the parts of the curriculum design model, write two questions you will need to answer to plan a course.

Case Studies

An important way to make use of this book on curriculum design is to examine case studies using the model introduced in this chapter. Choose a short case study of curriculum design (about three to six pages long). Look in the list of references at the back of this book for the items marked [20] and choose one of them, or choose a case study report in journals such as *English Teaching Forum, Guidelines, ELT Journal, System* or *English for Specific Purposes*. Analyse it to see how the parts of the curriculum design model described in Chapter 1 fit with the case study. See what is in the model and not in the case study. See what is in the case study and not covered by the model. Table 1.1 provides an example analysis based on the Nation and Crabbe (1991) article (available at I.S.P. Nation's web site).

Table 1.1 Examination of Nation and Crabbe (1991) case study

Parts of the curriculum design process	Nation and Crabbe's procedure
Environment analysis	The major constraints and their effects in ranked order were: 1 Limited time to invest in learning (therefore – focus on immediate needs; have very limited goals, i.e. vocabulary and only spoken use). 2 Must be useful for a wide range of people and countries (therefore – include only generally useful items).
Needs analysis	Future needs (necessities) were found by: 1 Interviewing people previously in the situation that the learners will soon be in. 2 Analysing the language section of guidebooks. 3 Personal experience. There was no need to look at present proficiency as it was assumed that the learners were beginners. Wants were not looked at.
Application of principles	The following principles were directly stated: 1 Learners should get an immediate and useful return for their learning. 2 Avoid interference. 3 Use thoughtful processing. 4 Get fluency practice.
Goals	The goal was to quickly learn a survival vocabulary.
Content and sequencing	The content included approximately 120 words and phrases classified according to topic. The learner can decide on the sequence of learning. The sections of the list are in order of usefulness. Advice is given not to learn related items together.
Format and presentation	Suggestions are provided for self-study, such as using vocabulary cards, using deep processing and practice.
Monitoring and assessment	Not dealt with.
Evaluation	The checking of the list against personal experience is one kind of evaluation.

Chapter 2

Environment Analysis

The aim of this part of the curriculum design process is to find the situational factors that will strongly affect the course.

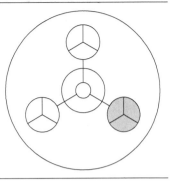

Environment analysis (Tessmer, 1990) involves looking at the factors that will have a strong effect on decisions about the goals of the course, what to include in the course, and how to teach and assess it. These factors can arise from the learners, the teachers, and the teaching and learning situation.

Environment analysis is also called "situation analysis" (Richards, 2001) or "constraints analysis". A constraint can be positive in curriculum design. For example, a constraint could be that the teachers are all very highly trained and are able and willing to make their own class activities. This would have a major effect on curriculum design as much of the format and presentation work could be left to the teachers. In some models of curriculum design, environment analysis is included in needs analysis.

Environment analysis is an important part of curriculum design because at its most basic level it ensures that the course will be usable. For example, if the level of training of the teachers is very low and is not taken into account, it might happen that the teachers are unable to handle the activities in the course. Similarly, if the course material is too expensive or requires technology and copying facilities that are not available, the course may be unusable. There are many factors that could affect curriculum design, so as a part of the procedure of environment analysis, the curriculum designer should

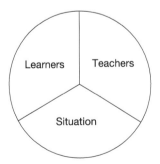

Figure 2.1 Factors in environment analysis.

decide which factors are the most important. The importance of a factor depends on:

1 whether the course will still be useful if the factor is not taken into account
2 how large and pervasive the effect of the factor is on the course.

An Example of Environment Analysis

Here is an example of an environment analysis on a course for young Japanese learners aged six to nine years old who had lived in English-speaking countries while their parents were posted there. During their time overseas they learned quite a lot of English in much the same way as native-speaking learners do. On their return to Japan, once a week for one and a half hours they attended a special class to help maintain their English. They all could speak Japanese and were attending Japanese medium schools in Japan.

The important constraints on the special second language maintenance class were as follows.

1 There was very limited class time and contact time with English.
2 There would be a drop in the learners' interest in learning English as they identified more strongly with Japan and being Japanese.
3 The learners knew that they could communicate more easily with each other in Japanese than in English.
4 There was a range of levels of English proficiency with some learners appearing to be very proficient for their age.
5 The learners had been learning English in much the same ways as native speakers acquire their first language.

These constraints could have the following effects on curriculum design.

1 Parents should be guided in giving their children some extra contact with English.
2 The activities should be fun so that the children look forward to doing them for their own sake.
3 Some of the activities should carry over to the next class so that the children look forward to continuing them.
4 The activities should be largely teacher-centred rather than group or pair work.
5 Most of the activities should be meaning-focused. Language-focused activities should mainly involve correction.

This would mean using activities like the following.

1 Listening to a serial story.
2 Reading comics and other high-interest material.
3 Listening and speaking games.
4 Writing to be "published" or read aloud.
5 Learners giving talks to the group, e.g. show and tell.
6 Reading at home and reporting to the class.
7 Diary writing to the teacher or a secret friend.
8 High-success quizzes and activities with awards.
9 Production of a newsletter where everyone gets a mention.
10 Pen pals.
11 Watching English movies and TV programmes.
12 Playing video games that use English.
13 Production of a play, etc.

The constraints faced by this course were very severe, and ignoring them would certainly mean failure for the course.

Environment Constraints

Table 2.1 lists a range of environment constraints. When designing a course, the table can be used as a checklist to help sort out the few that will be given most attention in a particular piece of curriculum design. Columns 1 and 2 list some constraints. Column 3 suggests some of the effects on curriculum design. There are numerous other possible effects. In the table the constraints have been presented as questions that curriculum designers can ask. Normally they would be framed as descriptive statements. For example, the first listed constraint could be expressed as "The learners are interested in a limited range of topics".

Table 2.1 Environment constraints and effects

General constraints	Particular constraints	Effects on curriculum design
The learners How old are they?	Are the learners interested in all kinds of topics? Can the learners do all kinds of learning activities?	Take account of learners' interests Use appropriate activities
What do they know?	Do they share a (first) language? Can their first language be used to help learning? What previous learning have they done?	Use teacher-centred activities Use some translation Use first language pre-reading activities Use reading input

Do they need English for a special purpose?	Will they use English for a wide range of purposes? Do they expect to learn certain things from the course? Do they have expectations about what the course will be like?	Set general purpose goals Include expected material Allow learners to negotiate the nature of the course
Do they have preferred ways of learning?	Are they interested in learning English? Do they have to learn English? Can they attend class regularly?	Use highly motivating activities Include relevant topics Recycle activities Use a spiral curriculum
The teachers Are they trained?	Can they prepare some of their own material? Can they handle group work, individualised learning . . .?	Provide ready-made activities Use group work activities . . .
Are they confident in their use of English?	Can they provide good models? Can they produce their own spoken or written material? Can they correct spoken or written work?	Provide taped materials Provide a complete set of course material Use activities that do not require feedback
Do they have time for preparation and marking?	Can the course include homework? Can the course include work which has to be marked?	Provide homework activities Provide answer keys
The situation Is there a suitable classroom?	Can the arrangement of the desks be changed for group work? Is the blackboard big enough and easily seen?	Use group work activities Use material that does not require the students to have a course book
Is there enough time?	Can the learners reach the goals in the available time? Is the course intensive? Can the learners give all their time to the course?	Set staged goals Provide plenty of material Set limited goals
Are there enough resources?	Can material be photocopied? Can each learner have a copy of the course book? Is there plenty of supplementary material? Are tape recorders etc available?	Provide individualised material Use teacher-focused material Match the content to available supplementary material Develop audio and video taped material
Is it worth developing the course?	Do learners meet English outside class? Will the course be run several times?	Provide contact with a large amount of English in class Put time into preparing the course

Sometimes it is necessary to consider wider aspects of the situation when carrying out an environment analysis. There may, for example, be institutional or government policies requiring the use of the target language in schools (Liu et al., 2004), or there may be negative attitudes towards the target language among learners in post-colonial societies (Asmah, 1992). Dubin and Olshtain (1986) suggest a useful way of thinking about the wider environment (Figure 2.2) that can have implications for language curriculum design. For example, the language curriculum in a situation where:

- the target language is recognised as one of a country's official languages (the political and national context)
- there are relatively few native speakers (the language setting)
- there are relatively few opportunities to use the language outside the classroom (patterns of language use in society)
- majority-language speakers doubt the target language has contemporary relevance (group and individual attitudes)

will differ greatly from that in a situation where:

- the target language is recognised as one of a country's official languages
- there are relatively few native speakers
- there are many opportunities to use the target language outside the classroom
- the target language provides employment and educational opportunities.

Understanding the Constraints

In order to understand a constraint fully, it is usually necessary to examine the nature of the constraint in the environment you are working in, and to examine previous research on the constraint. For example, let us look briefly at the constraint of class size. If this constraint is considered to be important for the particular course being designed, it is useful to know exactly how large the classes are. Do they contain 40 students or 140 students? Is it possible to change class sizes?

There has been considerable research on and examination of teaching large classes. This research has looked at the relative merits of group work and teacher-centred activities, the effect of class size on learning, and individualisation. There have been many articles and books on activities and techniques for large classes (Coleman, 1989; Hess, 2001), and on the principles of group work. Good curriculum design must take account of research and theory so that it provides the best possible conditions for learning that the state of the art allows.

Some of the major constraints investigated by research and analysis include the time available, cultural background, the effect of the first language on

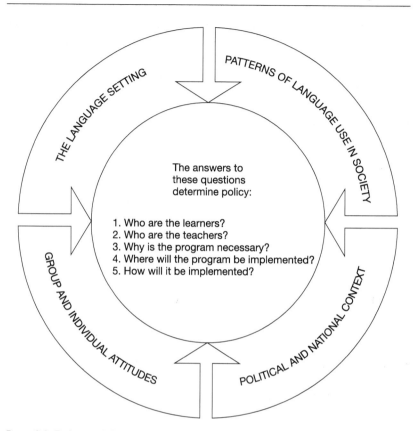

Figure 2.2 Dubin and Olshtain's (1986) model of sources of information for language program policy.

language learning and special purposes. The following section looks at time as an example of an important constraint in the environment, and provides information that would be useful in helping to plan the length of a course. This investigation of the time constraint provides a model of the application of the steps in environment analysis that can be applied to other constraints.

The Constraint of Time

In many courses the time constraint is very important. The time may be severely limited, or the desired goals might not fit into the time available. The steps followed include (1) examining the local environment, (2) looking at previous research, and (3) considering the effect of the constraint on the design of the course.

Local information from the environment

Useful information to gather about the constraint is how much class time is available, how much time out of class could be given to learning, and what the goals of the course are.

Research information

Useful research information would reveal what could be achieved within certain time periods. Pimsleur (1980), for example, presents estimates of the time taken to reach various levels of proficiency for learners of particular languages. The estimates are based on the idea that some languages are more difficult than others for native speakers of English to begin to learn. To reach an elementary level of proficiency in French or Indonesian for example would take approximately 240 hours of study, according to Pimsleur. To reach the same level for a more difficult language such as Hebrew or Japanese would take approximately 360 hours. These estimates derive from the considerable experience of teachers at the Foreign Service Institute of the Department of State in the United States. For further research on the time constraint see Collier (1987, 1989, 1995).

The effect of the time constraint on the design of the course

An environmental constraint can be approached in two ways – working within the constraint, and overcoming the constraint. To work within the constraint the curriculum designer could limit the goals of the course to fit the available time. This is what is suggested in the Pimsleur data. Another way of limiting would be to try to cover most of the language items and skills but at a rather superficial level, relying on later experience to make up for the quick coverage. Alternatively, very intensive study procedures could be used.

To overcome the constraint the curriculum designer might try to provide self-study options for work to be done outside of class time or if possible the time available for the course could be increased.

Steps in Environment Analysis

The steps in environment analysis can be as follows.

1   Brainstorm and then systematically consider the range of environment factors that will affect the course. Table 2.1 can be used as a starting point.
2   Choose the most important factors (no more than five) and rank them, putting the most important first.

3   Decide what information you need to fully take account of the factor. The information can come from investigation of the environment and from research and theory.
4   Consider the effects of each factor on the design of the course.
5   Go through steps 1, 2, 3, and 4 again.

Environment analysis involves looking at the local and wider situation to make sure that the course will fit and will meet local requirements. There is considerable research data on many of the important environment factors, including class size, motivation, learners of mixed proficiency and special purpose goals. Good environment analysis draws on both analysis of the environment and application of previous research and theory. In some models of curriculum design, environment analysis is included in needs analysis. Needs analysis is the subject of the next chapter.

Tasks

Task 1   The range of constraints

Brainstorm to create a list of constraints that may significantly affect the design of courses.

Task 2   Examining your teaching environment

1   List five important constraints facing you in your teaching situation. Use Table 2.1 at the beginning of this chapter to help you. Rank your constraints according to the strength of the effect that they will have on your course.

_____

_____

_____

_____

_____

2   Very briefly describe the most important constraint or strength and say why it is important.

_____

_____

_____

_____

3   What do you know or need to know about the constraint or strength? You may wish to know about the present situation and previous research.

_____

_____

_____

_____

4   How can you take account of the constraint or strength in your syllabus?
     (What parts of the syllabus will it most affect?)
     1 _____
     2 _____
     3 _____
     4 _____

5   Which of the solutions listed above do you most favour? Why?

_____

_____

Task 3 Comparing teaching environments

Discuss the second/foreign language teaching environments in two or more
different countries. To what extent can the differences be explained in terms
of Dubin and Olshtain's depiction of the situation (Figure 2.2)?

Case Studies

1   Look at the constraints listed in the Nation and Crabbe article. What
    other constraints are described in other parts of the article? What
    constraint had the strongest effect on their course?
2   Look at the SRA reading boxes. The SRA reading boxes were designed
    for native speakers of English. Each box consists of around seven levels
    with each level being distinguished by a different colour. Within each
    level there are 20 cards each containing a reading text with exercises.
    Each card of the same colour has a different text of roughly equal length
    and difficulty to others with the same colour. The levels gradually
    increase in terms of text length and text difficulty.

Each learner chooses a card of the appropriate level, reads it and does the
exercises, gets the answer key from the box, uses it to mark their answers to
the exercises, and then records their score on a graph. When the learner has
gained a high score on three consecutive cards at a level, the learner can then
move to the next level up.

What constraints do you think led to their design? List the constraints and
relate each constraint to an aspect of the design. The first one in Table 2.2 has
been done for you.

Table 2.2

Constraints	Aspects of design
1 Wide range of reading proficiency in a class	There are ten levels in one SRA box. Learners read at their own level and speed.
2. . .	Once the learners know how to use the reading box, the teacher does not have a lot of work to do.
3. . .	
4. . .	The learners mark their own work.
5. . .	The learners record their score on a graph.
6. . .	There are a lot of cards and a lot of levels in each reading box.
7. . .	There is a lot of reading material in one box. Many classes can use the same box.
	The teacher does not have to do much.
	Each card takes a short time to read and answer.
	There is a wide variety of interesting texts.

Chapter 3

Needs Analysis

The aim of this part of the curriculum design process is to discover what needs to be learned and what the learners want to learn.

Needs analysis is directed mainly at the goals and content of a course. It examines what the learners know already and what they need to know. Needs analysis makes sure that the course will contain relevant and useful things to learn. Good needs analysis involves asking the right questions and finding the answers in the most effective way.

The Various Focuses of Needs Analysis

The aim of this section of the chapter is to look at the range of information that can be gathered in needs analysis.

Hutchinson and Waters (1987) divide needs into *target needs* (i.e. what the learner needs to do in the target situation) and *learning needs* (i.e. what the learner needs to do in order to learn). The analysis of target needs can look at:

1 **Necessities** What is necessary in the learners' use of language? For example, do the learners have to write answers to exam questions?

Figure 3.1 Three types of needs.

2	**Lacks**	What do the learners lack? For example, are there aspects of writing that were not practised in their previous learning (L1, L2)?
3	**Wants**	What do the learners wish to learn?

Another way to look at needs is to make a major division between present knowledge and required knowledge, and objective needs and subjective needs. Very roughly, *Lacks* fit into *present knowledge, Necessities* fit into *required knowledge*, and *Wants* fit into *subjective needs* (see Table 3.1).

Information about objective needs can be gathered by questionnaires, personal interviews, data collection (for example, gathering exam papers or text books and analysing them), observation (for example, following a learner through a typical day), informal consultation with teachers and learners, and tests. Subjective needs are discovered through learner self-assessment using lists and scales, and questionnaires and interviews.

The outcomes of needs analysis must be useful for curriculum design. It is not worth gathering needs analysis information if no application can be found for it. It is therefore useful to do a pilot study first to check for this.

Table 3.2 covers many of the questions that are usually raised in an analysis of target needs (Munby, 1978; Hutchinson and Waters, 1987). They have been organised under four learning goals because needs analysis must lead to decisions about what will be learned during a course. The questions do not always match neatly with the goals and types of information. For example, a question like "Where will the language be used?" can result in information that affects language goals, content goals, skill goals and discourse or text goals. Table 3.2 can be used to make sure that a needs analysis is gaining information on a suitable range of learning goals.

Ongoing needs analysis during the course can make use of the pyramid procedure (Jordan, 1990). That is, the learners can be given a series of items that may describe their wants. They choose and rank these individually and then in pairs or fours, and finally as a group. When they report their ranking to the teacher, they also note the points that they individually ranked highly but could not gain group support for. This will help the teacher in planning a class program as well as arranging individualised or small group work. The items to rank can take this form:

Table 3.1 Types of needs

	Present knowledge	Required knowledge
Objective needs		
Subjective needs		

Table 3.2 Questions for focusing on needs

Goals	Questions	Types of information in the answers
Language	What will the course be used for? How proficient does the user have to be? What communicative activities will the learner take part in? Where will the language be used?	sounds vocabulary grammatical structures functions set phrases and set sentences tasks
Ideas	What content matter will the learner be working with?	topics themes texts
Skills	How will the learner use the language? Under what conditions will the language be used? Who will the learners use the language with?	listening speaking reading writing degree of accuracy degree of fluency
Text	What will the language be used to do? What language uses is the learner already familiar with?	genres and discourse types sociolinguistic skills

> I would like more group work activities.
> I would like more written feedback on assignments.
> . . .

This will be looked at more closely in the chapter on negotiated syllabuses. With a negotiated syllabus, learners negotiate with each other and with the teacher to determine the content and other aspects of the course.

The findings of needs analysis need to be balanced against constraints found in environment analysis, particularly the limitation of time.

Discovering Needs

Table 3.3 suggests a range of methods for discovering needs. It is organised around necessities, lacks and wants. Proficiency in column 2 relates to present knowledge and situations of use and involves the study of situations and tasks that learners will need to engage in using knowledge gained from the course. Self-report can take a variety of forms. It may involve written responses to a structured set of questions (as in the MAFIA example in Task 2 of this chapter) or to a sentence completion task. It may involve diary writing or some other form of extended written report. It may involve group activities such as voting, ranking, brainstorming, or problem solving. In its most organised form it may be a part of a negotiated syllabus.

Observation and analysis may involve process and product. Observation of skilled and unskilled writers performing target tasks may reveal important areas that need attention during a course. Analysis of the written products of target tasks such as university assignments or exams can reveal the type of language needed to perform the tasks well.

Table 3.3 can be used to check that a wide enough range of information-gathering methods is being used. Another set of methods of data collection can be found in Long (2005a).

Needs Analysis Tools

Table 3.3 briefly suggests a range of tools for using in needs analysis. Let us look at possible tools in more detail by taking the case of an English for academic purposes course which is preparing learners of English for university study. We will look at necessities, lacks and wants in that order.

Necessities

The first thing to look at in necessities is the demands of the target tasks. That is, what will learners have to do when they do university study? Among the things they will have to do is listen to lectures, take part in

Table 3.3 Methods and examples of needs analysis

Type of need	Focus	Method	Example
Necessities	Proficiency	Self-report Proficiency testing	Level of vocabulary knowledge (Nation and Beglar, 2007) Level of fluency e.g. reading speed
	Situations of use	Self-report Observation and analysis Review of previous research Corpus analysis	Analysis of texts (Nation, 2006) Analysis of exams and assignments (Friederichs and Pierson, 1981; Horowitz, 1986) Analysis of tasks (Brown et al., 1984) MICASE (http://quod.lib.umich.edu/m/micase/)
Lacks	Proficiency	Self-report Testing	Vocabulary tests
	Situations of use	Self-report Observation and analysis	Examiners' reports Analysis of tasks (Ellis, 1986)
Wants	Wishes	Self-report	
	Use	Observation	Records of choices of activities Teachers' observation

tutorials, write assignments and tasks, and sit exams. If we take assignments as one example of the things they have to do, we could analyse the kind of language needed to do an assignment as a way of working out what the learners would need to know. We could do this by doing a vocabulary analysis of good assignments, using a program like the Frequency programme or the Range program. Is it necessary to have a large vocabulary to write a good assignment, or can an assignment be well written in a limited vocabulary? We can also look at past assignment topics to see the kinds of discourse that learners would have to handle. Are the assignments mainly descriptions, analyses, comparisons, persuasive pieces of writing or instructions? We could interview university staff who are involved in setting and marking such assignments to see what they expect in a good assignment. Perhaps they are not concerned with the grammatical accuracy of the writing but are more concerned that the writer writes like a geographer or an economist or a political scientist. Another source of information about this would be to look in course outlines and other departmental information to see if there are any guidelines on writing assignments. If we have access to assignments from successful students in previous years, these could be a useful source of information. We could also look at the timeframe involved in writing an assignment. Do the learners have time to prepare notes, a rough draft, and a further draft? If they know the assignment topics well before the assignment is due, then the English for academic purposes course could focus more strongly on the process of assignment writing.

Presumably, this is not the first time that this English for academic purposes course has been taught. Can we see any evidence that the course has helped the assignment writing of learners who studied it in previous years? What kind of improvement did the course make? Did learners who studied on the course do well in their later study? If there were positive effects then this part of the course needs to be kept largely as it is.

Many of these suggestions are applicable for the design of an EAP course within a particular context. When more generic courses are being designed, or when information is not available locally, we could also look at publicly available corpora, especially specialised corpora, for language needs analysis purposes. These may become an increasingly valuable tool as more and more corpora become available and search engines become more powerful and more user-friendly.

Lacks

An important part of needs analysis involves looking at where learners are at present. How good are the learners at writing assignments now? One way to investigate this is to look at an assignment or two that the learners have just written. The assignment can be analysed from an information perspective, from a grammar perspective and from the discourse perspective. Another way to look at an assignment is to look at the parts of the writing process and to see what degree of skill in each part is reflected in the assignment (see Nation (2009) for such an analysis). Yet another way is to look at the learners in the process of writing an assignment. The quality of an assignment often depends on the conditions under which it was written. Observing students writing can give some insight into these conditions and the learners' control over parts of the writing process. There is however always the danger of the observer paradox where the observation changes the nature of the task.

Another source of information about lacks could come from the university lecturer who marks such assignments. What do they see as the strengths and weaknesses of the assignment that the learner has written? This information could be gathered using a think-aloud protocol as the examiner marks the assignment, or it could be gathered by getting the examiner to reflect on the assignment they have just marked.

The learners themselves are also a very useful source of information about lacks. How does the learner interpret the assignment task? One way of gathering information about this is to question the learner about the assignment task using a carefully prepared set of interview questions. Another way is to get the learner to talk about the assignment task encouraging them to say what they think they have to do to answer the assignment.

The ways of investigating lacks which have been described above focus on an assignment task. However, learners' general proficiency contributes to the way they handle any language task. To gather data about the learners' general proficiency, we can interview them, get them to sit tests such as vocabulary tests, grammar tests, writing tests and comprehension tests, or we can get them to do self-assessment using a specially prepared checklist. Learners' scores on standardised proficiency tests like the TOEFL test or the IELTS test can be a very useful source of information particularly when they provide information about separate aspects of language proficiency such as writing or speaking.

Wants

Learners have their own views about what they think is useful for them. At the very least, information about this is useful in working out whether the learners' views and the needs analyst's views are the same or not. If they are not the same, then the curriculum designer may need to rethink the results of the needs analysis or persuade the learners that there is a more useful view of what they need. We can gather such information through an interview or a questionnaire. Questionnaires are notoriously difficult to design well. However a well-designed questionnaire can be a very useful source of information which can be reused for later courses. We could ask the learners what they think will improve their assignment writing and what they want to be able to do regarding assignment writing by the end of the English for academic purposes course.

The main point behind looking at this example is to show that there is a wide range of tools that can be used to analyse needs. They include text analysis, talking with students both past and present, surveying the environment, looking at pieces of work, talking with teachers, employers and assessors, and using personal experience and commonsense. Because needs analysis is basically a kind of research it is important to get the research questions right as soon as possible and use these to guide the choice of methods of data gathering.

Good needs analysis thus covers a range of needs using a range of data-getting tools. Needs are not always clear and are always changing so it is important that needs are looked at from a variety of perspectives at a variety of times. The perspectives can vary according to the type of need (lack, necessities, wants; or present knowledge, required knowledge, objective and subjective needs), the source of information (present learners, past learners, teachers, present tasks and materials, future tasks and materials, future colleagues or future assessors or teachers), the data-gathering tools (text and discourse analysis, frequency counts, interviews, questionnaires, observation, negotiation and discussion, reflection on experience), and the type of information (learning goals, preferred styles of learning, learners' commitment to learning).

The times of needs analysis can include needs analysis before a course begins, needs analysis in the initial stages of a course, and ongoing needs analysis during the running of the course. If a course is to be repeated with different learners, then needs analysis at the end of a course is useful.

Evaluating Needs Analysis

Needs analysis is a kind of assessment and thus can be evaluated by considering its reliability, validity and practicality.

Reliable needs analysis involves using well-thought-out, standardised tools that are applied systematically. Rather than just observing people performing tasks that learners will have to do after the course, it is better to systematise the observation by using a checklist, or by recording and apply standardised analysis procedures. The more pieces of observation and the more people who are studied, the more reliable the results.

Valid needs analysis involves looking at what is relevant and important. Consideration of the type of need that is being looked at and the type of information that is being gathered is important. Before needs analysis begins it may be necessary to do a ranking activity to decide what type of need should get priority in the needs analysis investigation. The worst decision would be to let practicality dominate by deciding to investigate what is easiest to investigate!

Practical needs analysis is not expensive, does not occupy too much of the learners' and teacher's time, provides clear, easy-to-understand results and can easily be incorporated into the curriculum design process. There will always be a tension between reliable and valid needs analysis and practical needs analysis. A compromise is necessary but validity should always be given priority.

Issues in Needs Analysis

There are several issues in needs analysis that have been the focus of continuing debate. Three are briefly discussed here.

1   **Common core and specialised language** What are the content selection stages that a special purposes language course should follow? From a vocabulary point of view (Nation and Hwang, 1995; Sutarsyah *et al.*, 1994) there is evidence to support the idea that learners should first focus on a common core of 2,000 words, then focus on general academic vocabulary common to a wide range of disciplines (Coxhead, 2000) if their goal is academic reading and writing, and then focus on the specialised vocabulary of their particular disciplines (Chung and Nation, 2004).

   Study of vocabulary occurrence shows that this sequence of goals is sensible and generally gives the best return for learning effort. If goals are very focused, it is possible to shorten each step a little, focusing on around 1,600 word families of the common core and about 650 general academic words (Sutarsyah, 1993). It is likely that there is a similar progression for grammatical items, perhaps of two stages with stage 1 consisting of high-frequency widely used grammatical items, and stage 2 focusing on those particular to the text types of the discipline (Biber, 1990). This kind of progression should not be rigidly kept to. It is possible to focus on the content of the discipline using common core vocabulary and a few general academic and technical items. Most of the very-high-frequency content words in a particular discipline are from the common core and general academic vocabulary, for example *price, cost, demand, curve, supply, quantity* in Economics (Sutarsyah *et al.*, 1994).

Table 3.4 Vocabulary stages

Specialised/Technical (approximately 1,000 word families)	Stage 3
General academic (570 word families)	Stage 2
Common core (2,000 word families)	Stage 1

2   **Narrow focus – wide focus** Detailed systems of needs analysis have been set up to determine precisely what language a particular language learner with clear needs should learn (Munby, 1978). The arguments in favour of a narrow focus include the faster meeting of needs, the reduction of the quantity of learning needed, and the motivation that comes from getting an immediate return from being able to apply learning. Hyland (2002) finds support for a narrow focus in social constructionist theory, arguing for the importance of successful communication within a specific discourse community. Such a focus, however, runs the risk of teaching "parole" and not "langue" (De Saussure, 1983), that is, of not teaching the language system so that learners can be flexible and creative in their language use. If language learners have more than very short-term goals for language learning, it is important that their language learning not only satisfies immediate needs but also provides the basis for the development of control of the wider language system.

3   **Critical needs analysis** Benesch (1996) points out with some striking examples that needs analysis is affected by the ideology of those in control of the analysis. That is, the questions they ask, the areas they investigate, and the conclusions they draw are inevitably influenced by their attitudes to change and the status quo. For this reason, it is worth considering a wide range of possible viewpoints when deciding on the focus of needs analysis, and seeking others' views on where change could be made.

Needs analysis makes sure that a course will be relevant and satisfying to the learners. This is such a basic requirement that it is worth giving careful thought to needs analysis procedures. To neglect them is to run the risk of producing a course that does not meet the needs of its users.

Summary of the Steps

1   Discover learner needs by considering lacks, wants and necessities or some other framework.

2   Decide what course content and presentation features will meet these needs.

Needs analysis makes sure the course meets the learners' needs. Environment analysis looks at the way the course needs to fit the situation in which it occurs. Looking at principles makes sure that the course fits with what we know about teaching and learning. That is the subject of the next chapter.

Tasks

Task I Needs analysis for a writing course

You have been asked to design a writing course for learners of English who intend to go on to university study in English. As a part of the fact-finding stage you have decided to carry out a needs analysis (Table 3.5).

(a) Decide what kind of information you are looking for and classify it into necessities, lacks or wants.
(b) Decide where you will look to find the information.
(c) List three ways that you will use to gather the information for the writing course (questionnaires etc.).
(d) For each of these three ways prepare some sample items or describe the procedure you will use.

You have now done your needs analysis and have decided how to gather the information you need.

1   List your findings here.

2   List three important principles about how you think writing should be learned.

3   Write the general goal for your course.

Table 3.5

Type of information	Source of the information	How the information will be gathered

4   Choose three types of activities that you will use in your course.

_____

_____

_____

5   Take one of these activities and show how it will fit into your course.

_____

_____

_____

_____

_____

6   Look critically at your needs analysis to make sure that it is not limited
    by your own perspectives or a set institutional viewpoint.

Task 2 Evaluating a needs analysis scheme

You recently came across the following scheme (Table 3.6) which is designed
to help learners do needs analysis on themselves to guide their own learning.
You want to find out if this is a good scheme or not. Note that this is a needs
analysis tool that the learners answer themselves. Check the MAFIA focuses
and questions against the needs analysis subdivisions of lacks, wants and
necessities.

Supporting the learner in self-instruction

1   What questions do you need to ask yourself to evaluate the questions
    asked in the MAFIA scheme?
2   What do you think of the process of needs analysis used in the MAFIA
    scheme?

Task 3 Discovering needs

You have been given the job of designing a reading course for ten-year-old
primary learners of English. They can read in their own language which uses
a similar (but more regular) writing system.

1   List two needs analysis questions you wish to answer.

_____

_____

2   List the three most important ways that you will use to do a needs
    analysis.

    a _____

    b _____

    c _____

Table 3.6

Motivation	What is your attitude towards the community whose language you want to learn? How much does it matter if you don't succeed? Do you need to learn the language to be able to achieve certain specific tasks or do you want to learn enough to be accepted as a member of the foreign community?
Aims	What do you want to be able to do in the language? Do you want to communicate in the written or the spoken language? or both? Will it be enough if you just understand the language (at least in the first instance)? For you, is it sufficient to learn just enough language for communication to occur?
Functions	What use will you be making of the language? What kind of situations will you have to perform in? (telephone? lectures? seminars? shops? etc.) What functions of language will you primarily need? (explaining, persuading, seeking information, contradicting etc.) What will your relationship be with the people you will be dealing with? (friends, inferiors, superiors, etc.)
Information	What kind of linguistic information do you need to meet your needs? Which are the most important: technical vocabulary? the precise meaning of intonation? correct pronunciation? a set of ready-made sentences to get by with?
Activities	What do you need to do to learn what you want? How much time can you devote to it? What are your learning habits? Do you like working on your own? Is the Language Lab suitable? Do you need help? (Dictionary, radio, newspapers, grammars, contact with native speakers, etc.) Do you know native speakers who would agree to talk with you in their own language? Do you make full use of other possibilities, e.g., the radio? sub-titled film? etc.

3   Choose one of these ways and give two examples of the procedure, items or questions that you would use.

_____

_____

_____

_____

4   Choose one of the ways you listed to do a needs analysis and justify your choice of this method.

_____

_____

_____

_____

Case Studies

1   Case studies of needs analysis can be evaluated by looking at (1) the range of types of information gathered in the needs analysis (for example, were objective and subjective needs examined?), (2) the reliability, validity and practicality of the needs analysis procedures, and (3) the quality of the application of the findings of the needs analysis to the other parts of the curriculum design process (that is, were the results of the needs analysis used effectively?). Look at a case study of needs analysis and using the three aspects just mentioned evaluate the quality of the needs analysis. Here are some sample case studies: Bawcom (1995), Bello (1994), Sharkey (1994).

2   **Necessities: examples of needs analysis for a writing course**

(a)   Friederichs and Pierson (1981) collected 507 distinct question patterns from Science exam papers and classified them into 27 categories such as *Discuss, Explain, Describe, List, Show by what manner/means*. This was used to guide the making of writing exercises for EFL university students.

(b)   Horowitz (1986) gathered actual writing assignment handouts and essay examinations given to students in their classes. The 54 tasks gathered were classified into 7 categories:

1   summary of reaction to reading [9 items]
2   annotated bibliography [1 item]
3   report on a special participatory experience [9 items]
4   connection of theory and data [10 items]
5   case study [5 samples]
6   synthesis of multiple sources [15 items]
7   research project [5 items].

The information was used to create procedures, strategies and tasks to help ESL students with academic writing.

(c)   Shaw (1991) and Parkhurst (1990) examined the writing processes of science writers through the use of interviews and questionnaires.

Chapter 4

Principles

The aim of this part of the curriculum design process is to decide how learning can be encouraged.

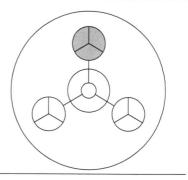

Methods and Principles

Very few teachers or researchers now follow any particular method or approach in their language teaching. Practitioners of a method soon find a remarkable similarity between methods that are supposed to be quite different from each other, particularly in the selection and sequencing of the items that make up a course. This same similarity leads us to suspect that the various published courses are either drawing on the same findings of research and theory or are unquestioningly repeating what other courses have repeated from some previous poorly based piece of curriculum design. When we find, for example, that a "modern" course is using a syllabus that differs in only minor detail from one used by Berlitz in the 1890s and that does not agree with the findings of substantial research in this area on the frequency of grammar items (George, 1963a, 1963b), then our worst suspicions are justified.

A "method" approach to curriculum design seems to result in some aspects of curriculum design being well thought out and well founded on research but in many aspects being ignored or not well thought out. Richards and Rodgers (1986) have demonstrated this point most clearly in their analysis of methods like Total Physical Response and Silent Way. When such methods are looked at closely, some of them are only suggesting small changes in format and presentation with no changes in the selection of what is to be taught or in how it might be monitored and assessed.

The basis of the problems described above is that *all* the various aspects of curriculum design have not been systematically based on research and theory. This is not because of an absence of suitable research and theory. It is more because of an unwillingness to look at what is already known and to apply it to curriculum design without being distracted by the need to adhere to a method.

The purpose of this chapter is to show that a sensible basis to guide teaching and to help in the design of courses rests on following principles. These principles must be based on research and theory, and must be general enough to allow variety and flexibility in their application to suit the wide range of conditions in which language is taught.

The Twenty Principles

The principles described here are based on a pedagogical perspective, focusing on curriculum design and teacher training. A similar list could be made from a learning perspective. It would also be possible to take a more philosophical stance on principles considering the nature of language, the nature of learning, and the role of culture.

Each principle in the list is there because it is supported by research and theory in any of three fields: second or foreign language learning, first language learning, and general educational research and theory. None of the principles is unique to language teaching, but could equally well apply to the teaching of mathematics or motorcycle maintenance. Their application, however, must draw as much as possible on research and theory within their field of application.

In Table 4.1 each principle is given a name to clarify its focus and to help it be remembered.

Table 4.1 Twenty principles of language teaching

Content and Sequencing

1   **Frequency:** A language course should provide the best possible coverage of language in use through the inclusion of items that occur frequently in the language, so that learners get the best return for their learning effort.

2   **Strategies and autonomy:** A language course should train learners in how to learn a language and how to monitor and be aware of their learning, so that they can become effective and independent language learners.

3   **Spaced retrieval:** Learners should have increasingly spaced, repeated opportunities to retrieve and give attention to wanted items in a variety of contexts.

4   **Language system:** The language focus of a course needs to be on the generalisable features of the language.

5   **Keep moving forward:** A language course should progressively cover useful language items, skills and strategies.

6   **Teachability:** The teaching of language items should take account of the most favourable sequencing of these items and should take account of when the learners are most ready to learn them.

7   **Learning burden:** The course should help learners make the most effective use of previous knowledge.

8   **Interference:** The items in a language course should be sequenced so that items which are learned together have a positive effect on each other for learning and so that interference effects are avoided.

Format and Presentation

1 **Motivation:** As much as possible, the learners should be interested and excited about learning the language and they should come to value this learning.

2 **Four strands:** A course should include a roughly even balance of meaning-focused input, language-focused learning, meaning-focused output and fluency activities.

3 **Comprehensible input:** There should be substantial quantities of interesting comprehensible receptive activity in both listening and reading.

4 **Fluency:** A language course should provide activities aimed at increasing the fluency with which learners can use the language they already know, both receptively and productively.

5 **Output:** The learners should be pushed to produce the language in both speaking and writing over a range of discourse types.

6 **Deliberate learning:** The course should include language-focused learning on the sound system, spelling, vocabulary, grammar and discourse areas.

7 **Time on task:** As much time as possible should be spent using and focusing on the second language.

8 **Depth of processing:** Learners should process the items to be learned as deeply and as thoughtfully as possible.

9 **Integrative motivation:** A course should be presented so that the learners have the most favourable attitudes to the language, to users of the language, to the teacher's skill in teaching the language, and to their chance of success in learning the language.

10 **Learning style:** There should be opportunity for learners to work with the learning material in ways that most suit their individual learning style.

Monitoring and Assessment

1 **Ongoing needs and environment analysis:** The selection, ordering, presentation, and assessment of the material in a language course should be based on a continuing careful consideration of the learners and their needs, the teaching conditions, and the time and resources available.

2 **Feedback:** Learners should receive helpful feedback which will allow them to improve the quality of their language use.

The principles have been divided into three groups. These three groups represent the three major divisions of the central circle in the curriculum design diagram.

The first group of principles deals with content and sequencing. That is, they are concerned with what goes into a language course and the order in which language items appear in the course. The aim of these principles is to make sure that the learners are gaining something useful from the course. It is possible to run a language course which is full of interesting activities and which introduces the learners to new language items, but which provides a very poor return for the time invested in it. This poor return can occur because many of the lessons do not contain anything new to learn, because the new items have very little value in the ordinary use of the language, or

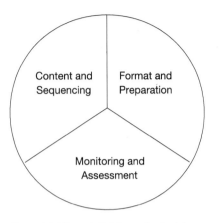

Figure 4.1 The subdivisions of principles.

because they set out interference conditions which result in a step backwards in learning rather than a step forwards.

The second group of principles deals with format and presentation. That is, they are concerned with what actually happens in the classroom and during the learning. Most practically, they relate to the kinds of activities used in the course and the ways in which learners process the course material. It is in this aspect of curriculum design that teachers may have their greatest influence on the course.

The third group of principles deals with monitoring and assessment and to some degree evaluation.

In each of these groups, the principles have been ranked in order of their importance, so that the first principle in the group is the most important of that group, the second principle is the next most important and so on.

It is worth looking at other researchers' lists of principles to see how they differ from the list in Table 4.1, and where they overlap. Useful lists can be found in Ellis (2005), Brown (1993), and Krahnke and Christison (1983).

Content and sequencing

1   **A language course should provide the best possible coverage of language in use through the inclusion of items that occur frequently in the language, so that learners get the best return for their learning effort.**

Many years of research on vocabulary frequency, the frequency of grammatical structures, and English for Special Purposes needs analysis have resulted in a substantial amount of information about the frequency of occurrence of various types of items and of the coverage of text provided by knowledge of the most frequent items. The most striking figures are for vocabulary, with

knowing ten items providing coverage of 25 per cent of written text, 100
items 50 per cent, 1,000 items 70 per cent and 2,000 items over 80 per cent.
It is possible to state a few general rules about frequency, coverage and types
of items.

1   A small number of high-frequency items will cover a large proportion of
     a text.
2   After the few most frequent items are known, a very large number of
     low-frequency items must be known to cover the remainder of the text.
3   Typically, high-frequency items are simple in their form (but not neces-
     sarily in their meaning!).

These rules can be applied to the selection of material for language courses
in the following ways.

1   A language course should give most attention to the high-frequency
     items of the language.
2   Low-frequency items should be dealt with only when the high-
     frequency items have been sufficiently learned. It may be more efficient
     to teach the learners strategies for learning and coping with low-
     frequency items rather than for the teacher to present the low-frequency
     items themselves.

Most courses do not have a sensible selection of frequent items. The selection of items seems to be opportunistic and traditional (based on the Berlitz
course of 1889) rather than principled and with a concern for frequency of
occurrence.

There are arguments against using frequency of occurrence as the *only*
criterion for the selection and ordering of items. But, if frequency is ignored
as a criterion, as George (1972) has shown, lack of a good return for learning
effort is not the only bad result.

A language course can be checked to see if it focuses on the high-frequency
items of the language by comparing it with available frequency lists. For
vocabulary, the list could be West's *General Service List* (1953), the *Cambridge
English Lexicon* (Hindmarsh, 1980) (though this does not provide frequency
figures), or a more recent frequency count like Kučera and Francis (1967)
or Carroll, Davies and Richman (1971). Nation (1990) provides more
information on this.

Verb form frequency can be checked against George's (1963b) verb-form
frequency count.

If a course contains a mixture of high- and low-frequency items that does
not give the best available return for learning effort, a teacher may wish to do
the following things:

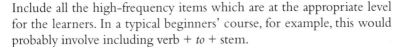
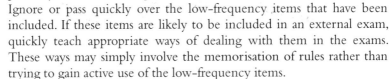

1   Include all the high-frequency items which are at the appropriate level for the learners. In a typical beginners' course, for example, this would probably involve including verb + *to* + stem.

2   Ignore or pass quickly over the low-frequency items that have been included. If these items are likely to be included in an external exam, quickly teach appropriate ways of dealing with them in the exams. These ways may simply involve the memorisation of rules rather than trying to gain active use of the low-frequency items.

3   Provide substantial amounts of practice of the high-frequency items both in and out of class. This can include the use of graded readers, graded listening to stories, guided and free writing, and guided speaking.

2   A language course should train learners in how to learn a language, so that they can become effective and independent language learners.

There has been considerable research on the characteristics of good language learners (Wong Fillmore, 1983; Naiman *et al.*, 1996) and on the strategies that can lead to effective language learning.

Learning and coping strategies can include the following:

> *Learning strategies*
>   Deep processing of language and content
>   vocabulary learning cards
>   word part strategies
>   mnemonic strategies, e.g. keyword
>   predicting
>   notetaking strategies
>   Gaining input
>   peer interaction strategies
>   strategies for controlling the teacher
> *Coping strategies*
>   Inferring vocabulary from context
>   Coping with complex sentences

Cotterall (2000) has suggested five principles for promoting learner autonomy that teachers and curriculum designers should consider. These principles relate to:

- learner goals
- the language learning process
- tasks
- learner strategies
- reflection on learning.

Cotterall and Cohen (2003) demonstrate how these principles can inform a teaching programme in a later account of scaffolding academic writing tasks in a university preparation course. Teachers can aim at developing autonomy within their courses (Cotterall, 1995).

3   Learners should have increasingly spaced, repeated opportunity to give attention to wanted items in a variety of contexts.

The evidence to support this principle comes from studies of the effects of repetition on learning (Kachroo, 1962; Saragi et al., 1978) and the levels of processing theory (Craik and Tulving, 1975).

A few course books check to make sure that they provide repetition but these are exceptional. It is too difficult and time-consuming for an individual teacher without the text available on a computer to do such checking. The simplest and possibly the most useful way to check is to test frequently whether wanted items are learned.

Another possibility is to choose a small group of very useful, but likely to be neglected, items and to keep a note of the repetition of these. The group should probably not contain more than 20 items to make checking manageable.

4   The language focus of a course needs to be on generalisable features of the language system.

This principle does not imply that all of the attention of the teacher and learners is directed towards formal features of the language. What it means is that where attention is directed to language features these features should be predominantly regular features. A command of these features will enable the learners to make "creative" use of the language. That is, to say or write things that they have not met or produced before, and to understand things that they have not met or produced before. If the teacher wants to check that this principle is being applied in a particular lesson, then the teacher should ask this question, "Does today's work help the learners to deal with tomorrow's task?" If the answer is yes, then the principle is being applied. Let us look at a few examples.

1   When explaining or teaching the meaning of an unknown word, the teacher should try to include the underlying concept of the word rather than just focus on the meaning the word has in one particular context. If the learners have some idea of the underlying meaning they will be better able to interpret the word when it occurs in a new context. For example, *sweet* should be explained so that *sweet taste, sweet music* and *a sweet smile* could be related to the explanation.

2   When setting questions to check learners' comprehension of a reading text, it is better to make the questions focus on language features like

cohesive devices, prediction clues, text coping strategies like guessing words from context and sentence interpretation strategies (Nation, 1979), and topic-type schemata (Johns and Davies, 1983; Franken, 1987) rather than on message aspects. Understanding today's text about the communication system of bees will help little towards understanding tomorrow's text about the discovery of penicillin. If however generalisable language features and strategies are focused on today, reading tomorrow's text will be a little easier.

The principle can be applied at all levels of language. The following list indicates areas of focus:

Vocabulary
    high-frequency vocabulary
    underlying meaning
    word parts

Structure
    frequent structures

Discourse
    topic type
    rhetorical structure
    cohesive devices

To check if the principle is being applied in a course, a teacher needs to look at particular lessons to see the learning goal of the lesson and then to evaluate that goal in terms of the uses that the learners will make of the language. This evaluation needs to check that the goal of the lesson is allowing the learner to make the widest possible use of the language features involved.

If a course does not do this well, teachers can change the focus of the course by adapting the exercises and activities.

5 A language course should progressively cover useful language items, skills and strategies.

This principle means that the course should have explicit language teaching goals and that there should be some way of ensuring that there is opportunity for the goals to be reached.

This principle is applied in a variety of ways by different language teaching methods. Aural-oral courses and many others assign particular structures, functions, or vocabulary to particular lessons. Good examples of this can be found in courses like the *Cambridge English Course* which lists the items to be learned in each lesson in its very detailed table of contents.

In order to check if a course is progressively covering useful items, skills and strategies, it is necessary to have lists of useful items to check the course against. This point is taken up in more detail in the section on attainment goals.

The most effective way of making sure that the principle of progressive coverage is applied is to make sure that each learning task has a goal which fits with the plan for the course. Before using a new task teachers should decide what the learning goal of the task is. When doing this it should be remembered that learning goals can include language items, content material (ideas), skill elements including the development of fluency with language and skill items that have already been met before, and discourse features such as text structure or dialogue maintenance strategies. It is often useful to inform learners of the learning goal for the task. If a course includes activities that do not have an obvious learning goal or that have a goal that does not fit the overall goals of the course, it is worth adapting or replacing the task.

An additional way of keeping the course directed towards learning goals is to have regular goal-directed tests. These can have a positive effect on the teaching and learning.

6   The teaching of language items should take account of the most favourable sequencing of these items and should take account of when the learners are most ready to learn them.

Pienemann and his colleagues (1988) and others have conducted research into the sequence in which language items are learned in second language acquisition and into the effects of this sequence on teaching a second language.

The psychological complexity of a structure depends on the amount of rearranging that is needed when the message that the speaker wants to communicate is expressed in language. For example, if a speaker wants to ask someone a question about the arrival of a friend (the message), it is necessary to express this idea in language: "When will John arrive?" This sentence however has a particular word order which has to be learned. We know from studies of young native speakers of English that it is likely that the order of ideas in the message is: "John arrive when?" Between this order and "When will John arrive?" two rearrangements are needed. This means that the sentence "When will John arrive?" is more psychologically complex than "Will John come?" Notice also that the rearrangement needed to produce "Will John come?" is also needed, along with another rearrangement, to produce "When will John come?" The learning of the rearrangement to produce "Will John come?" can be considered a prerequisite to learning "When will John come?"

On the basis of this kind of analysis and on evidence from second-language acquisition studies, Pienemann and Johnston (1987) have made a sequenced list of structures. The sequence of the items in the list is the same as the sequence in which second-language learners learn them.

The sequence of the structures in this list is not simply a result of the number of arrangements required but also the type of rearrangements (initial to final and vice versa, internal to final and vice versa, sentence internal operations).

Pienemann has also looked at this sequence with classroom second-language learners. His conclusion is that "classroom second-language learners follow a fixed order of stages in their acquisition of L2 grammatical forms and, even more importantly, that these forms can only be learned in a particular order" (Pienemann *et al.* 1988: 220). In his later work, Pienemann (1998) developed the Processability Theory in an attempt to formally predict which structures can be processed by learners at a given level of development.

The Teachability Hypothesis simply states *the course of second language development cannot be altered by factors external to the learner*. In this statement "the course of second language development" refers to the list of prerequisites as outlined in Table 4.2. "Factors external to the learner" refers mainly to teaching. So the Teachability Hypothesis says that teaching cannot change the sequence in which the structures are learned. As explained in the previous section, this is because a structure learned at one stage is a necessary prerequisite for later stages. However, teaching can have an effect if it occurs when learners are at the right stage to learn the particular item which is being taught.

Let us look in more detail at the implications of this hypothesis for teaching and curriculum design:

1   A course which does not present the items in this sequence will result in teaching which has little effect.

Table 4.2 Structures in order of acquisition

Structure	Example
1. single words, formulae	how are you?
2. SVO, SVO?	*The tea is hot?
3. ADVERB PREPOSING	*Yesterday I work
4. DO FRONTING	Does he work?
5. TOPICALIZATION	This I like
6. NEG + V(don't)	*He don't eat meat
7. PSEUDO-INVERSION	Where is my purse?
8. YES/NO-INVERSION	*Have he seen it?
9. PARTICLE SHIFT	*He turn the radio on
10. V-"TO"-V	We like to sing
11. 3RD-SG-S	She comes home
12. DO-2ND	They did not buy anything
13. AUX-2ND	Where has he seen you?
14. ADV-LY	They spoke gently
15. Q-TAG	It's expensive, isn't it?
16. ADV-VP	He has often heard this

2 It is important to know what stage in the sequence a learner is at because, to be effective, teaching has to be directed at the next stage.

Ellis (1985) includes most of these ideas in his 11 hypotheses about second-language acquisition. Research by Eckman, Bell and Nelson (1988) concludes that the order of grammatical items in the sequence need not be finely detailed for teaching purposes. They found that by teaching relative clauses in one position in the sentence this learning was generalised to other positions.

The importance of all this research is that it provides a theoretical, logical and testable basis for syllabus construction, and that it indicates an effective, though restricted, role for teaching. The research is still ongoing (Gold-schneider and DeKeyser, 2005), with continuing debate about, for example, the influence of first-language background on acquisition order (Izumi and Isahara, 2005). We still have only an elementary list of sequenced grammatical items to guide teaching and do not have easily applied tests to indicate the learners' stage in the sequence of development (Pienemann *et al.*, 1988).

7 The course should help the learners to make the most effective use of previous knowledge.

Much of the previous knowledge that is brought to second-language learning comes from the learners' first language. The effect of this knowledge on second-language learning has been a matter of debate with some arguing that the first language has a major effect on second-language learning (Lado, 1957; Ringbom, 1987) and others arguing that second-language learning like first-language learning occurs without the influence of other languages. Part of the reason for the debate has been that second-language learning occurs in a variety of circumstances. Where the language is learned as a foreign language with little opportunity for contact and use outside the classroom, the effect of the first language is more noticeable. Where the classroom is only one of a range of sources for second-language input as with second-language learning of English in countries such as New Zealand, Australia, Britain and the United States, first-language influence is less noticeable.

There is plenty of evidence however that aspects of the first language can help learning. This help can occur at all levels within the language, with pronunciation, grammar, vocabulary and discourse. It can also occur with aspects of language skill and with content knowledge.

The principle is most obvious in relation to vocabulary. A splendid example of this occurs in the course book for learning Italian for English-speaking learners entitled *Teach Yourself Italian* (L. Vellaccio and M. Elston, Hodder and Stoughton, 1986, pp. 6–7). From the earliest lessons of the course each lesson contains a reading text in Italian which is at a level far beyond the material presented for spoken production. The vocabulary of the reading text, however, has been carefully chosen so that it is cognate with English vocabulary. As a result the reading is easily manageable. A few questions at the beginning of the text are designed to stimulate relevant knowledge. Here is an example.

Before reading this passage, look at the questions carefully, since they will give you some clues about the subject matter.

1   What sort of activities can an Italian engage in when he goes to a square?
2   What buildings might you find around the square?
3   Which Italian cities are mentioned as famous for their squares?
4   Which square has fountains on either side of it?
5   What is noteworthy about the square in Florence?

La piazza

In Italia la piazza rappresenta una parte integrante della vita, e una bella status o una bella fontana contribuiscono spesso alla sua bellezza. Per un caffè, per un appuntamento, per una discussione o per un po' di musica, un italiano va generalmente in piazza dove c'e spesso un teatro famoso, un monumento, una status importante, un bar o un ristorante con un'orchestra. Famosa in tutto il mondo e Piazza San Pietro a Roma, con il Vaticano e con una fontana a destra e una fontana a sinistra. A Venezia, Piazza San Marco e stupenda, e a Firenze Piazzale Michelangelo offre un magnifico panorama di tutta la citta.

If cognate vocabulary is included in a course, learners can make a lot of progress in a short time which is good for motivation. Further information on the relationship between vocabulary learning and previous knowledge can be found in Nation 1990, Chapter 3.

8   The items in a language course should be sequenced so that items which are learned together have a positive effect on each other for learning, and so that interference effects are avoided.

Research has shown that items which have loose indirect connections with each other (indirect free associates) are learned more effectively if they are learned at the same time. Items which have strong meaning relationships (opposites, near synonyms, free associates) interfere with each other and thus make learning more difficult (George, 1962; Higa, 1963; Nation, 2000). In view of this evidence and the very large body of evidence on paired associate learning, it is surprising that courses still present opposites and alternative expressions of the same idea (near synonyms) together. Unfortunately the order of items within the course reflects the associations in the curriculum designer's mind rather than what will help learning.

The easiest solution to this sequencing problem is to let the occurrence of items in naturally occurring spoken or written texts determine the order in which they occur in the course. This takes the control of sequencing away from the curriculum designer and thus avoids the word association that the curriculum designer may bring to sequencing.

An additional solution is to check the sequence of items in the course, particularly to see that strongly related items are not presented together. A further solution is to let frequency of occurrence guide sequencing. West (1955), in an interesting article related to this topic, referred to the tendency of putting related items together to teach as "catenizing". Some examples of catenizing are teaching all the parts of the body together, teaching a range of colours together, teaching the series of numbers together. West criticises this tendency of curriculum designers from several aspects but he focused mainly on frequency. In a very sensible, but controversial, example he showed that the frequency of occurrence of numbers is very different. The frequency of occurrence of *ten, one* and *five* in normal language use is much higher than the frequency of occurrence of *seven, nine* and *eleven*. If frequency was followed as the criterion for sequencing, then *ten, one* and *five* would be presented earlier in a course than *seven, nine* and *eleven*. This frequency-based approach to grading would help to avoid most interference problems. For example, with opposites such as *hot* and *cold*, one item is much more frequent than the other.

If a course book presents closely related items together, a teacher can attempt to overcome this by helping the learners master the most useful of these before the pairs or groups of items are met. So if *hot* and *cold* are presented together in the course book, the teacher can help the learners master *hot* before the book introduces *hot* and *cold*. If one item in a pair is already well known, interference is unlikely to occur. The longer the time between learning for example the two items in a pair of opposites, the better. The more secure the learning of the first item, the less chance there is of interference when the second item is met.

The general rule which underlies this kind of interference can be stated in this way. *If two items have some similarities in meaning or in form and yet are different in some ways from each other, and are presented for learning at the same time, the similarities between them will encourage their association and the differences between them will interfere with each other.* Let us look at an example to see how this rule works. Here is a particularly difficult example from the Indonesian language. On some toilets the men's and women's toilets are distinguished by the words *putra* (for *men*) and *putri* (for *women*). Let us list the similarities:

1   Similar form   :   *putr*
2   Related meaning   :   they both refer to sex
3   They are presented for learning at the same time.

These similarities encourage the association of these items in the minds of the learners.

Let us now list the differences:

1   Different ending   :   *i*   *a*
2   Different meaning   :   *men*   *women*

These differences will interfere with each other so that most learners will be very uncertain about whether the *i* ending indicates *men* or indicates *women*. The results of such interference can be embarrassing. One way of trying to remedy it once it has occurred is to find some mnemonic trick to distinguish them, for example the *i* of *putri* rhymes with *she*. Most examples are not as difficult as this one, that is they do not share similarities of both form and meaning. However, interference of related items can be easily avoided with sensible curriculum design and teaching.

Format and presentation

1   As much as possible, the learners should be interested and excited about learning the language and they should come to value this learning.

This principle stresses the importance of the learners' attitude to what they are studying. Motivation is a very important determinant of the amount of time, involvement and effect that learners give to learning. The best motivation is "intrinsic", springing from within the learner, rather than "extrinsic", coming from some outside integrative or instrumental reward. Intrinsic motivation can develop as a result of extrinsic motivation. Learning for reasons of gain can result in a genuine love of learning and involvement in the activity.

If learners are not interested in learning, it is worthwhile beginning by looking at ways to attract them and involve them in learning.

1   Make the subject matter of the lessons relevant and interesting to them. Surveys of wants and attitudes can help gather information to guide this.
2   Give the learners some control and decision-making over what they do. A negotiated or partly negotiated syllabus (see Chapter 10) is one way to do this.
3   Set tasks with clear outcomes and with a high possibility of the learners completing them successfully.

4 Set many short achievement tests to encourage the learners to work and to show them that they can be successful learners.

5 Show the learners how to keep records of their progress so that they can see their continuing success. These records can include speed reading graphs, standardised dictation scores, number of graded readers completed and movement through the levels, scores on split-information tasks and writing-accuracy graphs.

6 Help the learners become autonomous learners (Crabbe, 1993; Cotterall, 2000) by explaining the rationale and goals of particular classroom activities, by the teacher modelling autonomous behaviour and by learners modelling autonomous behaviour for each other.

7 Reward learners' efforts through publication in a class newsletter, through praise and through attention from the teacher.

8 Use tasks that contain built-in challenges such as competition, time pressure, memory and hidden puzzle-like solutions (Nation, 1989a).

9 Encourage learners to set achievable and realistic individual goals (Boon, 2007).

2   A course should include a roughly even balance of the four strands of meaning-focused input, language-focused learning (output) meaning-focused output and fluency activities.

This principle is concerned with the relative amount of time given to the four main strands of a language course – meaning-focused input, language-focused learning, meaning-focused output and fluency development.

The rough rule of thumb is that on average roughly equal time should be given to each of these four strands in the total language experience of the learner. That means that time in class and out of class can be considered if, during these times, the learner is gaining appropriate language activity that can be classified as fitting into these strands. For example, if a learner is doing a lot of graded reading outside class time and is gaining truly comprehensible input outside of class time, this would mean that the time allocation for meaning-focused input could be met outside class and so the time in class could be given to language-focused learning, meaning-focused output and fluency development.

At different stages of a language course the proportions of the strands may change, but not by a large amount. In the early stages of a language course about 30 per cent of the time may be given to meaning-focused input, about 30 per cent to language-focused learning, about 20 per cent to meaning-focused output and about 20 per cent to fluency development.

At an advanced stage it may become too difficult to separate meaning-focused input from meaning-focused output ("One person's output is another person's input") and about 50 per cent of time may be given to them. Language-focused learning may get around 20 per cent, while fluency development may get 30 per cent.

It is worth checking the relative proportions of these four strands to make sure that one strand is not dominating the course. Language-focused learning dominates classroom activity in some countries. In others every effort is made to exclude it. A balance is preferable.

Some classroom activities or language contact outside the classroom may not fit into any of these four strands, for example listening to foreign language television with minimal comprehension. Such activities should not be included in the time allocation.

If a course does not contain a suitable balance of the four strands, it may be necessary to change the nature of existing activities, convince teachers of the need to include neglected activities, and inform teachers and learners of the defining characteristics of the strands. Some teachers may think that an activity is meaning-focused when it is really a language-focused activity.

Balancing the four strands is a very important part of curriculum design. The neglect or over-emphasis of a strand is a major failing in many language courses.

3   There should be substantial quantities of interesting comprehensible receptive activity in both listening and reading.

In a very practical and well-conducted experiment, Elley and Mangubhai (1981) replaced part of drill-based English lessons for Fijian learners of English with self-directed reading of interesting children's books. Eight months later, with four English classes per week, it was found that the learners in the experimental group had made 15 months' progress on a variety of proficiency measures of English. The large amounts of reading that the learners did was not in addition to their usual English course. It replaced about one-third of the usual course. Other experiments, although not as large-scale or as well-designed as the Elley and Mangubhai study, indicate a similar effect for large quantities of listening. The theoretical justification for such an approach to language learning rests on the idea that learners need to build up and are capable of building up an understanding of the language system before they are called on to produce language (Nord, 1980).

The requirements of such an approach to learning are that the learners have access to large quantities of interesting reading or listening material at a roughly suitable level and that although the use of such material may be monitored by the teacher it is not the excuse for quantities of carefully checked follow-up exercises. Basically the learners read and listen for pleasure. Day and Bamford (2002) suggest ten principles to guide this approach to reading. In the Elley and Mangubhai study the learners' interest in reading was stimulated by using the shared book technique where the teacher reads an enlarged copy of an attractive book with the class. The Elley and Mangubhai study used children's books that were popular with native speakers of English. Incidentally, the ones that proved popular with the learners were ones that native speakers also find interesting. There are hundreds of titles of graded readers now available that are written and presented in attractive ways. Useful surveys of graded reader schemes can be found in Day and Bamford (1998) and Hill (1997, 2001, 2008). Further information can also be accessed through the Extensive Reading website at http://www.extensivereading.net/er/.

There are various ways in which teachers can build up class sets (not all of the same title) of reading texts. Here are some of them:

1   Seek funding from an embassy of an English-speaking country to finance such a library. A request like this has more chance of being successful if it contains a list of the required books, their total cost, and information about where they can be obtained.
2   Get each learner to buy one text each and then organise a system for temporarily exchanging the books amongst the members of the class so that each learner can read the books belonging to other learners in the class.
3   Build up a reading box of material taken from newspapers, written by learners, written by a group of co-operating teachers, and put on cards or in plastic bags.
4   Place a book in a glass-covered case. Each day turn one page so that the learners can read more of the story each day. (We are grateful to Tony Howe for this suggestion.)

Elley (1989) also conducted research on reading stories aloud to learners to see what effect this would have on vocabulary learning. He found that there was substantial learning of vocabulary from listening especially if the teacher briefly singled out a word for attention by writing it on the blackboard or by quickly giving its meaning.

Advocates of the comprehension approach to language learning (Winitz, 1981) and the natural approach (Terrell, 1982) stress the importance of large quantities of suitably graded listening. There are several ways of incorporating this into a language course.

1   Set aside a regular time in each language class for listening to a short story or a continuing story read by the teacher.
2   Provide taped stories that learners can take home or listen to in class.
3   Use quantity-based listening techniques like listening to pictures (McComish, 1982), listen and draw, padded questions (Nation and Newton, 2009).

It is easy to check if a course is providing enough interesting quantity-based receptive activity simply by calculating what proportion of class time is spent on such activity and by adding this to the amount of time learners *regularly* do such activity at home. It may be useful to get another teacher to calculate this for a class to make sure that the class teacher is not misled. At least 25 per cent of class time should be spent on such activity unless the learners are clearly doing a large amount outside of class time. This proportion could be greater in the early stages of learning.

If a course does not provide enough quantity-based activity, it is worth looking carefully at the causes of this. Here are some possible causes:

1   The teacher is not aware or convinced of the value of such activity.
2   The teacher does not know how to encourage such activity.
3   The teacher does not have the necessary reading or listening material.
4   The teacher has not set up organisational systems to make sure that such activity runs smoothly.

All of these causes can be overcome.

4   A language course should provide activities aimed at increasing the fluency with which the learners can use the language they already know, both receptively and productively.

Fluency is a part of the skill goal of language learning. Fluency activities do not aim to teach new language items but aim to give the learner ready access to what is already known.

The importance of fluency in language use is highlighted in first-language research on the relationship between vocabulary learning and reading comprehension. One of the several possible explanations for a lack of success of many studies in showing that pre-teaching vocabulary results in improved comprehension is that it is not sufficient just to know the meanings of new words in a text. It is also necessary to be able to retrieve these meanings quickly and fluently when their forms are met in the text. Many learners of English as a foreign language experience this difficulty. Their language knowledge of vocabulary and sentence patterns may be substantial, the result of several years' learning, but their ability to access and use this knowledge fluently is extremely low.

Fluency is often contrasted with accuracy (Brumfit, 1984), and is seen as a way of making consciously studied material become available for less conscious use. Ellis (1987) sees fluency activities as a way of making features of learners' "careful" style of language use become available in other less-monitored styles.

Fluency activities depend on several conditions to achieve their goal. In the 4/3/2 technique, learners work in pairs with one acting as the speaker and the other as listener. The speaker talks for four minutes on a topic while her partner listens. Then the pairs change with each speaker giving the same information to a new partner in three minutes, followed by a further change and a two-minute talk.

From the point of view of fluency, this activity has these important features. First, the user is encouraged to process a large quantity of language. In 4/3/2 this is done by allowing the speaker to perform without interruption and by having the speaker make three deliveries of the talk. Second, the demands of the activity are limited to a much smaller set than would occur in most uncontrolled learning activities. This can be done by control by the teacher as is the case in most receptive fluency activities such as reading graded readers or listening to stories, or can be done by choice, planning or repetition by the learner. In the 4/3/2 activity the speaker chooses the ideas, language items and way of organising the talk. The four- and three-minute deliveries allow the speaker to bring these aspects well under control, so that fluency can become the learning goal of the activity. Third, the learner is helped to reach a high level of performance. Usually this level would be measured in terms of quantity and rate of production rather than quality. However the research by Nation (1989a) and Arevart and Nation (1991) shows that, in the case of 4/3/2, increase in rate is accompanied by improvements in the quality of the talk as measured by hesitations, grammatical accuracy and grammatical complexity. This is a very important effect of fluency activities. Improvement in fluency is not simply improvement in speed of access. Speed of access to be of value must be able to occur under a variety of conditions and contexts and this means that the development of fluency will also involve the enrichment of knowledge of language items as known items are processed in new situations.

Fluency is important in the receptive skills of listening and reading as well as in the productive skills of speaking and writing. Table 4.3 indicates how fluency activities can be made across the four skills.

A teacher can check to see if a course gives sufficient attention to fluency by looking at the amount of time given to fluency activities.

Research on vocabulary statistics shows that only a relatively small amount of knowledge is needed for successful language use. It is important that this knowledge is available for use and therefore a part of class time should be given to fluency activities. Brumfit (1985) suggests that "Right from the beginning of the course, about a third of the total time could be spent on this sort of fluency activity, and the proportion will inevitably increase as time goes on."

How can fluency activities be included in a course? If fluency activities are included in each lesson and make use of new language items taught in that lesson, then these items should occur at a low density in the fluency material. In reading material this means that at least 85 per cent of the words (Dowhower, 1989) should be very familiar to the learners. A second

Table 4.3 Features of fluency tasks

Features	Ways of producing the features
Quantity (processing a large amount of language)	Set a goal of time or quantity
Limited demands (focusing only on fluency without having to cope with too many new language items or unfamiliar ideas)	Learner control: choice of topic, language, organisation Teacher control: controlled or supported material
Preparation, planning, seeking feedback	Set a goal
Repetition by the learner	A new audience A new goal
High rate of processing	Limited time A running record, e.g. a graph

alternative is to include fluency activities in each lesson that make use of items learned several days or weeks before. It is likely that the optimal spacing of fluency activities agrees with Pimsleur's (1967) memory schedule, where repetitions are spaced further and further apart. A third alternative is to periodically give large blocks of time to fluency activities. This suggestion corresponds to Brumfit's (1985) "syllabus with holes in it". These holes or gaps are times when no new material is presented and there are fluency-directed activities. Extensive reading for fluency development, rather than for language growth (Hu and Nation, 2000), is an example of such an activity.

This alternative corresponds most closely to Ellis's (1987) suggestion of a parallel syllabus approach. A parallel syllabus has "two separate strands, one for 'products' and the other for tasks, each graded and sequenced separately" (p. 188).

One of the biggest obstacles to fluency in a foreign language situation is the lack of opportunity outside the class room to use the foreign language to communicate. As teachers we should believe that every problem can be solved through informed and imaginative pedagogy. Teachers can not only help learners learn the language but can also help them reach a high degree of fluency in using it.

5   The learners should be pushed to produce the language in both speaking and writing over a range of discourse types.

While no writer about language learning would deny the value of large quantities of comprehensible input, there are several who say that it is not sufficient in itself for language learning. While input is undoubtedly very important and should precede output, there are strong arguments for making sure that learners are given the chance to produce language. Swain (1985) argues that the language knowledge needed to comprehend language is not the same as the language knowledge needed to produce language. For example, a learner of English needs only minimal knowledge of the article and preposition systems of English in order to gain a satisfactory understanding of spoken or written English. If the learner wants to speak or write however, then there are decisions about the choice of articles (or their omission) and the choice of appropriate prepositions that need to be made. These decisions require much more knowledge for language production than they do for language reception. Swain describes this difference as having to move "from a purely semantic analysis of the language to a syntactic analysis of it" (1985: 252).

There are clearly other differences too. Speaking and writing require the retrieval of form and the development of productive skills.

Biber's (1990) research shows the different occurrences and clusterings of formal features in different text types. To gain a balanced coverage of the formal features of the language it is necessary to make use of language across a representative range of discourse types.

Courses which aim at all four skills can be checked to see that about 25 per cent of the total learning time is given to activities involving language production. It is also worthwhile checking that either writing or speaking is not being neglected at the expense of the other. It is also worth checking that learners are having to produce language in both formal and informal settings, for transactional and interactional purposes and in a variety of social roles and power relationships. Munby (1978: 72) provides a useful list of equal and unequal relationships.

6   The course should include language-focused learning in the sound system, vocabulary, grammar and discourse areas.

Language-focused learning can occur when the learners' attention is on language items not because the learner wants to receive or communicate a message in a normal way but because the learner wants to learn some part of the language system.

Language-focused attention can be directed towards the sound system, the spelling system, the vocabulary, the grammar system and discourse patterns.

Reviews of research on language-focused learning (Long, 1988; Ellis, 1990; Spada, 1997) show that some language-focused learning in a language course has the following effects:

1   It can speed up learning.
2   It can help learners overcome barriers to their language development.
3   It can have a positive effect on meaning-focused learning.

In general, courses containing appropriate amounts and types of language-focused learning achieve better results than courses which do not include such learning.

Language-focused learning requires certain conditions to be effective.

1   The language features focused on must be reasonably simple.
2   The language features should not be influenced by developmental sequences or, if they are, the learners should be at the appropriate stage of development to benefit from the attention.
3   If the purpose of the learning is to make learning from meaning-focused input more effective, then it is sufficient to raise learners' awareness of the item and its use (Ellis, 1995).

The following activities are all examples of language-focused learning:

Dictation
Listening for particular words or phrases
Repetition and substitution drills
Memorizing dialogues and poems
Analysing cohesive devices
Learning to guess from context clues
Sentence-completion activities
Sentence combining and transformation
Guided composition
Distinguishing minimal pairs
Focusing on sounds, intonation and stress
Learning vocabulary on cards
Parsing
Re-arranging words in the right order to make sentences
Getting feedback on errors

Most courses need to reduce the amount of language-focused learning rather than increase it. Generally it should take up about 25 per cent of the time in a language course.

For most items, language-focused practice does not lead directly to the implicit knowledge of language that is needed for normal communication. It is therefore very important in a language course that language-focused learning is seen as a support rather than a substitute for learning through meaning-focused activities.

7   As much time as possible should be spent using and focusing on the second language.

This principle is based on the research finding that one of the best indicators of how much will be learned is how long the learners spend on appropriate learning activities. The more time learners spend on language learning, the more they learn. The principle gains some support from the correlation between length of time spent living in a country where the foreign language is spoken and proficiency in the language.

Research on the proportion of time the teacher uses the foreign language in the classroom shows that (1) teachers have an inaccurate idea of how much information they give in the foreign language and how much in the first language, (2) learners are not worried by having all the lessons completely in the foreign language, (3) if there is a policy to maximise the use of the foreign language and if teachers receive some training on how to do this, then teachers can devote all of the class time to the foreign language without having to make use of the first language.

Research on individual differences in language learning (Wong Fillmore, 1982) indicates that learners who are oriented to the source of language input tend to learn a lot of the language. In Wong Fillmore's study most of the input came from the teacher and so children who were adult-oriented learned more. In a classroom where the only common language shared by the learners was the second language, peer-oriented learners would presumably learn more.

How can a teacher check to see that learners are spending sufficient time "on task"? The usual way of measuring this in an experiment is to observe particular learners at set time intervals, say every 30 seconds during a lesson, and to note on a schedule if they are on task or not. It is difficult for a teacher to do formal observation of this kind while handling the lesson, so it may be useful to have a colleague come in and observe a few learners, or at least for the teacher to note briefly after each lesson how much time was spent with learners actually reading, writing, speaking or usefully listening.

If the learners are not spending a lot of time on task, there could be several reasons for this:

1   The teacher uses such a variety of techniques and lesson formats that learners are uncertain about what they should do. If the organisation of each lesson was more predictable and if familiar procedures or techniques were more regularly used, the learners could get on with the job.

2   The tasks that the learners are asked to do do not interest them. If the content of a task is not attractive to the learners and it cannot be changed, the teacher can try the following things:

   (a)   Add a competitive or a score-keeping element to the task. Learners may compete against each other or against their previous achievement. Graphs are one way of recording this achievement. For example, when doing a cloze exercise, the class can be divided into half. The learners in each half do the exercise individually, and then reach a group consensus on the answers. The correct score of each half of the class is then compared.

(b) Explain the learning goal and the way this goal is achieved to the learners. One way of classifying learning tasks is on a blind–informed–controlling scale. In a blind task, learners do the task without knowing why they are doing it and what it is supposed to achieve. In an informed task, the learners understand the goals of the task. In a controlling task, the learners know how to manipulate the task to suit their own requirements. For example, when doing a cloze exercise learners can be told of the role of cloze in developing prediction skills. Where the learners could not guess an item they could note what they could predict, such as part of speech, positive or negative meaning, cause of prediction difficulty.

(c) Provide a choice of activities by developing equivalents to a reading box for other aspects of language learning.

3   Individual learners have difficulty maintaining attention on one task. Such learners may need some special practice in remaining on task. As they often tend to interfere with the work of other learners, it is worth making some special supervised tasks for these learners and rewarding them for increased attention.

The "time on task" principle is important at all levels. Even with absolute beginners there are many opportunities to establish the target language as the main classroom language, by using it for greetings and farewells, instructions and other naturally recurring interactions (Davis and Pearse, 2000). This will help the learners to view the target language as a means of communication rather than an object of study. Also where English is learned for specific purposes, which may involve solely the development of a reading knowledge, substantial time needs to be spent on the reading skill.

8   Learners should process the items to be learned as deeply and as thoughtfully as possible.

The "levels of processing" hypothesis (Craik and Lockhart, 1972) proposes that the single most important factor in learning is the quality of mental activity in the mind of the learners at the moment that learning takes place. Items that are repeated without thoughtful attention will not be learned as quickly or retained as long as those that are related to past experience, result in some meaning-directed effort, or are thoughtfully analysed. Another way of expressing this principle is to say that "the quantity of learning depends on the quality of mental activity at the moment of learning".

Many teachers apply this principle without really being aware of it. They do it to keep the attention and interest of their learners. Applying the principle only requires a small change to normal teaching procedures. Here are some examples:

1   Instead of translating the meaning of a useful unknown word, the teacher describes its meaning using foreign-language explanations. So, to describe *allow* the teacher might say, "I will not allow my children to eat dirty food". While listening, the learners have to find the appropriate first-language translation. So instead of the teacher providing the translation and the learners making little effort, the learners make the effort and work to find the translation. This also gives the teacher useful feedback. Variations of this technique are described in Nation (1978).

2   While doing a substitution table activity, the teacher writes the items on the board. The teacher gives a spoken model and points to the appropriate parts of the table. The learners repeat. As the exercise continues, the teacher gradually rubs out words and phrases from the table so that the learners are repeating parts from memory.

3   Before the learners read a text the teacher shows them the first sentence of each paragraph. The learners look at each sentence and discuss it in groups in order to anticipate what will come next in the paragraph. After guessing, they then read the paragraph. Reading thus becomes a more thoughtful and informed activity.

It is possible to check how much a course applies the levels of processing principle by looking at the various exercise types that it uses and ranking them according to the depth of processing they require from the learners. Most courses regularly make use of only a small range of techniques and these are the ones that should be considered rather than the "one-off" activities. It is not straightforward to rank diverse activities according to a single scale of depth but it is worth doing so, particularly if one considers that each activity used takes time that might be more profitably spent doing some other activity. The following scale for depth of processing (Table 4.4) is offered as a starting point for such ranking. The learners' level of proficiency and the relevance of their first-language knowledge will have a strong effect on the positions of items on the scale.

If a course does not allow for adequate depth of processing, a teacher can make up for this lack by making use of a new range of teaching techniques

Table 4.4 Continuum of depth of processing with techniques

	Type of processing	*Techniques*
Superficial processing	formal repetition	drill
	normal language processing at $l+l$	reading graded readers
	deduction to examples	relating to experience
	reproduction involving long-term memory	dicto-comp
	inductive analysis	What is it?
	prediction	self-questioning scales
Deep processing	use of mnemonic devices	keyword

that encourage such processing, and by training the learners to apply depth of processing strategies to their own learning.

Here is a list of useful learner strategies that add quality to vocabulary learning:

1 Mnemonic devices such as the use of word parts or the keyword technique
2 The guessing from context strategy
3 The use of cards with the foreign-language word on one side and the first-language translation on the other.

9 The course should be presented so that the learners have the most favourable attitudes to the language, users of the language, use of the language, the teacher's skill in teaching the language and their chances of success in learning the language.

Recent research and thinking about second-language learning have given an important role to "affective" factors. Affective factors refer to feelings and attitudes and include such things as motivation, shyness about speaking a strange language (or "language anxiety"), opinions about native speakers of the second language and attitudes towards the teacher. If learners have negative attitudes towards the language and its users, or if they feel personally threatened by having to use the language, this will make it difficult for them to progress in learning the language. ·

Some of these affective factors may be influenced by the teacher and by the way the course is organised. For example, if the learners are confident users of current technology but the teacher does not make use of this technology, learners may develop unfavourable attitudes to the course. This may be one reason for the teacher to adapt the course book (see Chapter 11).

Among the range of motivation factors, the two that have received the most attention from researchers are integrative motivation and instrumental motivation. While the interests of researchers have not always had immediate relevance to teachers, Dörnyei (2001) addresses the question of how teachers can motivate learners and suggests that motivational teaching practice has four principal aspects:

1 Creating basic motivational conditions
2 Generating initial student motivation
3 Maintaining and promoting motivation
4 Encouraging positive retrospective self-evaluation.

Dörnyei identifies specific strategies and techniques for each of these aspects (Figure 4.2). A number of these can be seen operating in a classroom where the teacher sets up small groups in which each member has a clearly defined

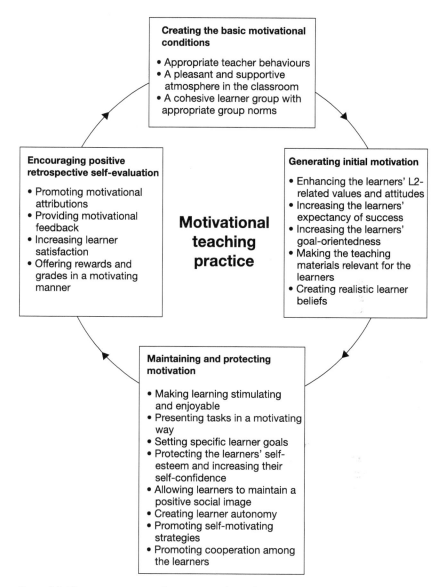

Creating the basic motivational conditions

- Appropriate teacher behaviours
- A pleasant and supportive atmosphere in the classroom
- A cohesive learner group with appropriate group norms

Generating initial motivation

- Enhancing the learners' L2-related values and attitudes
- Increasing the learners' expectancy of success
- Increasing the learners' goal-orientedness
- Making the teaching materials relevant for the learners
- Creating realistic learner beliefs

Maintaining and protecting motivation

- Making learning stimulating and enjoyable
- Presenting tasks in a motivating way
- Setting specific learner goals
- Protecting the learners' self-esteem and increasing their self-confidence
- Allowing learners to maintain a positive social image
- Creating learner autonomy
- Promoting self-motivating strategies
- Promoting cooperation among the learners

Encouraging positive retrospective self-evaluation

- Promoting motivational attributions
- Providing motivational feedback
- Increasing learner satisfaction
- Offering rewards and grades in a motivating manner

Motivational teaching practice

Figure 4.2 The components of motivational teaching practice in the L2 classroom (Dörnyei, 2001: 29).

role (creating the basic motivational conditions). The groups are given a task with a desired outcome, which the learners can expect to achieve through working together (generating initial motivation). This in turn promotes co-operation among the learners and makes learning stimulating and enjoyable (maintaining and protecting motivation). The teacher moves among the groups, offering advice and encouragement as they work towards the goal, and the learners experience feelings of satisfaction when they complete the task (encouraging positive retrospective self-evaluation).

10 There should be opportunity for learners to work with the learning material in ways that most suit their individual learning style.

Learners approach activities in a variety or ways depending on their personality, their previous learning experience, their expectations of how they will be tested on what they learn, and their view of the nature of the learning task.

Not all learners will feel comfortable with the same way of learning, and learners may learn more effectively if they can choose a style of learning that most suits them. An effectively designed language course allows for these individual differences and provides choices and flexibility in the way activities can be done. The following list suggests some of the choices that could be made available:

- group size: learning individually or with other learners
- speed and intensity: learning at a slow, thoughtful pace or at a fast, intensive pace
- medium: learning through aural input or written input
- representation of information: learning through language or through pictorial or diagrammatic representation
- mental process: learning holistically or through analysis
- understanding: learning through doing or through understanding
- use of first language: learning through translation or through the second language
- source of control: learning through activities planned and provided by the teacher or through self-access and negotiated procedures.

A course should take account of individual differences and learning styles in two ways: (1) by providing opportunities for learners to work to their strengths, and (2) by providing opportunity and training for learners to try other ways of learning. An effective language course not only produces effective learning but also produces effective learners.

Monitoring and assessment

1   **The selection, gradation, presentation and assessment of the material in a language course should be based on a careful consideration of the learners and their needs, the teaching conditions, and the time and resources available.**

This principle stresses the importance of doing environment analysis and needs analysis during the planning of a course.

2   **Learners should receive helpful feedback which will allow them to improve the quality of their language use.**

Feedback is a term from communication theory. After a message has been sent, the sender may receive information about various aspects of the message. Did the message say what it was supposed to say? Was it clearly received? Did it bring about the required action or response in the person who received it? All this information going back to the sender is called feedback. The receiver of a message may also get feedback about the degree of success of his understanding of the message.

Feedback from language use can come from the sender herself, from the people who receive the message, and from an observer of the communication process. Let us look at each of these three sources.

1   Learners can improve the quality of their language use by monitoring themselves. As Krashen (1981) has observed, this monitoring requires certain conditions. These conditions can exist during most reading and writing activities, and in the "careful" style of spoken language use (Ellis, 1987). Teachers can help learners with this monitoring in several ways. One way is to provide the learners with monitoring goals, namely particular points to monitor. This can be done simply as a suggestion, "When you present your talk, be particularly careful about . . .", or it can be a list or scale of points to look for in written work. Hillocks (1984) found that the use of monitoring scales had a significant effect on the improvement of written work. Another way that teachers can help learners with monitoring is to model the monitoring process for them. So, as well as providing lists of items for learners to monitor, the teacher can spend some time demonstrating the use of the lists on sample material.

2   Learners can provide helpful feedback in their communication with each other. One process involving feedback which is given great importance in some theories of second-language learning is called "negotiation". Negotiation occurs when the sender and receiver of a message exchange information about problems they have with the sending or receiving of the message. For example, the speaker may not be

able to find the right word needed to say something and may appeal to the receiver for help. Or, the receiver may not understand a word or expression in the message and may ask the sender to repeat or explain. Some negotiation like this can lead to language learning and to improvement in the skills of language use.

3   An observer of the communication process can provide useful feedback to those involved. Often this observer is the teacher. This feedback can focus on the result or product of communication, or it can focus on the process of communication.

Focus on the product of communication, particularly in reading and writing, can have a positive effect on language use. Feedback about the process of communication can bring about valuable improvement in formal speaking, and in writing (Franken, 1987). The giving and receiving of feedback, usually from all three sources, is an integral part of the process approach to writing. A key point for teachers to remember, however, is that the learners are required to do something with the feedback they receive (Chandler, 2003).

So far we have looked at focusing feedback on qualitative aspects of language. There is some evidence that providing positive feedback about quantity of language use can result in qualitative improvement. Feedback can have both positive and negative effects. The negative effects of feedback are reluctance by the learner to use the language because of fear of error (or feedback!), an overconcern with the form of the message so that the content of the message suffers, and the use of avoidance strategies so that language use is restricted to those parts of the language the learner feels secure with. It is thus very important that feedback is provided in ways that avoid these negative effects.

What can a teacher do to check that there is sufficient feedback in a course? The following checklist is intended as a guide to do this:

1   Do the learners have regular opportunities for careful language production?
2   Do the learners have appropriate checklists or scales to monitor their written work? Has the teacher set up a peer checking system to make sure that the scales are used?
3   Does the teacher have a realistic list of aspects of language use that learners can be encouraged to monitor?
4   Do the learners regularly do information gap or opinion gap activities which encourage peer negotiation?
5   Do the learners wish to receive feedback about their language use from the teacher?
6   Does the teacher make use of a process approach to writing and formal speaking?

7   Is the teacher aware of the aspects of the writing and speaking processes where the learners most need help?
8   Does the teacher make regular use of an informative and acceptable marking system for written work?
9   Do learners understand the marking system and make use of the feedback?

Using the List of Principles

The previous discussion of the twenty principles has attempted to explain the principles and to indicate their application in curriculum design. The list of principles however has a much wider range of uses.

1   It can be used to guide the design of language teaching courses and lessons.
2   It can be used to evaluate existing courses and lessons.
3   It can be used to help teachers integrate and contextualise information gained from keeping up with developments in their field. For example, when reading articles from journals such as *TESOL Quarterly, Language Learning, Applied Linguistics* or *RELC Journal*, teachers can try to decide what principle is being addressed by the article and how the article helps in the application of a principle.
4   It can provide a basis for teachers to use to reflect on their practice and professional development. It may provide a basis for action research within their classrooms. It can help them answer questions like "Is this a good technique?", "Should I use group work?", and "Do my learners need to speak a lot in class?".
5   It can act as one of many possible reference points in teacher training courses.

Summary of the Steps
1   Choose the most important teaching and learning principles.
2   Decide how you will incorporate them in the course.

This chapter has suggested twenty principles of teaching and learning that can provide a basis for curriculum design and evaluation, and teacher development. The selection and ranking of these principles reflect a personal view of language teaching. We have tried to balance this by seeking suggestions from colleagues and by comparing the list with points made in articles in professional journals and with overviews of curriculum design and language teaching and learning. One of the values in using a principle-based approach to language teaching is that developments in theory and research can be easily accommodated by altering, expanding, removing or adding a principle without having to discard all the other principles. In this way our knowledge of language teaching can grow without being subject to the blanket acceptance or rejection that is typical of methods. The information gathered by considering principles, by doing needs analysis, and by doing environment analysis provides essential input for setting course goals and deciding what goes into a course, which is the subject of the following chapter.

Tasks

Task 1 Principles in a course

Look at a course and decide the extent to which the course puts one of the principles in this chapter into action.

Task 2 Activities and principles

Examine one teaching activity to see what principles it puts into practice. Let us use the example of comprehension questions to show how a technique can be examined to see what principles lie behind it. Here is the activity – a reading text is followed by some comprehension questions. The learners are not supposed to look at the text while they answer the questions. The questions require the learners to think about the text, not just repeat parts of it.

The analysis of the comprehension questions activity

The principle of retrieval is being applied here. Retrieval occurs when the learners are not able to refer back to the original text. So, they must retrieve the information needed for the answer from their memory. If the answer involves target vocabulary or grammar, then this retrieval could help language learning. It is important that the questions should focus on important ideas in the text rather than trivial details. Most readers do not have detailed memory of a text no matter how carefully they read, and so questions should look for reasonable comprehension.

The principle of deep processing is also being applied. Because the answer involves the learners making some changes to what is stated in the text, then this encourages a degree of generative use which involves deeper processing than word-for-word retrieval.

A third principle being applied is that comprehension is important. That is, the input should be comprehensible. A major aim of such questions is to check comprehension.

Because this simple activity applies three very useful principles, it is likely to be a worthwhile activity for language learners. It does not seem to involve any unnecessary busy work.

You could examine extensive reading, role play, ten-minute writing, 4/3/2, substitution tables or any other technique you wish to look at.

Case Studies

1   Ellis (2005) presents a list of ten principles which overlap with the list of twenty mentioned in this chapter. Which ones overlap? Write the number of the overlapping principle from Table 4.1 next to the principle below. Which of Ellis's principles are not in Table 4.1? Here are Ellis's principles:

1   Instruction needs to ensure that learners develop both a rich repertoire of formulaic expressions and a rule-based competence.
2   Instruction needs to ensure that learners focus predominantly on meaning.
3   Instruction needs to ensure that learners also focus on form.
4   Instruction needs to be predominantly directed at developing implicit knowledge of the L2 while not neglecting explicit knowledge.
5   Instruction needs to take into account the learner's "built-in syllabus".
6   Successful instructed language learning requires extensive L2 input.
7   Successful instructed language learning also requires opportunities for output.
8   The opportunity to interact in the L2 is central to developing L2 proficiency.
9   Instruction needs to take account of individual differences in learners.
10 In assessing learners' L2 proficiency it is important to examine free as well as controlled production.

2   Jones (1993: 457) lists the principles that could lie behind the evaluation of "teach-yourself" courses. What parts of the curriculum design process are covered by the listed principles? Can you see differences between these principles and principles of curriculum design for teacher-led classes?

Chapter 5

Goals, Content and Sequencing

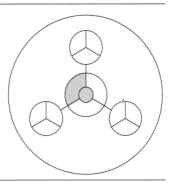

The aim of this part of the curriculum design process is to make a list of the items to teach in the order in which they will be taught.

Content and sequencing must take account of the environment in which the course will be used, the needs of the learners, and principles of teaching and learning. Table 5.1 lists some of the factors to consider.

Guidelines for Deciding or Checking the Content and Sequencing of a Course

Table 5.1 Content and sequencing guidelines

ENVIRONMENT	*Learners*	The ideas in the course should help learning in the classroom.
		The ideas in the course should suit the age of the learners.
		The content should take account of what learners expect to see in an English course.
		The sequencing of the content should allow for some learners being absent for some classes.
	Teachers	The language in the course should be able to be modelled and comprehended by the teacher.
	Situation	The number of lessons in the course should suit the school term or year.
		The ideas in the course should increase the acceptability and usefulness of the course outside the classroom.
NEEDS	*Lacks*	The content should suit the proficiency level of the learners.
	Wants	The content should take account of what learners want.
	Necessities	The content should be what learners need.
PRINCIPLES		See Chapter 4 for the relevant principles.

Goals and Content

The goals of a language lesson can focus on one or more of the following: Language, Ideas, Skills or Text (Discourse). It is possible to plan or evaluate the content of courses by looking at each of these four areas. Within each of these four areas, choices have to be made regarding the units for planning and checking the course. For example, in the area of language, the units may be based on vocabulary (as in *Advanced English Vocabulary* by Helen Barnard), verb forms and verb patterns (as in *101 Substitution Tables* by H.V. George), sentence patterns (as in *English 901* by P. Strevens), or language functions (as in *Orbit* by J. Harrison and P. Menzies). Often a combination of language units is used. The Longman Structural Readers Series combines vocabulary control with control of verb and sentence patterns. Some courses cover language items through organising lessons around topics.

Even if the selection of content for a course is based on topics, themes or situations, it is useful to check to see that the language items that are covered are the most useful ones.

Making sensible, well-justified decisions about content is one of the most important parts of curriculum design. If poor content is chosen, then excellent teaching and learning result in a poor return for learning effort.

Some curriculum designers break goals down into smaller well-specified performance objectives (Brown, 1995). As we will see in Chapter 7, this is especially useful for monitoring and assessing learners' progress. Even if a course designer does not want to go to this level of detail, there is value in setting smaller goals for the various strands or skill subdivisions of a course. The way these smaller goals are detailed will depend partly on the unit of progression for the course.

The Units of Progression in the Course

The units of progression in a course are the items that are used to grade the progress of the course. For example, if the starting point of a course was language items, and, in particular, vocabulary, the units of progression would be words, and at a broader level, word frequency levels which are similar to those used in grading the levels of simplified readers. Similarly the academic word list is presented in ten sub-lists ranging from the most frequent to the least frequent (Coxhead, 2000). If the starting point of a course was topics, then the units of progression would also be topics with progress through the course being marked by an increasing number of topics covered. Long and Crookes (1993: 9–19) call units of progression "units of analysis" and argue that the choice of the unit of analysis should be one of the starting points of curriculum design. Harden and Witte (2006) explore the different kinds of progression from a historical perspective, noting that "the notion of progression has undergone remarkable changes throughout the history of foreign language teaching methodologies" (p. 11).

The units of progression can be classified into two types – those that progress in a definite series, such as vocabulary levels, and those that represent a field of knowledge that could be covered in any order, such as topics. Table 5.2 shows units of progression for a range of starting points. The order of items within a field is determined by pedagogical considerations and constraints such as keeping the learners' interest, making use of available resources, and allowing for recycling of material. Harden notes (2006: 29) that there is a big difference between progress (learning) and progression (how the course moves forward) – "there seems to exist an enormous gap between the structure underlying a course and the one that individuals subjectively create for themselves."

Although certain units of progression may be used to select and sequence the material in a course, it is useful to check that other units are covered in the course and that other units are at an appropriate level. For example, a course that uses topics as its units of progression should also be checked to see that vocabulary is at the appropriate level for the learners and that there is reasonable coverage of useful vocabulary. It is not easy to check all these things in a course, so teachers must decide which are most important for the goals of the course and check on those.

What Will the Progression be Used For?

So far we have looked at designing a course as the aim for deciding on the units of progression in a course. However, units of progression can be used for a variety of purposes:

1   Units of progression can be used to set targets and paths to those targets.
2   Units of progression can be used to check the adequacy of selection and ordering in a course.
3   Units of progression can be used to monitor and report on learners' progress and achievement in the course.

Although a course may seem to have several units of progression, there is usually one on which the others are dependent. Thus a course may seem to have both a grammar and function progression, but a careful study of what changes in each lesson and what reoccurs may show that it is, for example, the grammar points that determine what functions will occur.

Let us now look briefly at units of progression to see what information is available to guide in the choice and sequencing of the items.

Table 5.2 Units of progression

Starting point	Type	Units of progression	Determinants of progression
Vocabulary	Series	Words	Frequency levels Occurrence in tasks
Grammar	Series	Grammatical constructions	Frequency Acquisition stages Complexity
Language use	Field	Functions	
Ideas	Field	Topics Themes	
Discourse	Field	Topic types Genre	
Situations and roles	Field	Situations Roles	
Component skills	Series	Subskills	Order of complexity
Strategies	Field	Strategies	
Outcomes	Field	Real life outcomes Task outcomes	

Vocabulary

There is considerable frequency-based research that provides clear indications of what vocabulary learners would gain most benefit from knowing. This research shows strikingly the value of ensuring that learners have good control of the high-frequency vocabulary of the language. Typically,

- the first 1,000 words account for 75 per cent of the successive words in a text
- the second 1,000 words account for 5 per cent of the successive words in a text
- 570 academic words account for 10 per cent of the successive words in an academic text.

Nation (2001) argues that the low-frequency vocabulary of the language (vocabulary not in the most frequent 2,000 words or in the academic word list) does not deserve teaching effort. Rather, strategies for dealing with and learning this vocabulary should receive the teacher's attention. A list of the 2,000 most frequent words in English can be found in West (1953), and in the rank list of frequency counts, such as Kučera and Francis (1967). As mentioned earlier, a list of the most frequent wide-range academic vocabulary can be found in Coxhead (2000).

The sequencing of vocabulary in a course can be loosely based on frequency levels as it is in series of graded readers such as the Longman Structural Readers or the Oxford Bookworms Library. The COBUILD course (Willis and Willis, 1989), as another example, consists of three books covering 700, 850, and 950 words apiece, making a total of 2,500 words.

The sequencing of vocabulary should not be based on lexical sets or the grouping together of opposites or near synonyms (Higa, 1963; Tinkham, 1993) (see Chapter 4 of this book for discussion of this). There should also be the opportunity for learners to meet the same vocabulary in a variety of contexts and across the four strands of a course.

Grammar

There are several frequency counts of verb form usage in English which can act as the basis for the selection and sequencing of items in a course (George, 1963b; Joos, 1964; Dušková and Urbanová, 1967). Appendix 1 contains a list from H.V. George's *Verb Form Frequency Count.*

George (1963b) suggests that a reasonable basis for Stage 1 of a course (1,500 to 2,000 words over roughly two years of five periods of English per week) would consist of the following verbs.

- Imperative
- Don't + stem (Imperative)
- Simple Present Actual and Neutral
- Verb + to + stem
- Simple Past Narrative and Actual
- Past Participle

This group of items accounts for 575 of every 1,000 successive verb forms in written English.

Stage 2 of a course could add the following items.

- Simple Past Neutral and Habitual
- Past Perfect from Simple Past Narrative
- Stem+ing in Free Adjuncts
- Noun + to + Stem
- Simple Present Iterative and Future
- Verb + to + Stem (Stem dominant)
- Verb + Noun + to + Stem
- Noun + Preposition + Stem+ing
- Stem+ed = Adjective in a Noun Group
- Stem+ing = Adjective in a Noun Group
- Stem+ing = Noun
- Can + Stem (immediately and characteristically able)
- May + Stem (possibility and uncertainty)

- 'll + Stem
- Must + Stem (necessity from circumstances)

Stage 1 and Stage 2 items together account for 756 of every 1,000 successive verb forms. Stage 2 verb forms occur more often than once in two pages of text and less often than once per page (George, 1963a).

Items for Stage 3 of a course do not occur frequently and their frequency depends on the type of material the learner is going to read. Many would be learned only for receptive use. Items like *verb + to + stem* occur early in the sequence because they allow learners to fulfil language needs (I like to sing; I want to go).

Many courses use grammar as the major unit of progression. Unfortunately the selection and sequencing of the items is at the best opportunistic and gives no consideration of the value of learning particular items. Courses thus include a strange mixture of very useful items and items that occur relatively infrequently in normal language use. Infrequent items can be usefully introduced in courses where they are needed to be learned as memorised phrases (lexicalised sentence stems) rather than as structures to focus on.

Functions

There is no standard list of language functions that is accompanied by frequency data. The most widely available list of functions can be found in Van Ek and Alexander (1980) and is organised under the six headings of:

1 Imparting and seeking factual information
2 Expressing and finding out intellectual attitudes
3 Expressing and finding out emotional attitudes
4 Expressing and finding out moral attitudes
5 Getting things done (suasion)
6 Socialising.

Dobson (1979) presents a similar brief list. Council of Europe (2001) builds on the earlier list, adding new emphases.

1 Imparting and seeking factual information
2 Expressing and finding out attitudes
3 Suasion
4 Socialising
5 Structuring discourse
6 Communication repair.

Some courses use functions as their unit of progression with each lesson focusing on a different function or set of functions. Often however courses are called "functional" but really have grammatical structures as their units of progression. Each new structure is described in functional terms but it is the sequence of structures determining the sequence of the lessons.

The danger with functionally based courses is that curriculum designers sometimes feel the need to present several different ways of expressing the same function, for example, several ways of refusing something. This can result in interference between these somewhat similar expressions, making them more difficult to learn because they keep getting mixed up in the learner's mind. In addition, learners usually feel little motivation for learning to say the same thing in several ways. This interference trap is easily avoided by initially presenting only the most useful way of expressing a function.

Discourse

Discourse as the basis for units of progression is more likely to be used in pre-university courses where learners systematically cover a range of relevant genres such as recounts, information reports and arguments. Attention to elements of spoken discourse, such as ellipsis between speakers and negotiation of discourse, may occur early in language courses but is rarely the unit of progression for a course.

Biber's (1990) work on the co-occurrence of language features in different types of texts indicates that curriculum designers should check the genres that are covered in their courses to make sure that learners are not getting a distorted view of language features. Biber found that certain text types are rich in certain language features, but contain few instances of others. If a learner is to gain a useful coverage of language features, the genres that occur in the course should match the genres that the learner will need to work with outside the course. For example, are learners getting plenty of narrative but very little of information report even though they will need to work with information report texts a lot in their academic study? Table 5.3 contains Biber's text types and these may serve as a simple checklist for a course. Biber (1990) also describes the grammatical features that cluster in these various groups.

Skills, Subskills and Strategies

Some courses use skills and subskills as their units of progression. Reading courses for example may focus on skills such as finding the main idea, reading for detail, notetaking, skimming, reading faster, and reading for inferences. There are three major ways of defining subskills. One is to look at the range of activities covered by a skill such as speaking and to use these as a starting point for defining subskills (see Munby, 1978: 176–184; Alderson, 1990; Weir et al., 1990). For example, speaking can be divided into interactional speaking and transactional speaking (Brown, 1978). Transactional speaking can be divided into monologue, dialogue etc.

Table 5.3 Text types and texts from Biber (1990)

Text type	Texts
Intimate interpersonal interaction	Telephone with friends Face-to-face conversation
Informational interaction	Telephone about business Face-to-face conversation Telephone with less close friends Spontaneous speeches Interviews Personal letters
Scientific exposition	Academic prose Official documents
Learned exposition	Official documents Press reviews Popular magazines Academic prose
Imaginative narrative	Fiction – romance, mystery, adventure, general Prepared speeches
General narrative exposition	Humour Press editorials Press reportage Non-sports broadcasts Religion Biographies Science fiction
Situated reportage	Sports broadcasts
Involved persuasion	Spontaneous speeches, interviews, professional letters Popular magazines

Another way is to look at the skill as a process and to divide it into the parts of the process. This is a typical way of approaching writing, dividing the writing process into parts. One possible division of the process is: (1) having a model of the reader, (2) having writing goals, (3) gathering ideas, (4) organis-ing ideas, (5) turning ideas into written text, (6) reviewing what has just been written, and (7) editing the written text. Process divisions can be applied in other skills.

A third way of dividing up a skill is to use levels of cognitive activity. The most well-known approach of this kind can be found in what is popularly known as Bloom's taxonomy (Bloom, 1956). Bloom divides cog-nitive activity into six levels of increasing complexity: (1) knowledge, (2) comprehension, (3) application, (4) analysis, (5) synthesis, (6) evaluation. These levels have often been applied to the construction of reading comprehension activities (see Kraus-Srebic *et al.*, 1981; Chikalanga, 1992; Day and Park, 2005).

There are now comprehensive lists of strategies for language learning and language use (Oxford, 1990; Brown, 2006: Chapter 5).

Ideas

A good language course not only develops the learners' control of the language but also puts the learners in contact with ideas that help the learning of language and are useful to the learners. The ideas content of a course can take many forms. The following list is adapted from Cook (1983). The ideas content of a course can be about:

1   imaginary happenings. The course could follow the typical activities or adventures of a group of learners or native speakers.
2   an academic subject. Examples would be linguistics or the special purpose of the learners such as agriculture, tourism, commerce or computing.
3   learner survival needs. These can arise from suggestions by the learners or investigation by the teacher. They may include topics like shopping, going to the doctor, getting a driver's licence, and making friends. Van Ek and Alexander (1980) provide a detailed list of topics under 14 main headings covering daily use of language.
4   interesting facts. These might include topics like the discovery of penicillin, whales and solar power.
5   culture. Adaskou, Britten and Fahsi (1990) divide culture into *aesthetic* which includes the study of literature, *sociological* which looks at norms of behaviour and cultural values, *semantic* which looks at word meaning and the classification and organisation of experience, and *sociolinguistic* which involves the appropriate use of language. Adaskou *et al.* see the greatest threat to the local culture coming from the sociological focus. However, all four aspects of culture could contradict and threaten the local culture. See Witte (2006) for a description of seven stages of "cultural progression" (sociological) moving from explicit knowledge of inter-related aspects of the native and non-native cultures (such as housing, eating, school) to markedly different conceptualisations between the cultures (such as notions of cleanliness and politeness) to understanding the culture from an insider's view and gaining a distanced view of one's own culture.

The following list of criteria can be used to guide and evaluate the choice of ideas in a language course. The criteria are in two groups, those that help the learning within the classroom, and those that make the language course acceptable and useful outside the classroom.

A   The ideas content of the course helps learning in the classroom because:

1   the ideas content makes the learners interested and motivated in their study of the language.

2   the ideas content encourages normal language use. That is, it involves ideas that can be talked about in a natural way in the classroom.

3   it makes learning easier because the ideas are already familiar to the learners and they can thus give full attention to language items.

4   the ideas content is familiar to the teacher and thus allows the teacher to work from a position of strength. For example, teachers of ESP courses in agriculture who are not trained in agriculture work from a position of weakness.

B   The ideas content of the course increases the acceptability and usefulness of the course outside the classroom because:

1   the ideas content helps in the learner's job, study or living. ESP, study skills and language survival courses aim to do this.

2   the ideas content develops awareness of another culture or cultures. It may promote international understanding and it may encourage learners to accept the norms and values of other cultures.

3   the ideas content maintains and supports the learners' own culture. This criterion and the preceding one (awareness of other cultures) are sometimes seen to be in conflict (see Adaskou et al., 1990; Alptekin and Alptekin, 1984), particularly where parents and teachers see the norms and behaviour of native speakers of English as a threat to the local culture.

4   the ideas content helps learners develop intellectually by making them aware of important and challenging ideas. Courses which focus on issues like conservation or on important discoveries try to do this.

5   the ideas content helps learners develop emotionally and socially. Courses which use a humanistic approach or make use of values clarification activities have this goal.

6   the ideas content of the course meets the expectations of the learners and their parents.

The justifications listed above can be reclassified according to the parts of the curriculum design model. For example, the last justification listed above regarding learners' and teachers' expectations relates to constraints. The second to last justification regarding emotional and social development relates to needs.

The choice of the ideas content of a course will have a major effect on the marketability and acceptability of the course. It needs very careful consideration and application of the findings of needs analysis and environment analysis.

Task-based Syllabuses

With the shift to communicative language teaching in the 1970s there was an increasing emphasis on using language to convey a message, and as a result increasing attention was given to the use of tasks in the classroom. The realisation that many so-called communicative language courses were still largely based upon a sequence of language forms in turn generated interest in task-based, rather than task-supported, syllabuses. Published experimentation with task-based syllabuses largely began with the work of Prabhu (1987), and the interest in this type of syllabus may be a result of the links that teachers and curriculum designers see between this approach and their own teaching and planning activity. All the same, the use of task-based syllabuses remains the exception rather than the rule, although tasks themselves are widely used.

One of the questions that arises is: what is a task? Many different definitions have been proposed. Ellis (2003b: 4–5) provides nine different definitions, one of which is especially succinct and useful for teachers: "A task is an activity which requires learners to use language, with emphasis on meaning, to attain an objective" (Bygate *et al.*, 2001). Here is a sample task from Prabhu (1987) which demonstrates how the learner needs to focus on and understand the meaning of the language in order to complete the task successfully.

1   Name the top corners of the square: B on the left and C on the right.
2   Name the corners at the bottom: D on the right and A on the left.
3   Continue AB and call the end of the line E.
4   Continue CD and write F at the end of the line.
5   Join EC.
6   What should be joined next?

In the on-going debate about the nature of a task, Willis and Willis (2007: 13) have provided six questions that can help the teacher and the curriculum designer determine the extent to which an activity is task-like.

- Does the activity engage learners' interest?
- Is there a primary focus on meaning?
- Is there an outcome?
- Is success judged in terms of outcome?
- Is completion a priority?
- Does the activity relate to real world activities?

These questions could be used in both task-based and task-supported syllabuses.

Advocates of a task-based syllabus, particularly Long and Crookes (1992), argue that pedagogic tasks provide a vehicle for presentation of appropriate language samples to learners and allow negotiation of difficulty (p. 43). They suggest that the most appropriate tasks are those that a needs analysis determines are most useful for the learners. The order of tasks should be determined by the difficulty and complexity of the tasks. Ellis (2003b: 220–229) draws together earlier suggestions relating to task complexity and suggests criteria that could be used for determining the sequencing of tasks. These criteria relate to the nature of the input, the conditions under which the task is performed, the cognitive operations required, and the task outcomes. Applying these criteria, a task using written input employing high-frequency vocabulary about a familiar topic and requiring a pictorial output would be easier (and therefore more likely to occur before) than a similar task requiring written output.

The adoption of a task-based syllabus is usually argued on the basis of the inadequacy of other types of syllabus (see Sheen, 1994, and the Bruton–Skehan exchange in *ELT Journal* 2002 vol. 56 no. 3 for discussion of the quality of the arguments). One of the concerns about task-based syllabuses, however, is that they focus on fluency at the expense of accuracy. This concern has been addressed by advocates of task-based learning. Ellis (2003a) suggests that tasks can either be focused or unfocused on form. A focused task would target a particular language feature in meaning-based communication. Willis and Willis (2007) point out that opportunities to focus on language arise naturally during a task cycle. The teacher may highlight necessary vocabulary at the outset, learners may focus on the language used to convey their meaning during the task, and the teacher may close the cycle with a focus on form. All the same, if a task-based syllabus is used it is particularly important that there are other ways of checking the coverage of content, particularly vocabulary, grammatical items and types of discourse. Good curriculum design involves the checking of courses against a range of types of content.

The choice of units of progression in a course is very important for curriculum design and the decisions regarding the selection and sequencing of these units must be guided by well-justified principles and the best possible research information – there is plenty of it available. Once the units of progression have been chosen and applied, it is important that the course material is checked against other units of analysis to ensure that a sensible coverage is made of the other aspects that go to make up knowledge of a language.

Sequencing the Content in a Course

The lessons or units of a course can fit together in a variety of ways. The two major divisions are whether the material in one lesson depends on the learning that has occurred in previous lessons (a linear development) or whether each lesson is separate from the others so that the lessons can be done in any order and need not all be done (a modular arrangement).

Linear Approaches to Sequencing

Most language courses involve linear development, beginning with simple frequent items that prepare for later more complex items. Such a development has the disadvantages of not easily taking account of absenteeism, learners with different styles and speeds of learning, and the need for recycling material. The worst kind of linear development assumes that once an item has been presented in a lesson, it has been learned and does not need focused revision. This view does not agree with the findings of research on memory (Baddeley, 1990) and there are variations of linear progressions which try to take account of the need for repetition. These include a spiral curriculum, matrix models, revision units and field approaches to sequencing.

1   The best known advocate of a spiral curriculum is Bruner (1962). Developing a spiral curriculum involves deciding on the major items to cover, and then covering them several times over a period of time at increasing levels of detail. In the following diagram, the spiral line represents the progression of the curriculum and the radial blocks represent the material to be learned, with the starting point at the centre of the spiral (Figure 5.1).

   If we apply this model to a language curriculum, the blocks of material could be:

   (a) lexical sets or areas of vocabulary with less frequent members occurring later in the spiral;
   (b) high-frequency grammatical patterns and their elaborations with the elaborations occurring later in the spiral;
   (c) groups of language functions with less useful alternative ways of expressing the function occurring later in the spiral;
   (d) genres with longer and more complex examples of the genre occurring later in the spiral.

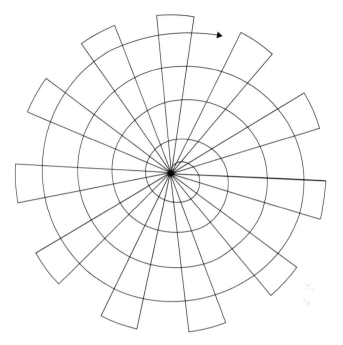

Figure 5.1 A spiral curriculum.

The advantages of a spiral model are that it provides easily monitored recycling of material, it allows for learners who were left behind to catch up at the next cycle, and it makes sure that the full value of the most important aspects of the language are dealt with.

2   A matrix model (Table 5.4) is somewhat similar to a spiral curriculum, the main difference being that the change when meeting old material again is one of diversity rather than complexity. In a matrix model one unit of progression is systematically varied against another, so that the same items are met with different contexts. For example the same grammatical items are focused on across a variety of topics.

Alternative matchings could include grammatical items and functions, vocabulary and genre, and vocabulary and grammatical items.

A matrix model has similar advantages to a spiral curriculum in that there are repeated opportunities to meet and enrich important items.

3   Revision units (Table 5.5) are simply an addition to a linear model. At certain points in the linear progression, time is spent revising previously met material. Logically, the relative amount of time given to revision should increase as the course progresses. This is because there will be increasingly more material to revise and material needs to be revised several times not just once. Ideally the revision activities should do more than just repeat previously met items but should enrich them in some

Table 5.4 A matrix curriculum

	Topic 1	*Topic 2*	*Topic 3*	*Topic 4*
Item 1	Lesson 1	Lesson 2	Lesson 3	Lesson 4
Item 2	Lesson 5	Lesson 6	Lesson 7	Lesson 8
Item 3	Lesson 9	Lesson 10	Lesson 11	Lesson 12
Item 4	Lesson 13	Lesson 14	Lesson 15	Lesson 16

way. Michael West (1955) saw the use of graded readers (which he called "supplementary readers") as an important way of recycling previously met vocabulary and grammatical structures. The revision unit model matches Brumfit's (1985) "syllabus with holes" which he proposed as a way of giving attention to fluency development, the holes being the time given to recycling old material and suspending the introduction of new material.

4   In a field approach the items to be covered are decided upon and then the learners can start anywhere with the material and end anywhere as long as it is all covered. A field approach to sequencing material involves: (1) deciding what items need to be covered i.e. make up the field, (2) providing a variety of opportunities to meet these items, (3) checking that each important item will be met sufficient times. If this approach was taken for vocabulary in a speaking course, then large quantities of activities would be designed which used the wanted vocabulary as part of the written input to the activities. A rough check could be made to see, for example, that each wanted vocabulary item occurred in the written input to at least five activities.

The appropriate use of a graded reading scheme (Nation and Wang, 1999) is a field approach. By reading at least five books at the same level all the new vocabulary introduced at that level should be met, some of it several times. That vocabulary will be met again in higher levels. Reading a book a week will ensure that learners have not forgotten the word when they meet it again. Nation and Wang suggest, however, that when moving from one graded reader level to another, there should be some direct teaching of new words as there may be quite a high proportion of unknown words in books at the next level.

While a field approach does not require as much initial planning as a spiral or matrix approach, checking later that there will be sufficient meetings may take more time.

Table 5.5 Revision units in a curriculum

New	Old	New	Old	Old	New	Old	Old

A Modular Approach to Sequencing

We have been looking at linear approaches to sequencing and ways of ensuring repetition within a linear approach. The second major type of approach, a modular approach, breaks a course into independent non-linear units. These units may be parts of lessons, lessons or groups of lessons. Each unit or module is complete in itself and does not usually assume knowledge of previous modules. It is not unusual for a modular approach to be accompanied by criterion-referenced testing with a high level of mastery set as the criterion.

In language courses the language could be divided into modules in several ways. The modules could be skill-based with different modules for listening, speaking, reading and writing, and sub-skills of these larger skills. The modules could be based on language functions, or more broadly situations, dealing with the language needed for shopping, emergency services, travel, the post office and the bank.

Modular courses often have some kind of division into obligatory or core modules, and optional or elective modules, or a division into level 1 modules and level 2 modules and so on.

Ellis (2003a, 2003b) proposes a modular approach for task-based language courses. In his proposal there are two unconnected modules. At beginner levels the sole focus is on a communicative, meaning-focused module. From intermediate level onwards attention is also given to a language- (or code-) focused module, with the intention of "drawing attention to form in order to destabilize learners' interlanguage" (Ellis, 2003b: 237) and thus avoiding fossilisation of language errors. This approach suggests a way to deal with the concerns mentioned above about a lack of attention to accuracy in some task-based language courses (Towell and Tomlinson, 1999).

Summary of the Steps

1 Describe the goals of the course.
2 Decide on the unit of progression for the course.
3 Choose and sequence the content of the course.
4 Check the content against lists of other items to ensure coverage.

The unit of progression in a course is usually what the curriculum designer sees as being important for learning. This means that it has an effect on the kinds of activities used which is a part of the format and presentation part of curriculum design. We look at format and presentation in the following chapter.

Tasks

Task 1   Verb form coverage in beginners' course books

Compare the verb forms in the first lessons of a commercially published course book with George's list (see Appendix 1).

Do it in this way.

1   List the items which are in the first 6 or 12 lessons of the course and which are in George's list. Add the frequencies that George gives for these items.

2   What items are frequent in George's list but are not in the first lessons of the course?

3   What items are in the course but are not frequent according to George's list? Why are they in the course?

4   How could you improve the course with regard to selection of verb forms?

Task 2   The ideas content of a course book

1   Look at some course books and see what the ideas content is (use Cook's list described above to help you). What justifications do the curriculum designers give for their choice of content? How effective, acceptable, and useful would such ideas content be for your teaching situation?

2   If you design a course, what ideas content will you use in your course? Give some examples of part of your ideas syllabus. Justify your choice. You may need to rank the criteria given at the beginning of the ideas section of this chapter to help you reach a decision.

3   If your ideas content was linguistics, survival needs, sociological culture, or interesting facts, where could you find items to include in your syllabus?

Task 3   Describing the goals of a course

The goals of English courses can relate to (1) Language, (2) Ideas or Content, (3) Skills and (4) Text or Discourse Types. Look at statements of goals in course books and then write no more than 50 words describing the general goals of your course. You may find it useful to begin your statement with "The main objective of this course is . . .".

If you have time, you should begin to operationalise your goals by describing the product or outcomes of your course. You may find it useful to begin your statement with "At the end of this course, learners should be able to . . .". Here is a sample statement for a survival language course.

The main objective of this course is to help learners gain fluent use of a small number of very important words and phrases that will allow them to fill the needs of travelling, buying, socialising, eating, and finding accommodation.

Case Studies

1   Look at a report of a curriculum design project. What type of content did they choose? What caused that decision?
2   Look at Savage and Storer (1992) for an example of a course where learners decided on the ideas content. How could you do this in your classroom?

Chapter 6

Format and Presentation

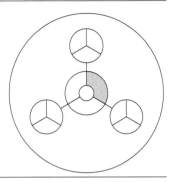

The aim of this part of the curriculum design process is to choose the teaching and learning techniques and design the lesson plans.

Format and Other Parts of the Curriculum Design Process

It is at the format and presentation part of the curriculum design process that the data gathered from needs and environment analysis, and the principles chosen to maximise learning come together in activities that involve the learners. Most of the decisions made regarding constraints, needs, principles, content and sequencing will only be indirectly observable through the format and presentation of the lessons. But these decisions must come through into the lesson format or the work done on these aspects of curriculum design has been wasted, and the course might not suit the environment or learners for which it is intended, and might not apply what is known about teaching and learning.

Guidelines for Deciding on a Format

Format and presentation must take account of the environment in which the course will be used, the needs of the learners, and principles of teaching and learning. Table 6.1 lists some of the factors to consider.

A problem facing the curriculum designer is how to communicate the reasons why each lesson is like it is. If both teachers and learners are aware of the goals of each activity, why they are useful goals, how the activity should be best presented to achieve the goal, what kind of learning involvement is needed, and the signs of successful involvement, then learning is more likely to be successful. There is plenty of evidence to show that teachers and learners do not share the same view of parts of a lesson (Block, 1994), and that the learners sometimes do activities in ways that defeat the purpose of the activity (Hosenfield, 1976). Information about the lesson can occur in several different places in a course. Probably the most useful place is in the headings and instructions for each activity in a lesson.

If the lessons always follow the same format, then the introduction to the course book can include some explanation of the goals and how they are best

Table 6.1 Format guidelines based on environment and needs

ENVIRONMENT	Learners	The layout of the content should attract the learners. The learners should have the skills to do the activities. The activities should take account of whether the learners share the same first language. The activities should be suitable for a range of levels of proficiency in a class. The activities should suit the size of the class. The activities should fit the learning styles of the learners.
	Teachers	The activities should be able to be presented and managed by the teacher [e.g. the teacher should be able to organise group work].
	Situation	The course book should be easy to carry. The material in the course or the course book should not be too expensive. The amount of material in a lesson should suit the length of a class. The activities should suit the physical features of the classroom [e.g. move desks for group work; sound proof for oral work].
NEEDS	Lacks	The learners should be able to successfully complete the activities.
	Wants	The activities should take account of what the learners expect to do in a language learning course.
	Necessities	The kinds of activities should be useful to the learners in their future use or future learning of the language [e.g. knowing how to rank; knowing how to negotiate].
PRINCIPLES	1	**Motivation:** As much as possible, the learners should be interested and excited about learning the language and they should come to value this learning.
	2	**Four strands:** A course should include a roughly even balance of meaning-focused input, language-focused learning, meaning-focused output and fluency activities.
	3	**Comprehensible input:** There should be substantial quantities of interesting comprehensible receptive activity in both listening and reading.
	4	**Fluency:** A language course should provide activities aimed at increasing the fluency with which learners can use the language they already know, both receptively and productively.
	5	**Output:** The learners should be pushed to produce the language in both speaking and writing over a range of discourse types.

(Continued overleaf)

Table 6.1 Continued

6 **Deliberate learning:** The course should include language-focused learning on the sound system, spelling, vocabulary, grammar and discourse areas.
7 **Time on task:** As much time as possible should be spent using and focusing on the second language.
8 **Depth of processing:** Learners should process the items to be learned as deeply and as thoughtfully as possible.
9 **Integrative motivation:** A course should be presented so that the learners have the most favourable attitudes to the language, to users of the language, to the teacher's skill in teaching the language, and to their chance of success in learning the language.
10 **Learning style:** There should be opportunity for learners to work with the learning material in ways that most suit their individual learning style.

reached. In some course books, for example *The Cambridge English Course* (Swan and Walter, 1985), a detailed table of contents ("a map of the book") indicates the various new points of focus. Many courses have a special teacher's book, which then gives the teacher the responsibility for informing the learners of the goals and how to learn.

The four strands

As we have seen in Chapter 4 on principles, it is important that a language course provides a balanced range of opportunities for learning. One way of trying to check this balance of opportunities is to see a course as consisting of four strands which are each given a roughly equal amount of time (Nation, 2007). These four strands are meaning-focused input, meaning-focused output, language-focused learning and fluency development.

Meaning-focused input

Meaning-focused input involves having the opportunity to learn from listening and speaking. Krashen (1981) would call it learning from comprehensible input. The conditions which are needed for such learning are a low density of unknown items in the language input, a focus on the meaning of the message, and a large quantity of input. In language courses, the most important way of providing a large amount of comprehensible input is to have an extensive reading programme. This involves the learners in reading books which have been specially written for learners of English in a controlled vocabulary. There are many series of such books and there are hundreds of such books. They are an excellent resource for meaning-focused input. For learners at elementary and intermediate levels an extensive reading programme is an essential part of any general English course. There also needs to be the listening equivalent of such a course. Many graded reading books now are accompanied by a CD. Learners can listen while they read, or read first and listen later. Where the listening is not accompanied by visual clues, it is more difficult to learn from listening than from reading. Repeated listening is thus a very useful activity, and Elley (1989) found that he had to provide three listening opportunities for the same story to be able to measure reasonable learning from listening input. Another major source of meaning-focused input in a course comes from interacting with others. One person's output can be another person's input. An advantage of interactive listening is that the listener can negotiate the meaning of the input with the speaker. That is, they can ask the meaning of words or constructions and they can ask for a repetition of poorly heard material. They can also control the speed of the input by asking the speaker to speak more slowly. A course can usefully include material which trains the learners in such negotiation. This training can include learning the phrases which are needed to seek information about input, and which can control the speed and repetition of the input.

It is important that a course should apply the "time on task" principle. That is, if reading is a goal of the course, there should be plenty of reading activity. If listening is a goal of a course, there should be plenty of listening activity. A problem with some reading courses is that they provide a lot of activities for the learners but not large quantities of reading.

Meaning-focused output

Meaning-focused output involves learning through speaking and writing. Learning by input alone is not sufficient because the knowledge needed to comprehend input does not include all the knowledge which is needed to produce output. A well-balanced language course spends about one quarter of the course time on meaning-focused speaking and writing.

Meaning-focused speaking should involve the learners in conversation and also in monologue. The conversation can have a largely social focus and can also be used for conveying important information. That is, there should be practice in both interactional and transactional language use (Brown, 1978). The conditions for meaning-focused output are similar to those for meaning-focused input. There should be a focus on the message (that is getting the listener or the reader to understand), the task should be demanding but not too demanding, and there should be plenty of opportunity for such activity.

If a language course has the goal of developing skill in writing, then there needs to be regular meaning-focused writing. This can involve writing letters to other students or to the teacher, keeping a diary, writing essays and assignments, writing brief notes to get things done, writing stories and poems, writing descriptions, writing instructions, and persuasive writing.

If the language course has the goal of developing skill in speaking, then there needs to be regular meaning-focused speaking. This can involve information gap activities, short talks, conversation while doing a task, problem-solving discussions and role plays.

Language-focused learning

Language-focused learning involves a deliberate focus on language features such as pronunciation, spelling, word parts, vocabulary, collocations, grammatical constructions and discourse features. Language-focused learning is an efficient way of quickly learning language features. It is an important part of any language course and about one quarter of the course time should be spent on such learning. In most courses too much time is spent on such learning, and this means that there is less opportunity for learning through the other three strands of the course. The answer is not to completely remove language-focused learning from the course, but to make sure that there is an appropriate amount of it.

Language-focused learning can have two major effects. It can result in deliberate conscious knowledge of language items. This explicit knowledge can be helpful in making learners aware of language features which they will meet in input. This awareness can help learning from input. Language-focused learning can also result in subconscious implicit knowledge of language items. This is the kind of knowledge which is needed for normal language use. Deliberate learning of vocabulary items can result in both kinds of knowledge (Elgort, 2007). For most grammatical features however deliberate learning is likely only to contribute to conscious knowledge. Such conscious knowledge can be useful when learners have time to check their production as in writing, but it is also useful as a stepping stone to implicit knowledge when the items are later met in meaning-focused input or fluency-development activities.

Here are some of the activities which could occur in the language-focused learning strand of course – intensive reading, pronunciation practice, guided writing, spelling practice, blank-filling activities, sentence completion or sentence combining activities, getting feedback on written work, correction during speaking activities, learning vocabulary from word cards, memorising collocations, dictation and the explicit study of discourse features.

There is a large variety of language-focused learning activities and many of them are effective in keeping the learners busy but do not make the best use of time for language learning. We will look critically at some of these activities later in this chapter.

Language-focused learning is a very important part of the language course, and there is now plenty of research to show that it can make very effective contributions to language learning.

Fluency development

The fourth strand of a course is a fluency development strand. Fluency involves making the best use of what is already known. Thus, the fluency development strand of a course does not involve the learning of new language features, but involves becoming fluent with features that the learners have already met before. The conditions for the fluency development strand are: (1) easy, familiar material, (2) a focus on communicating messages, (3) some pressure to perform at a faster speed, and (4) plenty of opportunities for fluency practice.

There needs to be fluency practice in each of the four skills of listening, speaking, reading and writing. Listening fluency practice can involve listening to stories, taking part in interactive activities, and listening to lectures on familiar material. Speaking fluency activities can involve repeated speaking where learners deliver the same talk several times to different listeners, speaking on very familiar topics, reading familiar material aloud, and speaking about what has already been spoken or written about before. Reading fluency activities should involve a speed reading course within a controlled vocabulary. Such courses can bring about substantial fluency improvement with just a few minutes practice two or three times a week for most learners (Chung and Nation, 2006). Such courses need to be within a controlled vocabulary because they should not contain vocabulary which is unfamiliar to the learners. It is very difficult to develop fluency when working with material which contains unknown language features. Other reading fluency activities include repeated reading where the learners read the same text several times, and extensive reading involving very easy graded readers. Writing fluency activities involve the learners in writing about things where they bring a lot of previous knowledge. A very useful activity in this strand is ten-minute writing. In this activity, two or three times a week, the teacher gets the learners to write under timed conditions, that is for exactly ten minutes. The teacher does not mark any of the errors in the writing but comments on the content of the writing perhaps suggesting what the learners should write more about next time. The learners record the number of words per minute they have written on a graph. Their goal is to increase the number of words per minute written. Other writing fluency activities include linked skills activities. Linked skills activities are very effective for fluency development in all of the skills of listening, speaking, reading and writing. A linked skills activity involves learners working on the same material while moving through a series of changes, for example, from listening to the material, to talking about it, and then to writing about it. Usually we would expect to see three skills linked together, such as reading, then writing, and then speaking. The last activity in a series of linked skills is usually a fluency activity, because by this time the learners are very familiar with the material and can work with it at a faster speed.

Table 6.2 summarises and expands on the conditions and activities for each of the four strands. A reasonably straightforward way to evaluate if a course is well balanced or not is to keep a list of activities done over a period of time recording how much time was spent on each activity. The activities should then be classified into each of the four strands and the amount of time added up for each strand. The amount of time for each of the four strands should be roughly equal.

For more detail on these activities, see Nation and Newton (2009), and Nation (2009).

Busy work

Most language-learning programmes only make use of a small number of different kinds of teaching techniques or activities. There is nothing wrong with this, because if there is too great a variety of teaching activities, the

Table 6.2 Activities and conditions for the four strands

Strand	Conditions	Activities
Meaning-focused input	A focus on the message Only a small amount of unfamiliar language features A large quantity of input	Listening to stories Extensive reading Listening while reading Communicative activities
Meaning-focused output	A focus on the message Only a small amount of unfamiliar language features A large quantity of output	Short talks Communicative activities Writing stories and assignments Letter writing
Language-focused learning	A deliberate focus on language features	Pronunciation practice Spelling practice Learning vocabulary from word cards Intensive reading Grammar study Substitution tables and drills Dictation Feedback and correction
Fluency development	Focus on the message No unfamiliar language features Pressure to go faster A large quantity of practice	Listening to stories Linked skills activities Easy extensive reading Repeated reading Speed reading Ten-minute writing

teacher may have to spend a lot of time explaining to the learners how the activity is done before they actually get on to doing the activity. When deciding whether a course is likely to be effective or not, it is useful to look very closely at a few of the major activities used in the course to see how they help learning and how much of the work involved in them is just busy work which is not making an effective contribution to useful learning. Let us look at some examples of this analysis, focusing on some very commonly used activities.

Comprehension questions

A very common activity in courses which focus on reading involves the learners answering comprehension questions of various kinds. These kinds can include pronominal questions, true/false questions, and multiple-choice questions. This kind of activity fits into the meaning-focused input strand, because the focus of the activity is on understanding messages. If the learners have to write original answers to pronominal questions, this part of the activity would fit into the meaning-focused output strand. How can such questions help vocabulary learning? Clearly, vocabulary learning is not the main goal of comprehension questions, but questions can be designed so that they also help vocabulary learning as well as provide feedback about comprehension. Questions help vocabulary learning if the answer to the question involves the use of target vocabulary, if the question itself includes the target vocabulary, and if the answer to the question involves the target vocabulary being used in generative ways. That is, the way the word is used in the question or the answer is not an exact copy of the way in which it is used in the text.

If the target vocabulary occurs in the questions, or the answers to multiple-choice questions, this can contribute to receptive knowledge of the words. If the target vocabulary occurs in the answers that the learners have to write for pronominal questions, then this encourages productive learning of the words.

If the target vocabulary occurs in the questions, or the answers to multiple-choice questions, the learners need to retrieve the meaning of this vocabulary and this retrieval can help the learning of the words. If the question context for the target vocabulary differs from the context of the word in the text, then the learner is meeting a generative use of this word and this will strengthen memory for the word. To answer the question the learner also has to comprehend the word as a part of the sentence and apply it to the real-world task of finding an answer. This involves a deep level of mental processing and will thus make a good contribution to the learning of the word.

Thus, when looking at a course, it is worth checking to see if the comprehension activities include the opportunity to make receptive or productive use of the target vocabulary.

When looking at an activity, it is always useful to consider how much of the activity involves typical language use and how much of it is game-like. "Game-like" means that the activity involves learners doing things which are not a part of normal language use, or of normal language learning. Sometimes these game-like elements may motivate the learners to do the activity because there is a kind of challenge involved in playing the game. This may be the case for example in crossword puzzles. In *Fill the blanks*, the game-like element involves deciding which word goes into the gap. When the learner fills the gap, the learners try to figure out the intended complete meaning of the sentence, and what word will fill the gap to make this intended meaning. The intended meaning does not come from the learner as in normal productive language use, but comes from the activity maker. How useful is this game-like element for learning? To fill the gap, the learner has to comprehend the target word, and has to comprehend the whole sentence. These activities can contribute to learning as they involve receptive retrieval. However, it is interesting to compare such an activity to a true/false activity including the target words and drawing on learners' general knowledge. Here are two examples.

Black is a colour which is always in fashion.
Goods which have been used are easy to exchange.

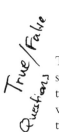

This activity does not involve a game-like element. Comprehension of such sentences is a normal part of language use. Evaluation of whether they are true or false is also a part of normal language use, as we do not always agree with what someone says. The activity involves retrieval of the meaning of the target word, and comprehension of the target word within the context of the sentence. Comprehension of the target word within the context of the sentence involves choosing the right sense or referent for the word. Both retrieval and comprehension help learning. In deciding between the two activities of *Fill the blanks* and *True/false questions*, the distinguishing point comes down to whether making a true/false decision is more useful for learning than deciding which word goes into a blank. We prefer the true/false questions.

Following a Set Format

When designing the format of a lesson, the curriculum designer needs to consider environment factors such as the length of time available for each lesson, the teachers' skill and role in the lesson, and the size of a typical class. In Chapter 1 we looked at the advantages of having a set format for lessons.

Deciding on the format of a lesson involves combining practical and principled considerations. Too often principles are ignored because of practical pressures. What occurs in a lesson and the order in which it occurs should reflect principles of teaching and learning. Let us look at one format as an example. The lesson format of this course divides into the following parts:

"Block"

1. Listening input usually with a meaning focus

2. Language-focused learning taking up points from the listening

3. Meaning-focused output, mainly speaking, often involving pair and group work and a game-like activity

Within each of these sections, especially the language-focused learning and meaning-focused output sections, there is no set order of activities and no strict limitation of activity types.

The principles at work in this lesson format seem to be:

1   There should be learning from comprehensible input as a basis for later activities.
2   Language-focused learning will contribute to the production of output.
3   Learners should have to produce language with a focus on the message.
4   Repetition is an important aid to learning and material should be recycled in a lesson.
5   Learners' interest can be engaged through short activities, attractive presentation using pictures, and a degree of unpredictability regarding the types of exercises.
6   Learners need not know why they are doing a particular activity.

Overall each lesson in this particular course has a set format with the three main sections but there is variety within some sections. The length and number of sections in a lesson may depend upon time constraints such as the usual length of a school lesson in the school or country where the lesson is taught.

Blocks and Threads

In a very interesting book entitled *Planning from Lesson to Lesson* (1995), Woodward and Lindstromberg describe two ways of planning a lesson. One way is called a "block" lesson where the lesson has a set format and is a separate block largely complete within itself. Typical block formats include the type of lesson looked at earlier in this chapter with listening and reading input, language-focused activity, and meaning-focused output. Another block format involves an experience-providing stage, a guided practice stage, and then a fluency-development stage. "Blocks" of these kinds provide support for the lesson planner in that once the type of block is chosen as being suitable for the goals that the teacher wants to achieve, the lesson itself requires very little planning because its parts are predictable and the later parts build on the previous parts of the lesson. [Vertical] [Horizontal]

The other way of planning a lesson is by making use of "threads". Threads are activities that run through a series of lessons. Threads are activities that can be used again and again with minimal planning and only small changes. For example, a teacher or curriculum designer might set up an interview thread that appears in a large number of lessons. In each lesson, the class interviews a different learner from the class. The types of questions remain the same and all that changes is that a different learner is interviewed each time. After the initial preparation and allocation of times, little further planning is needed. Alternatively, the learners interview each other in pairs with the members of the pairs changing for each lesson.

Table 6.3 lists a variety of threads. Column 1 gives the general learning goal of the activity. Column 2 gives the name of the activity and column 3 describes how the activity changes each time it is used. For example, the "It's my word!" activity involves a learner reporting to the class on a useful word that she found and researched out of class. The variation is that each time it is done in class, there is a different speaker reporting on a different word. Column 4 describes the preparation that the teacher has to do when setting up the thread. In the case of "It's my word!", the teacher needs to show the learners what information to gather about the word and how to report on the word. This could involve a simple table to fill in which acts as the basis for the spoken report and includes the pronunciation of the word, several examples of the word in context, some of the range of meanings of the word, its translations, its etymology and any constraints on its use. The report might also include tips on how to remember the word. Morning talks and the daily weather report are carried out in a similar way. Although it is not listed under teacher's preparation, several of the techniques require the teacher to make a schedule of whose turn it is to present the activity.

Column 5 indicates how the activity is carried out, individually, in pairs or groups, or with the whole class.

In "Talk and report", learner A addresses half of the class and learner B the other half. Then learners pair up with one from each half to report to their partner what they heard.

The reading and writing activities in Table 6.3 are all done as individual work. SSR means sustained silent reading where the learners (and teacher) quietly read their individually chosen books for a period of time. The

Table 6.3 Examples of threads across a range of skills

Goal	Activity	Variation	Teacher's preparation	Group size
Vocabulary	It's my word!	Speaker\word	Model procedure	Learner with the class
Listening and speaking	Morning talks	Speaker\topic	None	Learner with the class
	Interview	Partner	Model interview	Pairs
	Weather report	Speaker	Model procedure	Learner with the class
	Dictation	Partner	Learners bring a text	Pairs
	Report on a text	Speaker\text	None	Pairs or group
	Talk and report	Speaker\topic	None	Pairs
Reading	SSR	Text	None	Individual
	Speed reading	Text	Set of texts	Individual
	Information transfer	Text	Set of texts	Individual
Writing	Continuous writing	Topic	Topics	Individual
	Post office	New letter	Procedure for distributing letters	Individual

information transfer activity involves completing an information transfer diagram for a given text. Each time there is a different text to read and use to fill an information transfer diagram. The diagram can be based on topic types. The post office activity involves learners writing letters to each other and replying to letters received for a variety of purposes.

There can be threads within threads. For example, in a listening thread each learner can present their text for the others to listen to five times on five different days, once just to listen to, once to listen to and complete a cloze task, once to listen to and draw or fill an information transfer diagram, once as dictation, and once where the presenter questions the listeners.

There are two immediate values in spending time on an activity on a regular basis. Firstly, there is the opportunity for spaced repetition which is very important for learning. For example, by listening to a daily weather report learners will become familiar with the related vocabulary and the relevant constructions and collocations. Secondly, there is no need to keep explaining new techniques and procedures to the learners. By using the same techniques over and over again they become good at using them and do not need to keep dealing with procedural problems. Learning and classroom management are thus done more efficiently.

Threads can be part of blocks. Whereas blocks approach the lesson as a vertical unit, threads see lessons as made up of horizontal parts that link with other lessons. The use of threads and blocks reduces the need for detailed planning and organisation.

Techniques and Activities

A large variety of techniques and activities can be drawn on when designing lessons. These can be divided into four major types, each type having its own cycle of activities, favoured learning goals, and principles of learning (see Table 6.4 for a range of techniques). Sometimes, of course, an activity can be a combination of two or more types (a guided activity involving pair- or group-work, for instance) and sometimes two or more types are used in sequence (such as an experience activity before an independent activity). Let us look briefly at the four types.

1   Experience activities try to keep as much as possible of the knowledge needed to perform the activity within the learners' previous experience. This can be done in several ways:

   (a)   The teacher, curriculum designer or materials writer carefully controls the language, ideas, skills, etc. so that they will be largely already familiar to the learners. Simplified or graded reading texts are like this.

   (b)   The knowledge needed to do the activity is provided through previous lessons or previous activities within a lesson. Speaking activities near the end of a lesson, or the listening activities at the beginning of a lesson may be like this. This results in a lesson format that builds up to a final activity or set of activities that are the main point of the lesson.

   (c)   The teacher helps the learners to share and recall previous experience to make the following activity easier. This results in a lesson format that may begin with teacher-led discussion or group work and ends with what otherwise may have been quite a demanding task. Examples include discussion of a topic followed by each learner writing about it, and semantic mapping of a topic followed by speaking about it.

   Experience techniques allow the learners to perform tasks with apparent fluency because of the preparation and control that has preceded them. They are most often meaning-focused tasks with a fluency goal.

2   Shared activities involve the learners achieving through group work

what they could not achieve by working alone. Nation (1989b) describes four major kinds of group work:

(a) the learners in a group have equal access to the same information;
(b) each learner has a different piece of information essential to the completion of the task;
(c) one or more learners have all the information that the others need;
(d) the learners share the same information but each has a different task to do.

Shared activities are usually complete in themselves and can thus be fitted into any part of a lesson format. They provide a break from teacher-led activity and have several advantages, such as allowing negotiated meaning-focused communication, keeping all learners active, and providing substantial quantity of language input and output. They also allow learners to work at a level beyond their normal level of proficiency. Shared activities pose problems where learners all share the same first language, but these can be overcome through the design of the activity, explaining the goals to learners, and setting up monitoring and reward mechanisms.

3   Guided activities involve the learners doing already partly completed tasks. For example, completion activities, substitution activities, matching activities, repetition activities, and ordering activities all involve the teacher or curriculum designer providing part of what is needed so that the learners' task is made easier and less likely to result in error. In a substitution activity, the model is provided, and the items to substitute may be provided. The learner simply has the task of putting the item in the appropriate place and repeating the sentence. Guided activities usually involve language-focused instruction, though they may lead to a kind of meaning-focused activity where for example learners produce sentences based on a model that involves them saying things that are meaningful to them, for example describing themselves. Some lesson formats are almost completely dominated by language-focused instruction to the unfortunate exclusion of meaning-focused activities. This may be satisfactory if learners have many opportunities for meaning-focused language use outside class. Usually language-focused guided activities are used to prepare learners for meaning-focused experience activities. They therefore are found early in a lesson. A very common format for learning spoken language is as follows:

(a) The presentation of the model piece of language. The presentation may be meaning-focused, but the fundamental purpose of the model is to provide a look at the goal of the lesson and suggest items for learning and practice.

Table 6.4 Teaching techniques for listening, speaking, reading and writing classified according to the type of task

	Listening	Speaking	Reading	Writing
Experience	Listening to a graded reader read aloud Linked skills	4/3/2 Ask and answer Talking about a very familiar topic Best recording Expert groups Prepared talks Pyramid procedure Oral book reports	Reading a graded reader Easy extensive reading Issue logs Linked skills Repeated reading Speed reading course	Reading, discussing and then writing Draw and write Project work Ten-minute writing
Shared	Ranking Strip story	Brainstorming Find the differences Split information	Pause, prompt, praise Paired reading	Group composition Peer feedback Writing with a secretary Reformulation
Guided	Dictation Information transfer Listen and choose Listening to pictures Picture ordering	Dicto-gloss Retelling Running dictation Substitution tables Surveys What is it?	Comprehension questions Intensive reading Sentence completion True/false sentences	Delayed copying Dicto-comp Blackboard composition Picture composition
Independent	Reading an unsimplified text Taking part in a friendly conversation Notetaking	Giving a talk Telling a joke Taking part in an interview	Reading subtitles to a film Reading the newspaper Reading a novel	Writing a letter Writing an assignment

NB: Most of the techniques in this table can be found in *Teaching ESL/EFL Listening and Speaking* (Nation and Newton, 2009), and *Teaching ESL/EFL Reading and Writing* (Nation, 2009).

(b) The learners do guided tasks on parts of the model to prepare for the next section of the lesson.

(c) The learners do activities like role plays or discussions resulting in meaning-focused production of language that is like the model.

4   We have looked at experience, shared and guided activities. Experience tasks rely on support from previous knowledge. Shared tasks rely on support from other people and guided tasks rely on support in the activity itself. The fourth kind of activity, independent activities, is the ultimate goal of the other three. In independent activities the learners work with no assistance or preparation. They can draw on their skills and make use of other resources, but essentially they are in control of their own learning. Independent activities tend to occur late in a course and at advanced levels.

The four types of activities can all be used in a course and it is desirable that they are. This is because each provides a different kind of learning goal and means of learning. Each kind of activity makes use of a different set of principles and it is useful to look carefully at major activity types within a course to examine these principles and see if they agree with principles based on research and theory.

Tasks and Presentation

The previous chapter considered tasks as one of the units of progression in a syllabus. The arguments that task-based learning advocates like Long and Crookes (1992) presented against other types of syllabus are mostly arguments about the presentation of material rather than the selection of content. As mentioned in the previous chapter, tasks can be present in either a task-supported or a task-based syllabus. In a task-supported syllabus, the task is likely to be the final stage in a conventional Present–Practise–Produce unit of work; the task may be designed to focus on the language structure that has been presented. In a task-based syllabus, however, the task is likely to be the unit. Willis (1996) describes the task-based learning framework as consisting of three phases – pre-task, the task cycle and language focus. Considerable variety and variation is possible within this framework, and, the task need not focus on a specific language structure.

Summary of the Steps

1   Decide on the main teaching techniques and activities.
2   Plan the format of the lessons.
3   Check the format against principles.
4   Write the lessons.

In this chapter we have looked at the format and presentation part of the curriculum design process. For those unfamiliar with the curriculum design process, the format and presentation part is what they think of as curriculum design – designing lessons in sets of lessons. Some "methods" of language teaching like Total Physical Response (TPR) or the oral-aural approach were largely innovations solely or largely in the format and presentation area, with little or no contribution to content and sequencing or monitoring and assessment.

The outer circles of principles and environment analysis contribute most strongly to format and presentation. The kinds of activities we do in the class need to help learning by applying proven principles of learning, and the kinds of activities we use need to suit the current teachers, learners and classrooms.

The most important principle to consider in format and presentation is the provision of a balance of learning opportunities across the four strands of meaning-focused input, meaning-focused output, language-focused learning and fluency development. There should be a usefully limited range of teaching and learning activities used that spend roughly equal time on each of the four strands. Having a wide variety of activities is not nearly as important as having a proper balance of activities. The most important job of the language teacher is to plan, and the second most important kind of planning is to provide a balance of opportunities for learning across the four strands (the most important kind of planning is to focus on the most useful language features (content and sequencing) for learners considering their present level of proficiency (monitoring and assessment)).

Planning is made easier by having a clear format to lessons, possibly in the form of blocks or threads.

Classroom activities can be of several types and in this chapter we have looked at experience, shared, guided and independent activities. There is no need to have a balance of these types, but it is useful to understand how each of them helps learning. Experience tasks help learning by making the task a very familiar one because it is close to the learners' previous experience. Shared tasks help learners to learn from each other. Guided tasks work because the teacher has already done part of the work for the learner in the design of the task and so the learner simply, for example, has to complete a sentence, make a substitution, transform a sentence, or put sentences in order to do the activity.

So far, we have looked at the outer circles of the curriculum design model which provide valuable information to guide the application of the processes in the large inner circle. We have also looked at goals, content and sequencing, and in this chapter, format and presentation. In the next chapter we will complete our coverage of the large inner circle by looking at how teachers can see where learners are in their learning and whether they are making progress – monitoring and assessment.

Tasks

Task I Examining the format of a lesson

Go through the following steps to study the format used in a course book:

1   Take a course book and briefly describe the typical format of a lesson. Describe the job of each part of the format (introduce new items, contextualise items, provide practice, test . . .). How many different kinds of techniques are used?
2   How strictly is the format followed?, i.e. does every lesson follow exactly the same format? Are the same techniques used in every lesson? Do the lessons contain "threads"?
3   (a) What form does the syllabus take (linear or modular)? How is repetition accounted for?
    (b) How does the format reflect this?
4   What is the content of the course based on (texts, situations, topics, functions . . .)?
5   Choose the three learning principles that are most important for that course and briefly describe how they are applied in the lessons. Look carefully at the format of the lesson and describe the principles that the lesson assumes. See the section "Following a set format" in this chapter for an example.
6   Choose an important constraint that exists in your teaching and say how the format would cope with it.

Task 2 Examining teaching techniques

1   Choose your favourite or most commonly used teaching technique. Write its name or brief description here.

_____

_____

2   Does this technique work well in your situation?
    (a) Why do your learners like it?

_____

    (b) Why is it easy for you and your learners to use it?

_____

    (c) Would other teachers of different subjects in your school think that this was a strange technique? Why?

_____

3   Why do you use this technique?
    (a) What learning goal does it achieve?

    _____

    (b) What theory of learning does it follow?

    _____

4   How does this activity fit into your course?
    (a) How does it help meet the general goals of your course?

    _____

    (b) In what ways is it like and different from the other techniques you
         use?

    _____

5   How do you check to see if it has had a good or bad effect?

    _____

6   After these questions have been answered, try to fit the answers into
    the curriculum design diagram.

Case Studies

1   Compare the format of three published course books. Is the difference
    in format the major difference between the books?
2   Examine a case study of the design of a format. What justifications are
    given for the format which was chosen?

Chapter 7

Monitoring and Assessment

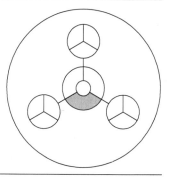

The aim of this part of the curriculum design process is to decide what to test and how to test it.

The outer circles of the curriculum design model (environment, needs and principles) provide data to guide the planning of the processes in the inner circle. Thus, monitoring and assessment must take account of the environment in which the course will be used, the needs of the learners, and principles of teaching and learning. Table 7.1 lists some of the factors to consider.

Guidelines for Monitoring and Assessment

In Table 7.1, we can see that monitoring and assessment can have both informational and affective goals. That is, monitoring and assessment can provide a teacher and learners with information about the learners' present knowledge and progress, and it can also be a means of encouraging involvement and participation.

Types of Monitoring and Assessment

The purpose of the monitoring and assessment part of curriculum design is to make sure that the learners will get the most benefit from the course. This involves carefully observing the learners and the course, and suggesting changes to the course and the way it is run. Assessment may also simply be expected to be a normal part of curriculum design. The person designing the course may also be expected to design the assessment for the course. Let us look at the major types of monitoring and assessment that can occur as part of a course.

1   **Placement assessment** The learners are assessed at the beginning of a course to see what level of the course they should be in. The aim of this testing is to ensure that the course is not going to be too easy or too difficult for the learner.

2   **Observation of learning** While the course is running, the activities that the learners do are carefully monitored to see if each particular

Table 7.1 Monitoring and assessment guidelines

ENVIRONMENT	Learners	The learners should feel good about their progress.
	Teachers	The teacher should be able to assess and correct the outcomes to the activities. The teacher should have time to assess and correct the outcomes to the activities.
	Situation	The assessment should be economical. The assessment may need to match with the external testing set by the education department, a government ministry or testing agency.
NEEDS	Lacks	The course should show that the learners are increasing their knowledge of the language.
	Wants	The course should show the learners that they are learning to do what they want to do.
	Necessities	The course should show that the learners are getting better at tasks they will need to do after the course.
PRINCIPLES		Two of the principles described in Chapter 4 have particular relevance to monitoring and assessment. • As much as possible, the learners should be interested and excited about learning the language and they should come to value this learning. • Learners should receive helpful feedback which will allow them to improve the quality of their language use.

activity is likely to achieve its learning goal. This involves technique analysis and classroom observation.

3   **Short-term achievement assessment** At regular intervals during the course, the learners may be monitored to see what they are learning from the course. These pieces of monitoring may take the form of weekly tests, the keeping of achievement records such as graphs of reading speed, charts of writing improvement and self-assessment records. This short-term assessment can occur on a daily or weekly basis. It is called "achievement" assessment because it examines items and skills drawn from the course.

4   **Diagnostic assessment** In order to plan a programme, it is useful to know where learners' strengths and weaknesses lie and where there are gaps in their knowledge. Diagnostic assessment tries to diagnose or locate areas of need. It can be done through interpreting the results of placement tests, achievement testing and proficiency testing, through observing the learners in learning tasks and language use tasks, interviewing learners and learner self-assessment, and through the use of

diagnostic tests. The aim of diagnostic assessment is to find the gaps and weaknesses and provide a remedy for them.

5   **Achievement assessment** Usually at the end of a course, and perhaps at one or two other points during the course, the learners are assessed on what they have learned from the course. This may have the purpose of examining the effectiveness of the course as much as testing the learners.

6   **Proficiency assessment** Proficiency assessment is based on items drawn from the language as a whole rather than from the content of a particular course. It tries to measure a learner's language knowledge in relation to other learners who may have studied different courses, or in relation to areas of language knowledge that are based upon an analysis of the language. Proficiency assessment has the goal of seeing where learners have reached in their knowledge of the language. Some of the better-known proficiency tests include the TOEFL test (the Test of English as a Foreign Language) and the IELTS test (the International English Language Testing System). These tests are offered for a fee on a regular basis throughout the world. They are often used to help decide if international students can be admitted to an English-medium university. The Vocabulary Size Test (Nation and Beglar, 2007) is a proficiency measure of vocabulary size. Teachers can make their own proficiency tests, however, and proficiency can be assessed through scales and checklists.

Let us now look at each of these six kinds of assessment in more detail and see the range of assessment options available for each of them. While doing this we will look briefly at important considerations in assessment such as criterion-referenced and norm-referenced tests, tests of language knowledge and language use, performance objectives, and determining the reliability, validity and practicality of assessment instruments. These are all issues of considerable importance in assessment but can only be touched on here. They are all worth following up in more detail in more specialised texts on language testing.

Monitoring and assessment is an important part of the wider field of course evaluation which is taken up in the next chapter.

Placement Assessment

Placement assessment is used to decide what level of the course a learner should enter, what class the learner should join, and whether the learner should join the course at all.

Placement assessment usually occurs under environment constraints. It often has to be done just before a course begins. The results have to be available quickly. The learners are largely unknown and may be confused about the course they wish to do. The learners may not perform their best

[margin notes: Characteristics of Placement Tests; Placement tests focus on RAW Potential knowledge; Placement Tests can be used as Diagnostic vice-versa]

on a placement test because they are unfamiliar with some of the test formats, because their knowledge of the language is "rusty" through lack of opportunity to use it, or because they are anxious about the test. The assessment may be the learners' first meeting with the teachers and course and could affect their attitudes to the course. The time available for assessment may be limited. The assessment needs to be reasonably accurate because it often proves difficult to move learners to other groups once they have joined a group. All this means that placement assessment needs to be: (1) familiar, friendly and relaxed, (2) reasonably brief and easy to mark and interpret, and (3) focused on gathering the most relevant information. This often means that placement tests focus on knowledge of language items rather than skill in language use. Let us look at this situation in more detail.

Tests which focus on language items include pronunciation, vocabulary and grammar tests. For example, a placement test designed for the Council of Europe (Meara and Buxton, 1987) consists of a computerised yes/no test where the learners see individual words without context from various frequency levels and have to indicate whether they know the word or not. About one-third of the words are nonsense words which are used to correct for over-estimation by the learner. A grammar-based test could ask the learners to complete sentences, choose appropriate items from multiple-choices, locate the items referred to by reference words in a text, or complete a cloze test or dictation. In most cases, it is reasonably clear what is being measured and the assumption is that knowledge of these items is a prerequisite for effective language use. If learners do not do well in these tests then considerable learning would be needed to achieve effective language use.

Tests which focus on language use include interviews, role plays, listening tests with message-focused questions, reading passages with message-focused questions and composition writing. These involve complex skills and if learners do not do well on such tests, there could be a variety of causes. Some of these may be apparent from careful analysis of the learners' language use, such as their compositions, but this requires time.

The results of tests involving language use may be difficult to interpret, difficult to score (especially those involving productive use) and time-consuming to sit (especially those involving written skills). They thus may not meet many of the requirements for an effective placement test. Teachers should therefore not feel that they have to include mainly language use tests in a placement test, and should feel comfortable with making use of tests focusing on knowledge of language items.

Let us now look at possible placement tests:

1   The Eurocentres Vocabulary Test has already been mentioned. This test takes about ten minutes to sit and is automatically scored by the computer

that administers it. It is reported to work well as a placement test (Meara and Buxton, 1987).

2   The Vocabulary Levels Test (Nation, 1990; Schmitt *et al.*, 2001) was designed to see where learners needed to develop their vocabulary knowledge and thus is basically a diagnostic test. Because knowledge of vocabulary is an important component of language use, it has however been effectively used as a placement test.

3   Structured interviews are often used as a placement test. In a structured interview, the learners are interviewed individually. The interviewer has a series of questions, beginning with common short questions such as "What is your name?" and moving gradually to more complex questions or commands such as "Tell me about the places you have visited in New Zealand".

4   A cloze test, particularly one where the deleted words are selected by the test maker, can be a useful placement test. Although the cloze is considered to be a reasonable test of general language proficiency, a selective cloze can focus on particular aspects of vocabulary and grammar. It is not a test of language in use because the conditions in sitting a cloze test do not closely parallel meaning-focused reading.

CLOZE TEST

5   Sentence completion tests can also be used as placement tests. Allen's (1970) "thumbnail test of English competence" is a modest example of this. Here are some example completion items.

> I have been here _____.
>
> Since you are late we _____.

Placement tests need continual monitoring to make sure that they are doing their job properly. Often their effectiveness is seen within a few days of their use and it is worth setting aside time soon after to review their performance so that they can be improved before the next administration.

Observation of Learning

Monitoring learners' progress in a course can occur at the level of the learning activity. This monitoring does not assess the learners but is directed towards the tasks that they do. The purpose of the monitoring is to see if it is necessary to make changes to the learning activities in order to encourage learning. There are four questions that should be asked when observing learning activities (Nation, 2001: 60–74).

1   What is the learning goal of the activity?
2   What are the learning conditions that would lead to the achievement of this goal?

3   What are the observable signs that these learning conditions are occurring?

4   What are the design features of the activity that set up the learning conditions or that need to be changed to set up the learning conditions?

For example, in a spoken fluency development activity, the following learning conditions need to occur. The learners are focused on the meaning of the task. The task involves very limited language demands, i.e. all the language needed to do the task is familiar to the learners. There is some kind of pressure to perform at a higher than normal level of performance. The signs that the teacher should look for when monitoring the activity are an involvement in communicating with a partner, a reasonably high speed of speaking with a small number of hesitations, and some signs of comprehension by the listener. The design features include opportunity for preparation, a chance to repeat the task several times to different listeners, a familiar topic and an involved listener, and time pressure.

Monitoring can occur in other ways. Learner diaries or logbooks written for the teacher are a useful source of information (Savage and Whisenand, 1993). Learners talking in small groups to provide feedback for the teacher is another way.

Short-Term Achievement Assessment

Monitoring looks at activities as they occur and is essentially process-oriented. Short-term achievement assessment looks at the product of activities or a small set of activities. The purpose of this assessment is to see if the learners are making progress on a daily or weekly basis. It provides feedback to the teacher and the learners. In an intensive course a weekly test is a common way of carrying out this kind of assessment. In the test the learners are assessed on the work that they have done that week. Short-term assessment can also have motivational purposes, to make learners do required work and to give them feelings of achievement through success on the tests. In courses where there are fewer classes, this kind of assessment is not feasible, but there are several other ways of carrying out short-term achievement assessment.

For activities like speed reading, written composition, extensive reading, and dictation, the learners can record their performance on a graph each time they complete an activity. This shows the learners the progress they are making and allows the teacher to see who needs help and who is progressing well.

Short-term achievement is more easily assessed if there are clear performance objectives for some of the learning goals. A performance objective is a statement consisting of five parts (Brown, 1995). It describes (1) who should achieve the objective (the subject), (2) what the person should be able to do (the performance), (3) under what conditions the performance should occur (the conditions), (4) how the performance will be tested (the measure), and (5) what level of performance must be reached (the criterion). Here is an example performance objective with its five parts numbered:

> (1) The learners should be able to (2) quickly read and comprehend a 550 word text (3) containing only well-known vocabulary and constructions (5) at a speed greater than 250 words per minute and with at least 70 per cent comprehension (4) as measured by ten four-item multiple-choice questions. (3) The learners should not refer back to the text while they answer the questions.

Here is another performance objective:

> The learners should be able to write a 1,000 word composition based on an academic topic in their field of study requiring reference to at least three different source materials and obtain a grade of at least 3 on a 5-point scale for accurate use of language, at least 3 on a 5-point scale for quality of the content and argumentation, and at least 3 on a 5-point scale for clarity of organisation and observance of the conventions for bibliographical reference, use of subheadings, and acknowledgement of sources.

There has been considerable debate about the value of performance objectives (see for example Tumposky, 1984), but Brown (1995) in an excellent discussion shows that while many of the criticisms are true for poorly made objectives, there is considerable value in using performance objectives to clarify goals for both teacher and learners, and to monitor progress. At the least, curriculum designers should write performance objectives for some of the goals of the course, particularly where there might be misunderstanding of what is to be learned and where focused repeated practice is needed to reach the goals.

Good short-term achievement assessment should provide a clear record of progress that is easily interpreted. As much as possible it should be in a form to motivate learners to keep working towards the course goals. It should not occupy too much class time, but should be a regular expected part of class activity. Clarke (1989) suggests that some of the work of short-term achievement testing can be handed over to the learners.

Diagnostic Assessment

Diagnostic assessment is used to find the gaps and weaknesses in learners' knowledge so that something can be done about them. More positively, it is used to find what learners know well so that time is not wasted on teaching that. Diagnostic assessment is thus a very important part of needs analysis both before a course begins and during the course. The findings of diagnostic assessment are used to determine what goes into a course, so good diagnostic assessment is accurate and easy to interpret in terms of what should be done as a result. Diagnostic information can often be obtained from assessment intended for other purposes, such as proficiency tests, achievement tests or placement tests. There are however tests designed especially for diagnosis.

The vocabulary levels test (Schmitt *et al.*, 2002) is an example of a diagnostic test. This test helps a teacher decide whether learners should be focusing on high-frequency vocabulary, academic vocabulary or low-frequency vocabulary. This is a very important decision, because high-frequency vocabulary and low-frequency vocabulary require quite different teaching strategies. For high-frequency vocabulary, every word deserves individual attention in a variety of ways. For low-frequency vocabulary, the focus should be on the development of vocabulary coping and learning strategies that learners can use independently of a teacher. Each low-frequency word does not deserve individual attention from the teacher, but the strategies of guessing from context, using word parts to remember meanings, and using mnemonics and decontextualised learning do deserve attention. The findings of diagnostic assessment can thus have a major effect on the design of a course.

Diagnostic assessment can take other forms. These include analysis of language use such as written compositions, reading tasks, spoken performance, observation of learner performance such as the process of writing, notetaking, and conversational activity. Technological advances can facilitate such analysis; for example, the potential of vocabulary profiles based on samples of student writing to provide valid, reliable and cost-effective diagnosis (Morris and Cobb, 2004).

Learner self-assessment is another possible form of diagnostic assessment. Self-assessment usually involves learners working with checklists or scales to indicate their perceived areas of strength and weakness. The problem with self-assessment is that it is often difficult to separate the learners' subjective concerns from objective judgement.

One effect of diagnostic assessment can be to help learners set personal goals for a course. Diagnosis invariably reveals a range of needs and many of these may be best filled by giving learners responsibility for some of them. These personal goals can be put in a written form where each goal is accompanied by a schedule of work that will help learners achieve the goals.

Achievement Assessment

Achievement assessment measures both the achievement of learners during a course and the effectiveness of the course. Depending on the length of the course, there may be a final achievement test at the end, and perhaps one or two tests part of the way through a course. The tests part of the way through a course may have the purpose of picking up learners who are not achieving, so that something can be done to help them learn. These tests may also assess material that will not be assessed at the end of the course, thus allowing a greater spread of assessment of the material covered in the course.

Achievement tests have the following characteristics:

1   They are based on material taught in the course.
2   Learners usually know what kinds of questions will be asked and what material will be covered.
3   They are criterion referenced. That means that there will be a standard or criterion set which will indicate whether learners have achieved enough to be given a pass for the course. So the learners are not assessed in relation to each other, but in relation to a pre-determined criterion.

Achievement tests may be mastery tests. In a mastery test, a high criterion is set. The pass grade for example may be 80 per cent or 90 per cent. Learners can be given repeated opportunities to study the material and sit the tests until they reach the criterion of mastery. Mastery achievement tests usually focus on a small area of knowledge so that learners are clear about what has to be learned and so that they can set themselves a series of short-term goals to eventually cover the area of knowledge.

The thinking behind mastery tests is (1) that if something is to be learned, it should be learned well, (2) that every learner is capable of achieving mastery, some may require more time to do so than others, (3) that the teacher's responsibility is to the students and to learning and thus every learner should have the chance to learn well, and (4) that mastery of an area is rewarding and motivating for both teacher and learners.

There are opposing views, particularly at the university level. The thinking behind these views is (1) that the teacher's responsibility is to the subject matter and not to the students. The content of courses should not be reduced to suit the average level of the students, (2) that one role of courses is to indicate to employers and those responsible for admission to further education that some learners are more capable than others. Mastery learning hides these dissimilarities and thus the grades of a mastery course may misinform employers, and (3) that learners are responsible for their learning and the management of their learning.

There is no doubt that using achievement testing that is based on mastery brings about dramatic improvements in teaching and learning and it is worth considering its use for at least some parts of a language course.

Achievement assessment is not all done by tests. Some aspects of achievement are better done in other ways. Assessing skill in composition writing is a good example. To obtain a reliable measure of writing skill, it is necessary for learners to write more than one composition. This is usually not feasible in the limited time available during a test. It is thus better to base assessment of writing on several pieces of work done in class.

An issue to consider in achievement testing is how closely the form of the questions in an achievement test copy the types of activity done in the classroom. There are arguments for making them at least slightly different in that language learning is supposed to be able to transfer to a variety of uses and achievement tests should test for this.

Achievement assessment is a very important element in curriculum design. It not only provides important feedback for teachers, learners and curriculum designers, but also can affect teaching and learning in that the tests motivate and guide learning. This is sometimes called the "washback" effect of testing on teaching, and we will look at it a little more in proficiency assessment.

Proficiency Assessment

A test of language proficiency draws items for the test not from the course that the learners are studying, but from the language itself, independent of any course. The reason for this is that the purpose of a proficiency test is to show how much the learners know of the language or a particular part of the language. If the selection of language items and skills to go in a course has been based upon a valid analysis of the language then there may not be a big difference between what is in a proficiency test and an achievement test, except perhaps that the proficiency test is likely to cover a larger range of items and skills.

Sometimes, a proficiency test, such as the TOEFL (www.toefl.org/) or IELTS (www.ielts.org/) test, awaits a learner at the end of a course. This test may be working as a criterion-referenced test to determine whether a learner goes into an English-medium university or not. TOEFL is offered in three formats, and for the widely used internet-based test this criterion is usually set at a score of 79 or 80 out of a possible 120 for entry to an undergraduate course, depending on which university is setting the criterion. The IELTS test uses a 9-point scale with a score of 6, 6.5 or 7 usually being necessary to gain entrance to a university. Sometimes the test may simply act as a norm-referenced test which shows learners at which percentile of proficiency they are in relation to others.

A proficiency test like TOEFL which is used as a criterion-referenced test can have a profound washback effect on a language course that precedes the sitting of the test. It can be a major environmental factor affecting the course. It can have the effect of making the content of the course resemble the content and test item formats in the test. It can have the effect of encouraging learners to drop out of the course if the course does not clearly and directly address the requirements of the test. Courses which try to predict what will be in the test and which copy the format of the test in their learning activities are in effect trying to make the proficiency test be like an achievement test, except that instead of the test drawing items from the course, the course is drawing items from old tests. The presence of such a test at the end of a course cannot be ignored. Studies of washback (Alderson and Hamp-Lyons, 1996; Watanabe, 1996) reveal that the effects of a test on the classroom are by no means simple. Different teachers are affected in different ways, and the quality of the channels of communication between the test designers and users and the teachers and learners is crucial. Wall (1996) shows the value of regarding the introduction of a new test and the management of its washback effects as being an example of educational innovation. Thus, it is useful to consider washback effects using the framework and questions used in innovation theory. We look at this in Chapter 12.

There are several responses to the constraint of the test at the end of a course:

1   Make the course like the test. There are thousands of TOEFL and IELTS preparation courses like this, usually run as a commercial business. Each major publisher has its TOEFL or IELTS preparation course book for sale.
2   Make parts of the course like the test. This is a common compromise especially in university intensive English programmes where the proficiency test is obligatory for entry to university.
3   Remove the test. Some universities do this by allowing students who successfully complete their university's own intensive English programme to enter university without sitting an international proficiency test. The university's intensive English programme may have its own proficiency test which it administers and which fits more comfortably with its pre-university courses.

An important value of proficiency tests is that they are one source of evaluation data for a programme. They represent an independent measure of the relevance and adequacy of a language course. Elder and O'Loughlin (2003) provide data on how much change can be expected in an IELTS score as a result of doing an intensive English programme.

Achievement measures favour the course and favour learners who have done the course. But, it is possible that what is being done on the course, even though it is done well, does not represent what it means to know the language. A valid proficiency measure is one way of checking this.

Good Assessment: Reliability, Validity and Practicality

All assessment needs to be checked to see that it is doing its job properly and that it is not causing unnecessary work. Most investigative procedures, including the tools for needs analysis, course evaluation procedures, and tests and other measures for assessment can be examined by considering three criteria – reliability, validity and practicality. Here we will discuss these three criteria in relation to tests, but they can be applied to a far wider range of instruments.

Reliability

A reliable test gives results that are not greatly upset by conditions that the test is not intended to measure. After allowing for the practice effect, if the same person sat the test twice, they should get near enough to the same result. Statistically, reliability is measured by having the learners sit the test twice, or more commonly, by splitting the scores on the individual test items into two equal groups and seeing if the learners get the same score on both groups.

A test is more reliable if (1) it is always given under the same conditions, (2) it is consistently marked, (3) it has a large number of points of assessment, that is, many questions or as in a dictation many items that are marked, and (4) its questions and instructions are clear and unambiguous.

The conditions under which the test is given include the amount of time allowed for the test, whether the instructions are always presented in the same way, if it is a listening test whether the text is a recording to keep the speed and accent the same, and whether the recording can be heard equally well in all parts of the room.

A test may reliably tap learners' knowledge or performance, but if the marking is unreliable, then the results are unreliable. Reliable marking is consistent, and consistency is helped by having some kind of answer key or well-thought-out scoring procedure. Markers may need to be trained.

If a test has many questions or points of assessment, then if something is wrong with one or two of the points, this will not greatly influence the result. Usually at least 20 to 30 points of assessment would be desirable, but this is not always possible. A test which has four questions may still have 20 or more points of assessment if five or more things are looked for in each of the four answers.

An unreliable test cannot be valid.

Validity

A valid test measures what it is supposed to measure. A valid achievement test measures what has been learned on the course. A valid listening test measures skill at listening. The most practical ways for a teacher or curriculum designer to check the validity of a test are to look at its face validity and content validity.

Face validity simply means that if the test is called a reading test, does it look like a reading test? If it is called a vocabulary test, does it look like a vocabulary test? There is nothing very scientific about deciding on face validity, but face validity is important because it reflects how the learners and perhaps their parents, and other teachers will react to the test. For example the Eurocentres Vocabulary test that we looked at earlier in this chapter has rather low face validity – it presents words in isolation without a context, it does not ask for the learner to give a meaning, and it does not require the learners to use the vocabulary. This could affect learners' reaction to the test and their acceptance of its results. Similarly a test of speaking which does not require the learners to speak (Brown, 1983) has low face validity. A deeper understanding of how these two tests work and how they have been validated shows that these are valid tests, but their face validity, their appearance of being a certain kind of test, is still low. It is an advantage if tests look like the kind of test they are supposed to be.

Content validity is a little like face validity, except that the decision-making about validity is not made by looking at the test's "face", but by analysing the test and comparing it to what it is supposed to test. To find the content validity of an achievement test, we would have to look at the part of the course that was being tested and list the items and skills taught. Then we would have to look at the test and list the items and skills tested. If these two lists matched each other quite closely, or if the test involved a representative sample of the course list, we could say the test has content validity. Similarly, a vocabulary proficiency test could be analysed to see what particular vocabulary items and aspects of vocabulary knowledge it tested, and then we would have to consider what vocabulary knowledge in general includes and to compare this with the test. If the test includes the most important aspects and does not include too much of other skills and knowledge, it has some content validity.

One of the major obstacles in examining content validity is to find some well-supported description of what the language skills like reading and writing involve, or what knowledge of the language items like vocabulary and grammar involves. Often a commonsense analysis has to be done. Useful sources for the description of the content of language skills include Munby (1978), Richards (1983, for listening), Bennett (1972, for reading), Nuttall (1996, for reading). Validity exists when a test is used for the purpose for which it was designed. If it is used for another purpose, its validity needs to be checked for this new purpose.

There are other ways of measuring validity. Some of these involve statistical comparison with other measures. A long-term goal for the development of some of the more important parts of the assessment in a course, such as the final achievement test or the placement test, would be to check the validity of these tests in other ways besides face and content validity.

Practicality

Not only must a test be reliable and valid, it must also be practical. Practicality is examined by looking at (1) the cost involved in administering and scoring the test, (2) the time taken to administer and sit the test, (3) the time taken to mark the test, (4) the number of people needed to administer and mark the test, and (5) the ease in interpreting and applying the results of the test.

Tests can be made more practical by having reusable test papers, by being carefully formatted for easy marking, by being not too long, and by using objectively scored items such as true/false or multiple choice. The requirements of practicality and reliability and validity do not always agree with each other, for example short tests are practical but not very reliable or valid. Sometimes it is necessary to sacrifice some practicality to get a valid test (for example an individual oral interview for 200 people), or to sacrifice validity to make the test more practical (multiple-choice vocabulary tests). Where possible, reliability and validity should be preferred over practicality, but usually compromise is necessary. Improvements in practicality can often be found by giving careful thought to the test format and by doing a little pilot testing.

Summary of the Steps
1   Decide what kinds of assessment are needed and when they are needed.
2   Write the tests.
3   Check the reliability, validity and practicality of the tests.

Assessment is a major source of information for the evaluation of a course and thus its gradual improvement. Assessment also contributes significantly to the teacher's and learners' sense of achievement in a course and thus is important for motivation. It is often neglected in curriculum design and courses are less effective as a result. Curriculum design should include the planning of a well-thought-out programme of assessment of various kinds. We now go on to look at evaluation in the next chapter.

Tasks

Task I   Planning the assessment in a course

Think of a course you are familiar with or use the example of an evening course in English for non-native speakers of English, resident in an English-speaking country, who want to improve their written English. Plan six pieces of assessment in a course. Say where they would come in the course and what they would look for. Consider the means of assessment, including item types where relevant.

Task 2 Evaluating a test

Use the criteria of reliability, validity and practicality to describe how you would quickly evaluate a short-term achievement test of vocabulary which uses the following item type to test 15 words.

1   *blame*
2   *elect*   _____ *make*
3   *jump*   _____ *choose by voting*
4   *manufacture*   _____ *become like water*
5   *melt*
6   *threaten*

Task 3 Designing a placement test

Choose a course that you are familiar with or use the context of a pre-university course in English for foreign-language learners who want to go on to academic study in an English-speaking university. Design and evaluate a placement test with several parts to it.

1   Quickly decide on the course and the learners that the test is for. For example, a course for adult "false beginners" with three graded levels of classes.

   _____

   _____

2   Decide what skills and language items you need to test. Choose just one aspect to look at. For example, listening comprehension, vocabulary knowledge, reading skill.

   _____

   _____

3   Decide on an item type for each aspect you have chosen and make one or two sample items for each item type.

   _____

   _____

   _____

4   Evaluate the reliability, face validity, content validity and practicality of your test.

   _____

   _____

   _____

Case Studies

1 Upshur and Turner (1995) describe how to develop rating scales to assess various aspects of a course. Apply this approach to developing a rating scale for your learners' spoken performance.
2 Prodromou (1995) and Alderson and Wall (1993) describe the washback effect of external tests on teaching. List these effects and consider how they would apply to testing within a course.

Chapter 8

Evaluation

The aim of this part of the curriculum design process is to decide how to check if the course is successful and where it needs to be improved.

What is an Evaluation?

The broadest kind of evaluation looks at all aspects of curriculum design to see if the course is the best possible (this is why the outer circle of the model includes all the parts of the curriculum design process). Evaluation requires looking both at the results of the course, and the planning and running of the course. In reality, most evaluations are more narrowly focused and may be answering questions like the following:

- Is the teaching on the course of a suitably high standard?
- Is the course preparing the learners properly for their use of English at the end of the course (e.g. to pass the TOEFL test, to study in an English-medium university, to work as a tour guide)?
- Are the learners satisfied with the course?
- Is the course cost effective?

Carrying out an evaluation is like carrying out research, and it is thus critically important that the evaluator is clear about what question is being asked. That is, why the course is being evaluated.

Steps in an Evaluation

All of the early steps in evaluation aim at deciding why the evaluation is being done and if it is possible to do it.

1 Find who the evaluation is for and what kind of information they need.
2 Find what the results of the evaluation will be used for – to improve the course, to decide whether to keep or get rid of the course.
3 Decide if the evaluation is necessary or if the needed information is already available.
4 Find how much time and money are available to do the evaluation.
5 Decide what kinds of information will be gathered.

- Amount of learning
- Quality of learning
- Quality of teaching
- Quality of curriculum design
- Quality of course administration
- Quality of support services – library, language lab, etc.
- Teacher satisfaction
- Learner satisfaction
- Sponsor satisfaction
- Later success of graduates of the course
- Financial profitability of the course.

6   Try to gain the support of the people involved in the evaluation.
7   Decide how to gather the information and who will be involved in the gathering of information.
8   Decide how to present the findings.
9   Decide if a follow-up evaluation is planned to check the implementation of the findings.

A further step would be to evaluate the evaluation. Was the evaluation reliable, valid and practical?

Let us now look at some of the steps in evaluation in more detail.

Purpose and Audience of the Evaluation

Kiely and Rea-Dickens (2006: 225–271) make a useful three-way scope distinction: (1) large-scale evaluations which "tend to focus on major educational innovations with significant financial backing with an underlying agenda", (2) teacher-led evaluations, and (3) management-led evaluations. A course evaluation can be an expensive and time-consuming procedure. For example, an evaluation of an intensive English programme involved talking to each of the thirty-six teachers on the programme for at least half an hour each and in some cases for five or more hours. An evaluation of a university department involved bringing in some outside evaluators as part of the evaluation team and paying their travel and accommodation expenses plus a fee for their services. Because of this investment of time and money, it is important that an evaluation is well focused and well motivated.

Most of the really important work in an evaluation is done before the data gathering begins. As in experimental research, you cannot fix by statistics what has been spoilt in design.

The first critical step is to find out who the evaluation is for and what kind of information they value. There are several reasons why this step is very important. Firstly, it helps determine the degree of confidentiality of the evaluation. Will the report of the evaluation be available to all involved or will it only go to the person or group commissioning the evaluation? Secondly, it helps determine what kind of information should be gathered and what kind of information should not be gathered. The person or group commissioning the evaluation may place great importance on learner satisfaction or on economic issues, or they may consider these irrelevant. In the initial stages of an evaluation, the evaluator needs to talk at length with the person commissioning the evaluation to make clear the goals and type of data to be gathered in the evaluation. An effective way to make this clear is to prepare a brief "mock" report based on false data with the purpose of showing the person commissioning the evaluation what the report may look like. People interested in commissioning an evaluation of a language course could include the learners, the teachers, the Director of the language centre or the owners of the language centre. Each of these interested parties will have a different view of what a "good" course is and will value different kinds of evidence. Thirdly, knowing who the evaluation is for is useful in determining whether the data to be gathered will be provided willingly or reluctantly.

At the same time, it is important to know why the evaluation is being done. Is it being done to improve the course or to guide a decision whether to maintain or get rid of the course? It is at this point that the evaluator should be most cynical. Is there a hidden purpose to the evaluation that is not made clear to the evaluator? For example, is the real goal of the evaluation to dispose of an unwanted staff member, or to provide an excuse to get rid of a course (the decision to get rid of it already having been made secretly)?

At the end of this preparatory stage of the evaluation, the evaluator should be able to tell the person commissioning the evaluation:

(a) whether the evaluation is worth doing
(b) whether the evaluation is possible
(c) how long it might take
(d) how much it might cost
(e) whether the evaluator is willing to do it
(f) what kind of evidence the evaluation will gather.

If all the people are in agreement, then the evaluation can continue.

The Type and Focus of the Evaluation

A distinction is made between formative evaluation and summative evaluation (see Table 8.1). The basis of the distinction lies in the purpose of evaluation. A formative evaluation has the purpose of forming or shaping the course to improve it. A summative evaluation has the purpose of making a summary or judgement on the quality or adequacy of the course so that it

Table 8.1 Formative and summative evaluation compared

	Formative	*Summative*
Purpose	Improve the course	Judge the course
Type of data	More likely to look at causes, processes, individuals	More likely to look at results, standards, groups
Use of data	Used for counselling, mentoring, professional development, setting goals, adapting material	Used to make decisions on adequacy
Presentation of findings	Presented to and discussed with individuals	Presented in a report

can be compared with other courses, compared with previous summative evaluations, or judged as being up to a certain criterion or not. These different purposes may affect the type of data gathered, the way the results are presented, and when the data are gathered, but essentially most data can be used for either of the two purposes. The formative/summative distinction is important when informing the people who are the focus of an evaluation about the purpose of the evaluation, in helping the evaluator decide what kind of information will be most useful to gather, and in using the information gathered. Table 8.1 compares formative and summative evaluation deliberately contrasting the differences to make the distinction clear.

Deciding whether the evaluation is summative or formative is one decision. Deciding if it is to be long term or short term is another (Beretta, 1986a, b). Most evaluations are short term. Some are conducted over a few days. Others may be long term. Long-term evaluation is most economically done if it is planned as a part of curriculum design and we will look at this later in this chapter. Some important features of a course cannot be validly evaluated in a short-term evaluation. These include quality of teaching and learner achievement. A teacher's quality cannot be reliably or validly assessed from watching one or two lessons. The lessons may be especially well prepared for the evaluation, or the teacher could be nervous and having a bad day. Teaching also involves the planning of a programme of work and carrying it through to its conclusion. One or two isolated observations may not show this. Stenhouse (1975) stressed the importance of "illuminative evaluation" where evaluation helps those involved understand what is going on in the programme, and this necessarily requires teachers to be active programme evaluators.

Along with formative/summative and short term/long term, a third distinction is process/product (Long, 1984). An evaluation can focus on the process of learning and teaching and it can focus on the product or result of

Process v. Product Observations

learning and teaching. Process observations of learning look at how engaged learners are in their tasks, the quality of the interaction between themselves and between the teacher and the learners, and the quantity and quality of the language used. Product observations of learning look at what was learned and how much was learned. Both kinds of data provide different but hopefully intersecting views of the same thing.

The last set of distinctions to look at here is whether the evaluation will include cognitive, affective and resource factors. Cognitive factors involve learning and teaching and the gaining of knowledge, and the application of that knowledge after the course has ended. Typical questions would be: "How much has been taught?", "How much has been learned?", "Has the course improved learners' work or study performance?". Affective factors involve feelings of satisfaction and attitudes. Typical questions would be: "Are the learners pleased with the course?", "Do the staff work well together?", "Do the teachers feel the course is effective?". Resource factors involve costs, profit, availability and quality of teaching and learning resources such as books, classrooms, visual aids, tape recorders, computers, library facilities, social services and administrative support. Typical questions would be: "Is the library adequate for the needs of the learners?", "Are the classrooms large enough?", "Does the course make a financial profit?".

It should be clear from this brief survey that a full-scale evaluation could be an enormous undertaking. It is therefore important to decide what the evaluation will focus on. Primarily this decision should not be based on practical factors but on the kind of information that is needed to achieve the goal of the evaluation. It is better to have a small amount of relevant data than a large amount of data that do not address the main concerns of the evaluation.

Gaining Support for the Evaluation

A course evaluation looks for strengths and weaknesses, but it is naturally the weaknesses that cause concern. Finding weaknesses carries with it the idea that someone or something is to blame for the weaknesses and this is clearly a threatening situation. If an evaluation is to proceed effectively, it is important that honest data are available. So, it is necessary for those involved in the evaluation, particularly those who are sources of information, to feel that the evaluation is worthwhile and not personally threatening to their "face" and their job security. This will require meeting with those involved and involving them in the planning and carrying out of the evaluation. For this reason, some evaluations involve a respected outsider who makes gaining the agreement and cooperation of the staff a prerequisite to doing the evaluation. That is, if the evaluator is unable to gain the cooperation of staff through meeting with them and explaining the purpose and likely procedure of the evaluation, then the evaluator decides not to proceed with the evaluation. The issue of stakeholder involvement in evaluation is an important one (Kiely and Rea-Dickens, 2006). Clearly there is potentially a very wide range of stakeholders, all with different kinds of connections to the programme. Actively involving a wide range of stakeholders can result in a better informed evaluation as well as a protective sharing of responsibility (working with others means you don't have to take all the blame yourself!).

Not all evaluations are potentially threatening and they may spring from the desire of staff to improve their programme. In these cases it may be necessary to convince other staff of the value of the evaluation and that there will be a worthwhile return for the time and effort spent on the evaluation.

A properly conducted evaluation can be an empowering and motivating activity. The assumptions behind an evaluation usually are that: (1) this course is worth improving, (2) the people running and teaching the course are capable of improving it, (3) the people involved in the course have the freedom and flexibility to make changes to the course, and (4) the improvements will make it a better course for all concerned.

Seen in this way, an evaluation is an activity that deserves support.

Gathering the Information

The tools of needs analysis and the tools of evaluation are somewhat similar to each other. This will be apparent in Tables 8.3 and 8.4. The purposes for which the tools are used differ and in an evaluation they are used to gather a much wider range of data. Let us now look at a few of the most useful information-gathering tools in more detail. Table 8.2 looks at a range of focuses for evaluation, suggesting several possible data-gathering tools to choose from for each focus.

Table 8.2 looks at evaluating teaching and learning. This can involve looking at the performance of teachers and learners, observing lessons and examining achievement. Evaluation can also look at the environment of the course, which may involve looking at administrative procedures, availability and quality of resources, and how outsiders view the course. Table 8.3 looks at a range of such focuses and possible tools.

Let us now look at some of these data-gathering tools in more detail.

Interviews

Interviews are usually conducted on a one-to-one basis, but it is sometimes useful to interview a committee or to use a staff meeting as a way of gathering data. Interviews can be structured (the interviewer has a procedure and a set of questions to follow and generally keeps to these) or unstructured (the course of the interview depends on the wishes of the interviewer and interviewee and is largely unpredictable). It is valuable for the interviewer to take

Table 8.2 Focus and tools for evaluation of teaching and learning

Focus	Tools
Amount of learning	Achievement and proficiency tests Learner self-report scales Analysis of course book content Interviewing learners
Quality of learning	Achievement and proficiency assessment Lesson observation Interviewing learners Teacher diaries Study of research reports
Quality of teaching	Systematic lesson observation Interviewing teachers – retrospective accounts Learner self-report scales Teacher self-report scales Study of research reports Achievement tests Listing of staff qualifications
Quality of course book	Systematic course book evaluation checklist Teacher and learner questionnaires
Quality of curriculum design	Systematic course evaluation checklist Analysis of the syllabus Evaluation of the course materials
Degree of later success of graduates of the course	Interviewing employers or using questionnaires Interviewing graduates or using questionnaires Later achievement records such as GPA
Teacher, learner or sponsor satisfaction	Self-report scales Questionnaires Interviews Learner re-enrolment statistics

notes, particularly where a large number of people will be interviewed and it may be necessary to work out some quantification system in order to be able to summarise and combine interview data on important issues, for example, how many people consider that the course assessment procedure needs changing.

Self-report scales

Questionnaires are of many different types and so it is useful to distinguish those that involve open-ended questions from those that are largely asking respondents to rate an aspect of the course on a predetermined scale. These can be called "self-report scales". Here is an example.

> The teaching on the course was:
>
> | 1 | 2 | 3 | 4 | 5 |
> |---|---|---|---|---|
> | very poor | poor | adequate | very good | excellent |

Self-report scales are very efficient where (1) there is a need to survey a large number of people, (2) there is a large number of pieces of information to gather, (3) there are very clear focuses for the evaluation, and (4) there is a need to summarise the data to get a general picture, to compare with previous evaluations or other courses, or to provide a simple summative evaluation to see if further data need to be gathered.

There are several dangers of self-report scales:

1   They tend to result in average results if the responses are simply added and averaged. This is usually avoided by also showing how many people responded with 5 (excellent), how many responded with 4 (very good) and so on.

2   Self-report scales involve pre-determined questions and types of answers. In reporting the results of the evaluation, this might be expressed as "60 per cent of the people considered that the teaching on the course was very good". This is partly a misrepresentation as the term "very good" and the focus "teaching on this course" was provided in the self-report scale. The respondents may really have wanted to say the teaching

Table 8.3 Evaluating the course environment

Focus	Tools
Externally perceived status of the course	Analysis of media reports Interviewing staff of other institutions Enrolment statistics Quality of staff publication
Financial profitability	Audit of profit and loss data
Quality of course administration	Interview or questionnaire to teaching staff and students Study of departmental memos, handbooks, minutes of meetings, etc. Observation of procedures Interview of administrative staff
Quality of support services – library, audiovisual and language laboratory, computer laboratory, self-access centre, classrooms	Observation with a checklist Teacher and learner questionnaire Teacher and learner interviews Support staff interviews

was a bit above average, and may have wished to comment on the poor teaching facilities, but there was not an item for that. Most question-naires involving self-report scales have a final section where the respondent is invited to comment on anything else they wish to. Not all respondents make use of this. Davies (2006), in his interesting discussion of class-specific questionnaires being used by the teacher-as-evaluator, provides an example of a questionnaire that includes both types of information-gathering.

3 Self-report scales are often used for student evaluation of teaching and they are administered in class, allowing the learners a rather short period of time to answer. They are often thus influenced by what has immedi-ately preceded them. This can be partly avoided by encouraging learners to reflect on the whole course and by allowing them to discuss in pairs or small groups before responding individually.

Block (1998) provides a very insightful analysis of students' comments on their responses to a questionnaire showing that there may be a wide degree of variety in their interpretations of the questionnaire items as well as in the reasons for assigning a particular rating. Block suggests that questionnaires should be trialled in an interview form with a few learners to make sure the questionnaire deals with what the learners consider most important in their particular learning culture.

Observation and checklists

Most aspects of a course can be evaluated to some degree through observa-tion and analysis. These include analysing the course book, observing learn-ing in lessons, observing teaching, analysing the coverage of curriculum design procedures, and observing the performance of learners after the course. This observation can be unstructured in that the observer or analyser tries to see what is there without too many preconceptions. Another kind of observation and analysis is where the observer or analyser has a checklist of features to look for and evaluate. Both of these kinds of observation are important. The unstructured observation may pick up features that are strikingly important and features that may not have been included in any checklist. The structured observation with a checklist makes sure that everything that was thought to be important to look at is looked at.

The checklists for the various kinds of analysis and observation are like tests or dependent measures in an experiment and need to be reliable, valid and practical. Table 8.4 is a simple checklist for observing the quality of teaching. Each item can be responded to with a Yes/No or scaled response, and a space could be left for comments on each item.

A checklist is likely to be reliable if the items on it can be clearly under-stood by each person using it, if the people using it are trained to use it, and

Table 8.4 Teaching evaluation checklist

1	Does the teacher get the learners involved and excited about learning?
2	Is most of the lesson conducted in English?
3	Do the learners need to use English in the lesson?
4	Is each learner getting a large amount of meaningful contact with English?
5	Do the learners have to think deeply about the work they do?
6	Is the teacher monitoring the learners' understanding and providing useful feedback for them?
7	Are the learners aware of the goals of the lesson?
8	Is the teacher providing enough repetition to help the learners remember?

if it contains several items. The teaching evaluation checklist in Table 8.4 contains eight items. Too many would make it too complicated to use. Too few would make a poor item or a poorly used item have too great an effect on the whole list.

A checklist is likely to be valid if it is based on a well-thought-out, well-researched system of knowledge that is directly relevant to what is being evaluated. The teaching evaluation checklist in Table 8.4 is based on the principles of presentation described in Chapter 4. Other evaluation checklists can be based on the parts of the curriculum design process (see Chapter 11 for designing a course book evaluation form), or on a well-researched and thought-out model of the aspect that is being evaluated.

A checklist is likely to be practical if it is not too long, if it is easy to use, and if it is easy to interpret its results. It is well worthwhile doing a small pilot study with a checklist, using it on one or two occasions, discussing it with colleagues who are prepared to be constructively critical, and trying to apply its findings. A small amount of time spent on such simple pilot testing avoids a large amount of future difficulty.

The disadvantages of checklists are that (1) they may "blind" the observer from seeing other important features that are not on the list, (2) they tend to become out of date as theory changes (consider the course book evaluation form designed by Tucker (1968)), and (3) many checklists are based on the assumption that summing the parts is equal to the whole.

The advantages of checklists are that (1) they ensure that there is a systematic coverage of what is important, (2) they allow comparison between different courses, lessons, teachers etc., and (3) they can act as a basis for the improvement of a course through formative evaluation.

Formative Evaluation as a Part of a Course

An important question in an evaluation is who will be involved in the evaluation. The involvement of curriculum designers and teachers in an evaluation can be an important part of professional development. Much of the discussion of evaluation in this chapter has assumed that a one-off evaluation is being done and that the evaluators may be from outside the course. However, if curriculum design is seen as a continual process, then it is important that evaluation is built into a course. In Chapter 10 on negotiated syllabuses we will look at some aspects of evaluation (particularly learner satisfaction and the quality of learning) becoming an essential part of the course. In more traditional courses than those based on a negotiated syllabus, formative evaluation can still be planned as a part of curriculum design. This can be done in the following ways:

1   Parts of the curriculum design can be negotiated between the teacher and the learners (see Clarke (1991) for an excellent discussion of this). This may include negotiation of classroom activities, some of the goals of the course, and some assessment procedures. This negotiation is a kind of evaluation with immediate effects on the course.
2   The course can include periodic and systematic observation of classes by teacher peers.
3   The staff hold regular meetings to discuss the progress of the course.
4   Teachers are required to periodically fill self-evaluation forms that they discuss with a colleague.
5   Learners periodically fill course evaluation forms.
6   Some class time is set aside for learner discussion of the course and providing feedback for teachers.
7   Occasionally an outside evaluator is invited to evaluate aspects of the course.

The Results of an Evaluation

When an evaluation has been done, the results need to be presented. This presentation involves ethical issues, particularly those of confidentiality and consideration for the feelings of others. Often people participate in an evaluation on the understanding that the information they provide will remain confidential, at least in the sense of where the information came from. The results of an evaluation may also be threatening to the individuals concerned, especially if weaknesses are revealed. The results of evaluations of teaching are usually only available to the teacher concerned and perhaps to the head of the department. They are not seen by colleagues. In such evaluations particular comments by students may be reported, but the names of the students who made these comments are not reported. In student evaluations of teaching conducted by a central body, there are usually data provided about school averages in such evaluations so that the person receiving the evaluation can determine how they compare.

An issue in evaluation is whether a comparison model should be used. Should evaluations be norm-referenced or criterion-referenced? If they are norm-referenced what is the comparison – previous courses, other existing courses, other courses that could replace the existing course? A report of an evaluation needs to indicate the quality of the course and it must be made clear what the standard for the measure of quality is.

Most evaluations involve a written report, or in some cases two written reports – one for the person or group commissioning the evaluation, and one for wider circulation. The written report will usually be accompanied by an oral report. This oral report has two purposes, (1) to make sure the written report is clearly understood, and (2) to say things that could not be put tactfully in writing.

The report, however, is not necessarily the end of an evaluation although it sometimes unfortunately is so. The report needs to be considered and then acted on. The evaluation procedure may involve some later follow-up to monitor the effects and implementation of the evaluation.

An evaluation needs to result in learning for those involved. This learning needs to be applied to the course or to the planning of future courses. Surprisingly it is not unusual for an evaluation to result in very little change. At times this may be the correct response, but often it is not and may be the result of weaknesses in the planning and carrying out of the evaluation. In Chapter 12 we look at introducing change.

Summary of the Steps

1   Discover the purpose and type of the evaluation.
2   Assess the time and money needed.
3   Decide what kinds of information to gather.
4   Gain the support of the people involved.
5   Gather the information.
6   Present the findings.
7   Apply what has been learned from the evaluation.
8   Do a follow-up evaluation.

Evaluation is an essential part of good curriculum design. It ensures that weaknesses in curriculum design are found and repaired. It allows for the adjustment of a course to a changing environment and changing needs. If evaluation is well planned, it can help teachers develop professionally and come to feel that the course is truly their own.

We have now covered all the eight parts of the curriculum design model. In the next chapter we look at the various ways in which the whole process of curriculum design might be carried out.

Tasks

Task 1 Focus of evaluation

Here are some questions that an evaluation might try to answer:

- Why do so many people drop out of the course?
- Are the learners achieving the course goals?
- Does the course provide for slower learners?
- Are the learners satisfied with the course?
- Is this course putting accepted principles of language learning into practice?
- Is the course book effective?
- Is the course preparing the learners for their use of the language outside the classroom?
- Is the 4/3/2 technique an effective technique?
- Is the course making a profit?

Can you add to these questions?

Choose one of these questions and (a) decide if the question is worth answering (give reasons), (b) decide on two sources of information where you will look to answer the question, and (c) decide what investigative techniques you will use.

Task 2 An evaluation checklist

Choose a focus for evaluation, such as the quality of teaching or the quality of curriculum design as listed in Table 8.2, and design an evaluation check-list. Get a colleague to comment on the reliability, validity and practicality of the checklist.

Task 3 An evaluation plan

Plan a simple evaluation for a course you teach. Set clear goals. It should involve the evaluation of at least four aspects of the course as listed in Tables 8.2 and 8.3. You can also choose to evaluate an in-service course for teachers, or this course about curriculum design.

Case Studies

1   Look at Brumfit (1984b) and Beretta and Davies (1985) for an evaluation of Prabhu's procedural syllabus. Were all the important aspects covered? In what ways was the evaluation "unfair"?
2   How was the Book Flood (Elley and Mangubhai, 1981) evaluated? What other kinds of evaluation could you use?

Chapter 9

Approaches to Curriculum Design

After working through this chapter you should be able to decide on a starting point for curriculum design, and a way of covering the steps.

Models of Curriculum Design

This book is based on a model of curriculum design which is represented by the curriculum design diagram. This diagram is intended to be easy-to-remember, so that teachers can use it whenever they face curriculum design issues or are reading articles on curriculum design. How adequate is the model? One way to answer this question is to compare it with other models to see where they overlap and where they don't. Figure 9.1 is taken from *Designing Language Courses* by Kathleen Graves (2000). This is a very readable, practical book on curriculum design which draws strongly on the experience of teachers.

Let us try to match the parts of Graves' diagram with the one used in this course. Column 1 of Table 9.1 lists the parts of the curriculum design model used in this book. Column 2 lists the corresponding parts of Graves' model.

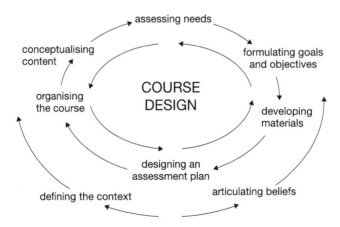

Figure 9.1 Graves' (2000) model of curriculum design.

From K. Graves, *Designing Language Courses*, 1st edn, © 2000 Heinle/ELT, a part of Cengage Learning, Inc. Reproduced by permission. www.cengage.com/permissions

Table 9.1 A comparative analysis of Graves's model of curriculum design (2000)

Language Curriculum Design model	Graves's framework of course development processes
Environment analysis	Defining the context
Needs analysis	Assessing needs
Principles	Articulating beliefs
Goals	Formulating goals and objectives
Content and sequencing	Organising the course Conceptualising content
Format and presentation	Developing materials
Monitoring and assessment	Designing an assessment plan
Evaluation	Designing an assessment plan

We can see in Table 9.1, each of the models has eight parts and there is considerable overlap between the two models. There are two major differences.

1   Content and sequencing in the *Language Curriculum Design* model matches two parts of the Graves (2000) model – organising the course and conceptualising content.
2   Monitoring and assessment and evaluation in the *Language Curriculum Design* model are included in one part of the Graves (2000) model – designing an assessment plan. In her book Graves distinguishes evaluation from assessment, but deals with both in the same chapter.

Clearly there is a great deal of similarity between the two models. When looking at other models of curriculum design, it is worth doing such a comparison to see where the similarities and differences lie.

Let us look at one more model which is more noticeably different. Murdoch (1989) presents his model in two columns (Figure 9.2). The left-hand column covers the main factors to be considered in curriculum design (the outer circles of the model used in this book). The four boxes in the right-hand column relate to the practical aspects of curriculum design (the large inner circle in the model used in this book).

Table 9.2 compares the *Language Curriculum Design* model and Murdoch's model.

We can see in Table 9.2, four parts of Murdoch's model fit into environment analysis. Two parts of his model fit into needs analysis (lacks and necessities), and three parts into content and sequencing. Part of what is included

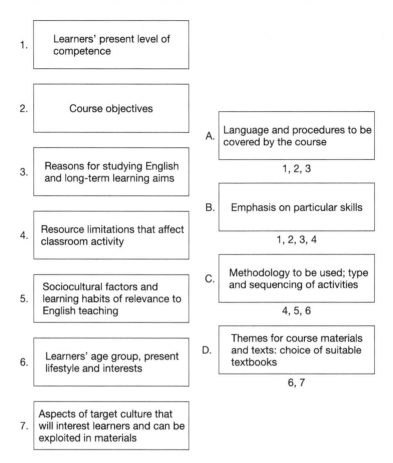

Figure 9.2 Murdoch's model of curriculum design.

in content and sequencing overlaps with format and presentation, that is, the choice of suitable textbooks.

Principles, monitoring and assessment, and evaluation are not included in Murdoch's model. These are possible weaknesses of his model. However, in his discussion of his model, it is clear that he intends that principles should be considered when dealing with several of the parts of his model.

There are numerous other models of curriculum design and it is interesting to compare them to see where their strengths and weaknesses lie.

Doing Curriculum Design

This book has taken the approach that curriculum design is best viewed as a process like writing where the curriculum design could begin at any of

Table 9.2 A comparative analysis of Murdoch's model of curriculum design (1989)

Language Curriculum Design model	Murdoch's model of curriculum design
Environment analysis	Resource limitations that affect classroom activity
	Sociocultural factors and learning habits of relevance to English teaching
	Learners' age group, present lifestyle and interests
	Aspects of target culture that will interest learners and can be exploited in materials
Needs analysis	Learners' present level of competence
	Reasons for studying English and long-term learning aims
Principles	
Goals	Course objectives
Content and sequencing	Language and procedures to be covered by the course
	Emphasis on particular skills
	Themes for course materials and texts: choice of suitable textbooks
Format and presentation	Methodology to be used: type and sequencing of activities
Monitoring and assessment	
Evaluation	

several places – needs analysis, materials writing, selection of principles, goals, etc. Some models of curriculum design see it occurring as a series of steps in a fixed order. Tessmer and Wedman (1990) describe this view as a "waterfall" model, where one stage of curriculum design, for example environment analysis, is done thoroughly, and then the next stage of needs analysis is done thoroughly, and so on in much the same way as the flow of water fills one container in a stepped–down series and then flows over to fill the next. If this does happen, it is probably rare. Most curriculum design occurs under constraints that make it almost impossible for a waterfall model to occur.

For example, in many English courses the teacher does not know who the learners will be until the first day of class. Needs analysis before the course begins is thus virtually impossible. The teacher needs to come prepared for the first class and so deciding on the content and format and presentation of the material may be a first step. The decisions made for the first day may have to be revised after meeting the learners.

Other constraints faced by curriculum designers include having very limited time to prepare the course, having to prepare a course for a largely unknown environment, having to design a course which can be marketed and used in a very wide range of environments, and having to prepare courses that will be taught by other teachers.

There are two main factors to consider when applying a model of curriculum design: (1) what is the starting point for the curriculum design process, that is, what is already available?, (2) how will we move through the process of curriculum design as shown in the curriculum design model? Let us now look at these two factors in detail.

Starting Points

Curriculum design begins either with no existing resources or some existing resources. The design of a completely new course may start from nothing except the knowledge of the curriculum designer. Most courses however have something more concrete to start from.

1   Curriculum designers and teachers can start from nothing and gather and write the material. This most often happens because of copyright issues with courses that are likely to be published, or where there is no existing course. The curriculum designer or teacher is thus responsible for all parts of the curriculum design process.

2   Curriculum designers and teachers can draw on a bank of existing materials from which they select the most appropriate material for the course. Such a bank could include (1) copies of activities prepared by themselves or other teachers for other courses or for previous deliveries of the course, (2) published supplementary materials such as graded readers, grammar activity books, and conversation texts, speed reading courses and so on, (3) clippings from newspapers or magazines, recordings from the radio or TV, or photocopied material from texts or course books. The curriculum designer or teacher chooses the bits and puts them together to make a course. The curriculum designer or teacher thus takes most responsibility for content and sequencing, and goals.

3   Some curriculum statements and some course books deliberately provide only some of the material needed for a complete course. Curriculum statements usually provide the content and sequencing, goals, and assessment parts of the course, and leave it to the teacher to decide on the materials to use to deal with format and presentation.

There are some course books that provide texts and some basic exercises, but leave it to the teacher to decide how to use these. For example, each unit of *Advanced English Vocabulary*, a pre-university English course by Helen Barnard (1980), contains a word list, word study material, pre-dictation activities and dictations, reading texts and a vocabulary test. The vocabulary in each unit has been carefully chosen and the number of times each target word appears in the whole course has been monitored.

The vocabulary learning goals of the course were determined by a very careful needs analysis based on university texts. It is the teacher's responsibility to prepare exercises for the reading texts and to use them and the dictations in any way that fits the environment and needs of the learners. The teacher must also determine how the course will be assessed.

The advantages of this split responsibility for different parts of the curriculum design process are as follows:

(a) The course can be made more suitable for the environment in which it is taught. This environment includes the resources available, the skill and teaching style of the teachers, and the time available.
(b) Adjustments can be easily made to suit a range of needs.
(c) The teacher is seen as a professional who has to make important curriculum design decisions, and who has the flexibility and skill to bring the material and learners together in the most suitable way.
(d) The material produced by the curriculum designer can be used over a very wide range of differing teaching situations.

The requirements of such an approach are well-trained teachers with the resources and time to perform their part in the curriculum design process.
4 The teacher chooses a published course book and uses that as the only material or the main material for the course. This starting point is the easiest if a usable course book is available. A usable book is one where at least half of the material in the book can be used in the course. This makes it worth buying the book and gives the curriculum designer time to work on extra material.

Much curriculum design begins with the results of someone else's curriculum design. That is, a teacher chooses a course book for a course and, as a result of teaching the course and using the books, becomes dissatisfied with the book. This results in making some changes to the book by skipping parts of it, spending a longer time than usual on some parts and by supplementing or replacing some of the material in the course book with other material. What may eventually happen is that the original course book or course materials are no longer used and the teacher works with the materials that were developed in response to the inadequacies of the original course.

This approach to a course has many advantages. Firstly, it allows a course to be initially taught without getting involved in an elaborate, poorly informed curriculum design process. The course is simply taught from the course book. Secondly, it allows for careful work to be done on aspects of the course that really deserve attention. This work can be done without the worry of neglecting the other, adequate parts of the course. Thirdly, it allows the teacher/curriculum designer to develop curriculum design skills in a safe, gradual way. Instead of having to have control of the whole curriculum design process, expertise in parts of it can be developed, applied and then supplemented.

There are dangers, and one of the most pressing could be that of copyright. If the teacher begins using a commercially produced course and starts altering and supplementing it, there is the danger that material from the original course may still be retained, perhaps in a slightly altered form in the later course. Secondly, in a process of gradual change and replacement, important aspects of the curriculum design process could be overlooked. In this approach to curriculum design, it is worth regularly evaluating the current state of the course by checking it against the parts of the curriculum design model. The curriculum designer thus needs to consider how the process of curriculum design will be followed. This is the focus of the next section of this chapter. Adopting and adapting a course book is examined further in Chapter 11.

The Process of Curriculum Design

In most approaches the main parts of the curriculum design process described in the curriculum design model will be covered, but they may be covered at various times, at various degrees of thoroughness, in various orders, and by various people. We will look at the ways of going through the process of curriculum design – the waterfall model, the focused opportunistic approach, and the layers of necessity approach.

Let us begin where conditions might seem to be ideal for curriculum design, where there is plenty of time, access to the intended learners, a known teaching environment and plenty of resources.

A "waterfall" model

Most reports of a sequence of carefully planned and produced curriculum design describe a progression from a study of the environment and needs (often they are not distinguished), to a consideration of important principles and the setting of goals, followed by the drawing up of a list of content items, and then the writing of the lessons. Macalister and Sou (2006) draw on a "waterfall" model in their description of a course's design. The output of one stage becomes the input of the next. Table 9.3 lists a sequence of steps that could be followed in this way in a variety of orders.

Murdoch (1989) describes a similar sequence, beginning with an analysis of learners' present proficiency and necessities, and a study of the learners' reasons for studying English and long-term learning aims (needs analysis). This results in a description of the content of the course. The limitations of the environment are then studied, particularly the resource limitations that

Table 9.3 Steps in curriculum design

Goals

1 List the goals and objectives for each lesson and the course.

Content and sequencing

1 Decide on the number and size of lessons or units.
2 Choose the ideas content.
3 Choose the language content.
    Start from the learners' present proficiency and wants.
    Choose regular, frequent language items where possible.
    Check on the proportion of the four strands.
    Check that there is the best coverage of the needed language.
4 Sequence the language items.
    Start with the items learners will find most useful and learners will be the most successful with.
    Separate opposites and other closely related items.
    Space and vary the repetitions.
5 Divide the language and ideas content into lesson units.
    Allow for the same items to occur in different units to get repetition.

Format and presentation

1 Decide on the form in which the material will appear.
    Consider the size and cost.
    Consider how much detail must be provided for the teacher.
2 Choose suitable activities.
    Consider the proportions of the four strands.
    Consider adaptability to class size and levels of proficiency.
    Consider learner and teacher training needs.
3 Decide on the lesson format.
    Fit the activities to the lesson length.
    Sequence the activities.
4 Produce the material.
5 Prepare a teachers' and learners' guide.

Monitoring, assessing and evaluating

1 Decide how each objective will be observed and/or measured.
2 Decide how the goals for the course will be monitored.
3 Decide how to evaluate the course and revise it on the basis of the evaluation.

affect classroom activity, sociocultural factors, learning style, the learners' age group and interest, and aspects of the target culture that will interest learners (environment analysis). This then allows the curriculum designer to decide on what skills to emphasise (content), what methodology to use (format and presentation) and what themes to exploit in the course materials (ideas content). The waterfall model is most likely to be applied in the design of the commercial course book, or in a well-funded curriculum design project. Both of these situations provide time and resources for systematic curriculum design, so that designers can do needs analysis, consider the environment and principles, and prepare a syllabus and lessons in advance of the actual teaching. Most teachers however do not have this luxury and have to design and teach courses without the chance to have fully planned and researched them. Development of the course occurs while and after the course is taught. A focused opportunistic approach is one way of managing this development.

A focused opportunistic approach

In a "focused opportunistic" approach, the format and presentation part of the curriculum design process is typically done first. That is, material is gathered or prepared to teach the course. Then, with each re-teaching of the course, one part of the curriculum design process is done thoroughly. Thus it might be that a proper needs analysis is not carried out until the third or fourth re-teaching of the course. Tessmer and Wedman (1990) warn against this approach, mainly from the point of view of efficiency in that working thoroughly on one aspect of curriculum design may result in wasted effort because the findings may not be able to be used in the other less-elaborated parts of the curriculum design process. The attractiveness of this model is that it allows a concentrated focus with possible high-quality improvements to a course. For example if, during one presentation of a course, assessment was focused on, or there was a careful needs analysis done, then these improvements could be done well.

This approach requires a tolerance of some inadequacies in other aspects of curriculum design, but if it is known that these will be eventually worked on, then they can be tolerated.

The major reason for taking this approach is time pressure. The learners have to be taught and there is not time to do a lot of data gathering or planning. Because teaching most immediately involves format and presentation, this is usually done first. That is, the course is taught using whatever material is available or can be made. During the teaching, the teacher may do some kinds of needs analysis to work out if the lessons need some adjustment. Assessment will also need to be developed as the course is taught. After the first teaching of the course, the teacher might consider content and sequencing on the basis of experience and make some changes so that the second delivery of the course is a bit more organised. This do-what-you-can-when-you-can approach is typical of most curriculum design carried out by teachers. It is clearly not ideal but is realistic. It can be effective if teachers have the opportunity to teach the same course several times, and if they know something about curriculum design so that they can make sensible decisions on where to focus the improvement of the course.

A "layers of necessity" model is somewhat similar, except that it tries to cover all the major parts of the curriculum design process at the same time.

A "layers of necessity" model

Tessmer and Wedman (1990) criticise sequential "waterfall"-type models because they require that each stage in the sequence should be done thoroughly in detail before proceeding to the next stage. This, Tessmer and Wedman argue, is difficult to do and often impractical. What is needed to meet the realities of most curriculum design situations is a model that allows for a 'good enough for now' level of quality to be reached.

In Tessmer and Wedman's model, curriculum design is seen initially as a choice between various layers. Each layer is complete in itself and includes the major parts of the curriculum design process – environment analysis, determining needs and goals, deciding on the instructional strategy (format and presentation), developing the materials, and evaluating and revising. But each layer differs in the detail and thoroughness with which each of these parts of curriculum design are carried out. The curriculum designer has to decide what layer of curriculum design will be chosen. This decision will depend on balancing the amount of time and resources available to do the curriculum design and the level of thoroughness needed.

If the time and resources available are very limited for example, the curriculum designer might choose the least detailed layer. This layer would involve all the following steps:

1   Decide on the most severe environmental constraint on the course and how it will affect the curriculum design.
2   Decide on the most urgent necessity that learners have to meet at the end of the course.
3   Make a short list of items to cover.
4   Decide on a simple lesson format that will make use of available material.
5   Gather the material for the course.
6   Decide on a simple form of assessment.

If more time and resources were available then a layer could be chosen which involved a more detailed set of steps like those in Table 9.1.

Tessmer and Wedman (1990) suggest some guidelines for using a "layers of necessity" model. Firstly, once the level of necessity has been chosen it is best to cover all the steps at that level with roughly the same degree of thoroughness. It is not efficient to perform one part of the curriculum design process at a much more detailed and more thorough level than the other parts. Secondly, at any level all the major parts of the curriculum design process should be touched. That is, there must be some needs analysis and environment analysis, rather than leaving them out. To these guidelines it could be added that the same piece of curriculum design can be done choosing a more detailed layer at a later time so that the previous curriculum design is made better. It is thus important that the difference between the layers is not seen as a difference between careful work and hasty work, but as a difference between the number of steps and points that are covered. In this way subsequent revisions can add to rather than replace previous curriculum design work.

Deciding on an Approach

We have looked at a range of starting points and different paths through the curriculum design process. Choosing which path to take will depend on the starting point, the time available for course preparation, the availability of needs analysis information, the availability of a usable course book, and the skill of the curriculum designer. We will assume that time is short and that only a small amount of needs analysis information is available.

Clearly the least demanding approach is to choose an existing course book as a source of material, and then apply a focused opportunistic approach to gradually improve and eventually replace it. We have looked at the advantages and disadvantages of this approach.

Whatever approach is chosen, the advantage of following a systematic approach to curriculum design involving all the parts of a model is that parts of the process are not missed out. Poor curriculum design misses important parts and does not deal with parts in a principled way.

Summary of the Steps
1   Decide on your starting point.
2   Decide what kind of path to follow through the process of curriculum design.

This chapter has looked at the meeting of the theory of curriculum design and the practical issues of putting curriculum design into practice. The approaches described here represent different ways of taking account of constraints upon curriculum design, particularly those of time, skill and the need for flexibility in using courses. With all of the compromises necessary, it is important to make sure that the various parts of the curriculum design process are given proper consideration at some point in the curriculum design activity. The main purpose of this book is to describe those parts and the steps involved in considering and applying them. An awareness of what they are should lie behind every piece of curriculum design no matter how small. In the following chapters we will look at how curriculum design applies to activities like choosing a course book, involving learners in curriculum design and teacher education.

Tasks

Task 1 Your curriculum design process

If you have never set up or designed your own language course, see if you can work with someone who has.

1   How much of the course did you have to design yourself? What parts were these?

_____

_____

_____

_____

2   At what place in the curriculum design model did you begin? Why did you begin there?

_____

_____

_____

3   Try to draw a simple flow diagram of the curriculum design process you went through. What approach to curriculum design would you classify your curriculum design under?

Task 2 Choosing an appropriate approach

1   Think of a piece of curriculum design you wish to do. For example you may wish to design a survival language course for non-native speakers of English who want to use English when they travel.
2   Decide which one of the approaches listed in this chapter will be most suitable.

_____

3   List the features that make this the most appropriate approach for your circumstances.

_____

_____

_____

4   Briefly say why the other approaches are unsuitable.

_____

_____

_____

_____

Task 3 Comparing models

Compare the following model of curriculum design with the model used in this book. Use a table like Tables 9.1 or 9.2.

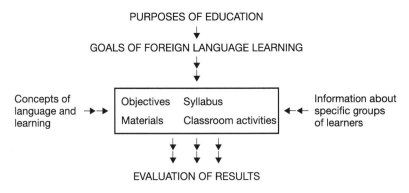

Figure 9.3 From Littlewood (1992).

Case Studies

1   Look at the Nation and Crabbe article (1991). List the steps followed in the curriculum design process.
2   Look at a published account of an example of curriculum design. See the items on the list of references followed by [20] for such descriptions. What starting point was used? What path through the curriculum design process was taken?

Chapter 10

Negotiated Syllabuses

After working through this chapter you should be able to give learners a say in the design and running of a course.

Negotiated Syllabuses

A negotiated syllabus involves the teacher and the learners working together to make decisions at many of the parts of the curriculum design process. It is a way of giving high priority to the recognition of learner needs within a course and to the need to continually adjust courses while they are running to suit changing needs and circumstances. Negotiated syllabuses are also called "process syllabuses" (Breen, 1987). The word *process* in the term *process syllabus* indicates that the important feature of this type of syllabus is that it focuses on **how** the syllabus is made rather than **what** should be in it.

Clarke (1991) sees the interest in negotiated syllabuses arising from humanistic methodologies like community language learning which are very learner-centred, from needs analysis which focuses on learners' needs, from work in individualisation and learner autonomy, and from learner strategy research which sees the learner playing a central role in determining how the language is learned. These are clearly strong reasons for having a negotiated syllabus. Breen and Littlejohn (2000b: 272–3) list situations where a negotiated syllabus is almost unavoidable:

1 Where the teacher and students have different backgrounds.
2 Where time is short and the most useful choices must be made.
3 Where there is a very diverse group of students and there is a need to find common ground.
4 Where initial needs analysis is not possible.
5 Where there is no course book.
6 Where the students' past experiences must be part of the course.
7 Where the course is open-ended and exploratory.

The strongest pressure for a negotiated syllabus arises when the learners have experience and skills which others in the class could learn from (see Norris and Spencer (2000) for a description of a course involving Indonesian tertiary teachers), and where the needs of the learners are not readily apparent to those teaching the course.

There is some debate over what aspects of the syllabus could be negotiated. Breen and Littlejohn (2000a: 30–31) see the range of decisions open to negotiation as including all the parts of the central circle of the curriculum design diagram, namely goals, content and sequencing, format and presentation, and monitoring and assessment.

> Purposes: Why are we learning the language? (Goals)
> Content: What should be the focus of our work? (Content and sequencing)
> Ways of working: How should the learning work be carried out? (Format and presentation)
> Evaluation: How well has the learning proceeded? (Monitoring and assessment)

Breen and Littlejohn (2000a: 34–38) point out that negotiation of the goals, content, presentation or assessment of the syllabus can occur at any level of detail or generality from negotiating a particular task in the course, to a sequence of tasks, a series of lessons, the whole course, or the wider curriculum (Figure 10.1).

A negotiated syllabus involves the steps of (1) negotiating the goals, content, format and assessment of the course, (2) implementing these negotiated decisions, (3) evaluating the effect of the implementation in terms of outcomes and the way the implementation was done. This then should lead to a return to step (1).

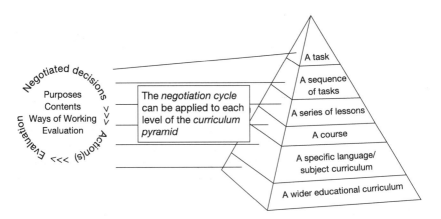

Figure 10.1 A process syllabus.

Let us look first at an example of a negotiated syllabus in action and then look more closely at the range of options available for a negotiated syllabus and its disadvantages and advantages.

An Example of a Negotiated Syllabus

[handwritten margin note: My class is beginner – intermediate – NOT related – for this negotiation]

The class is a group of adult graduate students preparing for post-graduate university study through the medium of English. They come from a wide variety of countries and will do their post-graduate study in a wide range of disciplines.

1   For the first two weeks of class the teacher follows a set programme involving a large variety of activities.

2   At the end of the two-week period the teacher tells the class, "Now that you have settled in and have experienced some typical classes, it is time for you to take an active part in deciding what we will do for the next two weeks."

3   The teacher and the class members list the activities and parts of the course on the board, and then working in small groups discuss what should be removed from the list, and what should be added to it. The groups report back and the list on the board is revised. If the learners wish they can discuss the list some more.

4   The next step is to rank the items in the list and fit them into the class timetable. This again is done in small groups and then with the class as a whole. During this discussion the learners negotiate with each other and with the teacher.

5   The resulting timetable with its activities then becomes the timetable for the next one or two weeks, when it is then renegotiated. The teacher sometimes calls on some of the learners to help with preparation and material for the class in order to cope with the short class preparation time that such negotiation sometimes results in.

This is a somewhat conservative example of a negotiated syllabus. It is conservative or cautious because the class did not start with a negotiated syllabus from the very first day of class. There were several reasons for this. First, many of the learners came from backgrounds where teachers are highly respected and would feel very uncomfortable telling the teacher what to do. In the first two weeks the learners can come to realise that the teacher can be trusted and that it is reasonable to negotiate with him. Second, most of the learners had not experienced a pre-university course before and so the teacher wanted to show them some of the range of goals and activities available, several of which might be new to them. This initial time of experience would inform and enrich the learners' later negotiations because they would have more to draw on. Third, the teacher wanted to show what he saw as important for the learners and what he taught well. This was partly with the hope of influencing the later negotiation. Fourth, the teacher wanted to develop credibility with the class before passing much of the control to them. If the syllabus had been negotiated on the first day, some learners may have reacted by thinking, "You are the teacher, can't you teach?"

All the same, there are many situations when negotiation begins when teacher and students first meet. Boon (2005) began on the first day because his fee-paying students were enrolled on a short course. Macalister (2007) was concerned with quickly meeting the ESP "wants" of engineering students, and used ranking and consensus-building activities in the first class to find out what their "wants" were.

After much trial and error, Irujo (2000) decided that negotiation of an MA teaching methodology course was best done by presenting course members with a draft syllabus in which some items were non-negotiable, but in which there were many items and procedures (methods of learning, assignments, etc.) that were negotiable. Adding to the draft necessarily involved removing something from it to provide a place for the new topic. This use of a draft syllabus satisfied course members who felt uncomfortable with a completely negotiated syllabus. It also made negotiation more focused and efficient, and dealt very effectively with the wide range of experience (or lack of it) that course members brought to the course.

Requirements for a Negotiated Syllabus

Breen (1987) describes the decisions to be negotiated in a negotiated (process) syllabus and the materials needed to make it work. The decisions include the following, and are made through discussion by the teacher and the learners.

1   **Negotiation procedure**. How will the negotiation be carried out? When will it be done? How often will it be done? Who has the responsibility for organising it? Who has the responsibility for checking that what is negotiated is actually done?
2   **Course planning: participation**. Who will work with who? The range of answers to this question includes individual work, pair work, groups working with the teacher, and the teacher working with the whole class.
3   **Course planning: procedure.** What kinds of activity will be worked on? The range of answers is many and may include role play, information gap tasks, guided writing, extensive reading, and oral drills. Mosback (1990) shows how nine different types of activity favoured by teachers, administrators and learners came to be incorporated into a curriculum in Sri Lanka as a result of negotiation over a two-year period. Additional decisions include how long each activity will be worked on, how it will be worked on, and how the results of the activity will be assessed.

4 **Course planning: learning goals**. What will be the focus of the work? The range of possible answers includes increasing speaking fluency, learning new vocabulary, learning how to organise written assignments, and learning how to understand and give directions.

The result of these decisions is a plan of work for a certain period of time. In order for the plan to be put into action there needs to be a choice of learning resources consisting of activities and tasks.

5 **Course evaluation**. The fifth, critical step in the negotiated syllabus is continual evaluation of the previous decisions and the learning resources. This evaluation should then lead to re-negotiation. The range of decisions to evaluate includes the kind of participation, the kinds of activities, the material used in the activities, and the learning outcomes. Breen (1987) sees the evaluation part of the negotiated syllabus as its "key element". Evaluation leads to re-thinking and re-negotiation. "The process syllabus thereby involves teacher and learners in a cycle of decision-making through which their own preferred ways of working, their own on-going content syllabus, and their choices of appropriate activities and tasks are realised in the classroom" (Breen, 1987: 167).

6 **Resources and materials**. A requirement of a negotiated syllabus is that there is a large amount of resource material available to draw on or which the teacher and learners can readily produce.

Syllabuses with Some Elements Negotiated

Breen's description of a negotiated syllabus is at one end of the scale. It is possible to have a syllabus within which some parts or some aspects are negotiated while others are left under the control of the teacher or curriculum designer (Clarke, 1989). There are several ways of dividing up the syllabus. Here are some of the possibilities.

1 A fixed lesson or time of the day is set aside for negotiated activities. For example, an hour each Friday afternoon is used for activities that the learners and teacher have negotiated.

2 One or more of the four types of decisions described above (participation, procedure, learning goals, evaluation) is open for negotiation. Clarke (1989) suggests encouraging learners to take over some of the assessment activity.

3 The classes for one or more language skills, such as free-speaking activities, are planned through negotiation. For example, the learners negotiate the types of reading activities that they will do.

4 One or more parts of the inner circle of the curriculum design diagram is open to negotiation. For example, the ideas content of the lessons can

be negotiated, while the teacher retains control of language focus, presentation and assessment.

The Breen and Littlejohn (2000a) collection of reports on the implementation of a negotiated syllabus provides a very valuable resource for teachers wishing to try such negotiation in their own classrooms. There are useful examples from all levels of the educational system, from five-year-olds to secondary school classes, students in tertiary institutions, and teachers-in-training.

Negotiating Assessment

Several of the reports focus on negotiation of assessment and evaluation, largely because this has direct effects on goals and ways of achieving these goals. Breen and Littlejohn (2000a: 40) point out that there are four major factors affecting feedback through assessment:

1   The extent to which students are aware of the criteria being used.
2   The relative emphasis given to what they have achieved as compared with what they have failed to achieve.
3   The coincidence between what the feedback focuses upon and what the students themselves have recognised as particularly difficult for them.
4   Whether or not they believe they can act on the basis of the feedback in a way that solves a recognised problem.

This is a very insightful list and the teacher needs to keep these factors in mind when negotiating assessment.

Smith (2000) describes a very effective way of negotiating assessment. The assessment is seen as including not only the results of tests and assigned tasks, but also participation in class, homework, and class projects. Table 10.1 provides a sample assessment form that was negotiated in two ways:

1   The components and percentage weightings of the components of assessment were negotiated with the class.
2   Each individual negotiated their particular marks with the teacher.

This negotiated assessment very effectively takes account of the four factors described above by including awareness of the criteria for assessment, and a positive, relevant, and formative focus. This informed and involved approach to assessment will clearly have positive effects on learning.

The idea of a negotiated syllabus raises questions about the role of the teacher and the role of the commercially produced text book (Richards, 1993). This issue will be looked at in the next chapter, which looks at evaluating a course book.

Table 10.1 Assessment scale

Component	Weight (%)	Pupil's mark	Teacher's mark
Doing homework	10	8	6
Level of homework	20	16	17
Participation in class	10	9	7
Individual progress	10	5	8
Projects	30	26	27
Test results (not negotiated)	20	15	15
Total	100	79	80

Even where a course uses a prescribed textbook, has an externally imposed syllabus, or leads up to an externally set test, there are still plenty of opportunities for negotiation, particularly as to how activities are carried out and how internal assessment is done.

Disadvantages and Advantages of a Negotiated Syllabus

The disadvantages of a negotiated syllabus are of two major types. The first is the result of a lack of knowledge or experience with such a syllabus. Learners may be reluctant to negotiate or to let their classmates negotiate because they feel it should be the teacher's expertise guiding the course. Gradual introduction of a negotiated syllabus can provide learner training to help overcome this problem. Learners may also not know enough of the range of options they could choose from and thus may make unimaginative choices. Teachers may feel that using a negotiated syllabus removes too much of their power and status. Learners may find it difficult to reach agreement about what they should be doing. The second major disadvantage is that a fully negotiated syllabus requires considerable teacher skill and time in accessing and producing resources. Where there are several teachers with similar classes, this load can be partly shared.

Table 10.2 divides the factors against implementing a negotiated syllabus into learner factors and teacher factors although some of them reach more widely than that. Some of the learner factors come from lack of knowledge. Some of them and some of the teacher factors touch a core issue, namely, will a negotiated syllabus serve the needs of the learners well? Each of the problems does have at least one possible solution. If the advantages of implementing a negotiated syllabus are seen as being great, then the disadvantages need to be dealt with.

Breen and Littlejohn (2000b: 273–281) have a very useful discussion of many of these factors. Learner factors in particular are very well illustrated in Holme and Chalauisaeng (2006)'s narrative of student responses to attempts

Table 10.2 Problems in implementing a negotiated syllabus

Learner factors

The learners have limited awareness of the possible activities.
The learners are perfectly happy to let the teacher teach.
The learners need training in negotiation.
With no course book learners do not feel a sense of progress.
Learners' wants are only a small part of learners' needs.
The needs of the learners are too diverse to reach agreement.
Cultural expectations make learners reluctant to negotiate with the teacher.
The learners lack confidence in negotiating with the teacher.
Negotiation will have a negative effect on students' attitudes to the course because the
    teacher is not taking control of the course.

Teacher factors

Negotiation uses valuable class time.
The teacher's workload is less if the teacher teaches exactly the same lessons to
    several different classes.
The school expects all learners in different classes to follow the same course.
What is done in your class needs to be similar to what is done in the rest of the school.
There are not a lot of teaching resources to draw on.
The teacher is not skilful enough to cope with short-term planning.

to negotiate an EAP reading course at a Thai university. For example, from believing that the teacher was responsible for their learning, students shifted to view learning as their own responsibility. They also point to another possible disadvantage of negotiating a syllabus, however, when they express concern that their approach "may focus the class too strongly on understanding how they had to learn to the detriment of learning itself".

Davies (2006) suggests using simple questionnaires, introduced and clarified through class discussion, to gather learners' opinions on what kinds of activities should be used in the course. Because these questionnaires are done at the local class level, changes are relatively easy to make within the course, and learners feel that their opinions are being considered and acted on.

The advantages of a negotiated syllabus come largely from its responsiveness to the "wants" of the learners and the involvement of the learners. Breen (1987) argues strongly that all courses have to adjust in some way to the reality of the teaching situation and the negotiated syllabus gives clear recognition to this. Involving the learners in shaping the syllabus has a strong effect on motivation, satisfaction and commitment to the course. It changes from being the teacher's course to the learners' course. The actual negotiation process has its benefits. If the negotiation is carried out in English, then this may be some of the most involving meaning-focused activity in the programme. The negotiation also develops learners' awareness of the goals of language-learning activities and how these goals can be achieved. This understanding may then make them better learners.

Summary of the Steps

1   Decide how the negotiation will be carried out.
2   Negotiate the participation, procedure and goals.
3   Begin to run the course.
4   Evaluate the effectiveness of the negotiated decisions.
5   Go through the steps again.

This chapter has looked at how learners can be involved in curriculum design. In the next chapter we look at a particular kind of evaluation, evaluating a course book.

Tasks

Task 1 Problems in implementing a negotiated syllabus

Look at the list of factors which may make it difficult to introduce a negotiated or partly negotiated syllabus in Table 10.1.

Think of your own teaching environment and decide on the top three factors creating the most difficult obstacles to overcome.

How could you overcome them?

Task 2 Partly negotiated syllabuses

What parts of the curriculum design process are most open to negotiation?

Task 3 Developing a negotiated approach to syllabus design

A bank of materials

1   How could you make your learners aware of the range of material, techniques, activities and tests that they could choose for the course?

_____

_____

_____

_____

Involving learners

2   How could you gather your learners' opinions about which materials, techniques, activities and tests they would like to use in the course?

_____

_____

_____

_____

Evaluation

3   How could you arrange for continual feedback for everyone involved and for adjustment of the syllabus?

_____

_____

_____

_____

Advantages and disadvantages

4   What do you need to be careful about in using a process syllabus?

_____

_____

Case Studies

1   Examine a case study of the implementation of a negotiated syllabus to see what parts of the curriculum design process were negotiated and what parts were not negotiated.

2   Examine a case study of a negotiated syllabus to see the steps that were followed in the negotiation. See, for example, Littlejohn (1983), Savage and Storer (1992), Boon (2005) or Macalister (2007).

Chapter 11

Adopting and Adapting an Existing Course Book

After working through this chapter you should be able to choose and adapt a course book in a systematic way, and justify your decisions.

Curriculum design is concerned with the creation of language courses and course materials, but it is also concerned with the selection of texts and other materials for courses, and with adapting and adding to existing courses. In this chapter we look at the relationship between the teacher and existing course books. This chapter aims to help teachers clarify the roles that they, the course book and the learners play in the curriculum design process, and aims to provide teachers with a rational approach to follow when deciding to adopt or adapt a course book.

The Course Book, the Learners and the Teacher

There has been considerable debate on the role of course books in a language course. Prabhu (1989) suggests that because teaching must be matched to the learners' current knowledge, course books will not be effective because they are not in touch with the state of this knowledge. Allwright (1981) sees textbooks as removing learners from negotiating the curriculum design process. These points underline the importance of having a flexible approach to the use of a course book and of choosing a course book which allows for flexibility.

Dividing the Parts of the Process

In order to take a systematic approach to looking at the possible roles of the course book, teacher and learners in the curriculum design process, it is necessary to look at each part of the curriculum design process.

Table 11.1 lists the areas to consider when deciding where the course book, learners and teacher will contribute to curriculum design. Each of these areas needs to be informed by considerations of environment, needs and principles. Column 3 needs to be filled according to who is given responsibility.

Table 11.1 Areas and agents in assigning responsibility for parts of curriculum design

Area of design	Questions	Responsibility: Course book Teacher Learners
Content and sequencing	What language content? What ideas content? How much covered? How often covered?	
Format and presentation	How presented? What format for the lesson? Who presents?	
Monitoring and assessing	What assessed? When assessed? How assessed? Who assesses?	

The Teacher and the Course Material

In this section we will look at a range of relationships between the teacher and the course material, ranging from strong reliance on a course book to the use of source books and the internet.

Strong reliance on the course book with minimal adaptation

Once a course book has been chosen, teachers may follow the course book very closely, making only small essential changes and additions. There are several reasons why teachers may follow the course book closely:

1   Their school or Ministry of Education requires them to follow it closely. This usually is because of a wish to standardise the quantity and quality of the education that all learners get and sometimes because of a lack of trust in the skills of the teachers.
2   The teacher may be inexperienced or largely untrained and there is security in following the set course book closely. The teacher may also have no idea about how to adapt the course book.
3   The teacher is convinced of the high quality of the course book.
4   The learners wish to cover every part of the course book.

The greatest areas of flexibility for a teacher when following a course book closely are in how the material is presented (format and presentation), and monitoring and assessment. The techniques that are used to present the material can be varied to suit the interests and proficiency of the learners. At its simplest this may involve varying the speed, number of repetitions, whether the learners have to use their memory by closing their books, assigning some parts of the lesson as homework, or getting learners to act out parts of the material. With more adaptation this may involve the teacher adding a game-like challenge to some of the activities by using competing teams, or by creating parallel situations to those in the course book to provide extra practice. Teachers who want to make the classroom activities more task-like can ask themselves the six questions proposed by Willis and Willis (2007) that were introduced in Chapter 4. For any question that gets a "no" answer, the teacher then considers a way to adapt the activity so that the answer becomes "yes".

Most course books do not provide a lot of guidance on monitoring and assessing progress, and teachers following a course closely may need to design tests to do this. Teachers also need to be aware of other ways of monitoring their success and their learners' success, such as watching learners as they do activities, asking learners how they did certain activities, and looking at the results of an activity.

Adapting a course book

Once a course book has been chosen, teachers may wish to make substantial changes to it. There are several reasons for doing this and these could be classified as responding to the environment, taking account of needs, or putting principles into practice. Here are some of them.

1   The course book does not include all the activities that the teacher has used successfully before.
2   The course book material does not fit comfortably into the time available for the course.
3   The course book contains content that is unsuitable for the learners' level of proficiency or age.
4   The learners' knowledge and skill do not match that involved in the course book (Prabhu, 1989).
5   The course book does not include language items, skills, ideas, discourse or strategies that the learners need.
6   The course book does not apply principles that the teacher feels should be applied.
7   The course book does not involve the learners in the curriculum design process (Allwright, 1981).

Because of these reasons or reasons like these, the teacher may wish to adapt the course book. In this example, the teacher does not have the option of abandoning the course book, perhaps because it is the required text for the course, the learners have already bought it, or overall it has more positive features than negative features.

The teacher can do the following things to adapt a course book. Note how the suggestions relate to the three parts of the central circle of the curriculum design diagram.

1   **Add or omit content.** The teacher adds exercises to give extra practice to items that are frequently used in the language or which require extra time to learn. The teacher skips over confusing or unimportant parts of a lesson, for example teaching only one item in pairs of words that might interfere with each other.

2   **Change the sequencing of the content.** The teacher introduces some items earlier in the course because they are needed to do added activities.

3   **Change the format.** Instead of beginning the lesson with a dialogue, the teacher puts it towards the end of the lesson and uses the other exercises in the lesson to prepare for it.

4   **Change the presentation.** The teacher uses different techniques than those used in the book. For example a 4/3/2 fluency activity is used to practise some of the dialogues.

5   **Add or omit monitoring.** The teacher encourages the learners to make tests to check each other's learning of what is in the lesson (Clarke, 1989).

6   **Add or omit assessment.** The teacher introduces weekly tests to encourage learners to do homework or to let them see their progress.

An example of the teacher adding content may be through the addition of an extensive reading component to the course. The teacher may decide to do this because she does not feel the course book is applying principles that the teacher believes are important. In this case the principles (from Chapter 4) are:

Comprehensible input: There should be substantial quantities of interesting comprehensible receptive activity in both listening and reading.
Fluency: A language course should provide activities aimed at increasing fluency with which learners can use the language they already know, both receptively and productively.
Time on task: As much time as possible should be spent focusing on and using the second language.

Tanaka and Stapleton (2007) describe the implementation and the results of this type of addition in a Japanese high school. As a means of preparing them for graded readers, students read teacher-made reading materials for a short time in class over a period of about five months. Reading speed gains were recorded for all students, and for those who also read graded readers reading comprehension also improved.

Progressive adaptation of a course book over several courses can be a safe way for a teacher to develop professionally through a modest amount of action research. As we have seen in Chapter 9, it is also a useful way of beginning to design your own course.

Using source books instead of course books

The proper role of course books in courses is a matter of debate (Richards, 1985). Prabhu (1989) suggests that learners would be better served if teachers did not use course books but assembled their courses by drawing on a variety of source books such as conversation books, timed reading books, intensive-reading books, listening texts, as well as teacher-made material. There are several reasons for doing this. They may be classified according to the outer circles of the curriculum design diagram.

1   A single course book does not meet the diverse needs of the learners in the class.
2   Drawing material from a variety of sources allows the teacher to keep each lesson as close as possible to what the learners need.
3   Learners can have a strong say in what kind of topics and what kind of material they work with. This allows teacher and learners to negotiate the syllabus during the course (Breen, 1984; Clarke, 1991).
4   Teachers have the chance to make greater use of their professional skills, such as material preparation, course planning, adaptation of activities, and multi-level teaching in one class.
5   The circumstances under which the course is taught make it difficult to find an appropriate textbook. For example, the teaching has been divided up so that one teacher deals with reading, another deals with writing and so on. Or, the class numbers are small so that learners of widely varying levels of proficiency have to be in the same class.
6   Current course books do not reflect "state of the art" knowledge in Applied Linguistics.

The biggest problems facing the teacher in a course drawing on source books are to provide systematic coverage of the important language and skills content of the course, and to make it seem like one unified course rather than a set of unrelated bits. Such courses are often organised around themes to provide this unity. Learners sometimes complain of not seeing any obvious progress when they do not have a set course book.

Generally, the more trained and experienced teachers are, the more likely they are to reject the idea of a single textbook. This means that they need to be aware of the various parts of the curriculum design process and need to be able to check that the greater freedom they have to draw on a variety of types of content, presentation and assessment is matched by monitoring of all parts of the curriculum design process.

Using computers and the internet

Technological innovations have always had an impact on teaching, not least because learners expect to use the new technologies in the classroom. The advent of the computer age has been no exception. It has had an impact on language teaching in four main ways:

1   the use of computers and computer software in self-access centres and language-learning laboratories
2   the use of computer-mediated activities in the classroom, most obviously in the teaching of writing (DiGiovanni and Nagaswami, 2001; Fedderholdt, 2001)
3   the use of the internet as a source of information (Yang, 2001)
4   the use of corpora such as the British National Corpus and the Corpus of Contemporary American English in language learning and to generate language-learning materials.

The extent to which teachers use computers and the internet is, however, going to be determined by the outer circles of the curriculum design diagram. Obvious environment constraints include a lack of money to purchase equipment, schools without electricity and teacher unfamiliarity with the technology. When the environment analysis and needs analysis favour the use of technology, it is most important that teachers consider how the use of technology fits with the course principles. One consideration is whether the new technology will contribute to the course goals more effectively than before. Salaberry (2001) suggests four major questions for teachers to consider about the pedagogical effectiveness and the use of technology:

- Does better technology result in better teaching?
- Which features of technology help teaching and learning?
- How can we use new technologies in the curriculum?
- Do new technologies result in an efficient use of human and material resources?

There are now very useful computer-based and web-based learning tools available at sites like the Compleat Lexical Tutor (www.lextutor.ca), J.P. Loucky's site (www.call4all.us/home/index2.php) and Laurence Anthony's web site (www.antlab.sci.waseda.ac.jp/). There are also large corpora of English available for searching to find out how words are used and the collocations they take. An excellent starting point is Mark Davies's site at http://corpus.byu.edu.

Evaluating a Course Book

Every year teachers choose course books to use in their courses and learners spend considerable amounts of money buying them. Once a course book has been chosen and bought there is then an obligation to make use of it even if it turns out to be not very satisfactory. It is thus worth spending some time considering in a systematic way what is the best book available and whether it is good enough to recommend making it the text for a course.

A systematic approach to course book evaluation can be based on the parts of the curriculum design process:

- Does the course book suit the environment in which it will be used?
- Does the course book meet the needs of the learners?
- Does the course book apply sensible principles of teaching and learning?
- Do the goals of the course book match the goals of the course?
- Does the content of the course book suit the proficiency level of the learners and reflect sensible selection and sequencing principles?
- Is the course book interesting and does it use effective techniques?
- Does the course book include tests and ways of monitoring progress?

Essential features: Reducing the list of possible books

Very early in the evaluation procedure, the teacher needs to decide what features are absolutely essential for the wanted course book. Any course book without these essential features would not be worth considering further. Here are some possible essential features:

- The book should be at the right vocabulary and grammar level for the learners.
- The book should focus on the language and skills that are the goal of the course.
- The book should be below a certain price.
- The book should be readily available.
- The size and number of lessons in the book should suit the length of the course.
- The book should not include behaviour and topics that would offend the religious or cultural sensitivities of the learners and their parents.

A source of some features to consider can be found in Chapter 2 on environment analysis. It is also useful to go systematically through the parts of the curriculum design process to find such features. The aim is to make a very short list of two or three absolutely essential features that can be used to quickly eliminate books that are not worth considering further. For example, if the course begins in a week's time, then the availability of the book is essential. If there is time for orders to be placed and filled, availability is not an essential feature. Similarly, most course books are not too expensive, but if the learners are particularly poor or the school has a very limited budget, a low cost could be an essential feature.

Choosing and weighting the features

The list of features to consider in Table 11.2 is taken from the chapters on content and sequencing, format and presentation, and monitoring and assessment. Three things need to be done to this list:

1   Add features that you consider important but which are not on the list. Try to do this systematically by considering the various parts of the curriculum design process.
2   Take away features from the list so that it contains a manageable list of features, leaving preferably no more than 10 or 12. Because it is not possible to include all the principles of teaching and learning on this list, it will be necessary to decide which of those principles are really important enough to include. This will probably mean choosing no more than two or three from the list of twenty.
3   Divide the features in the list into two or three groups in order to decide which features are very important, which are important, and which are desirable but not so important. This list of features does not include the absolutely essential features which should be listed separately. There are several reasons for dividing the features into groups. Firstly it helps to clarify priorities. Secondly, it provides some indication of how much time should be spent on examining a particular feature in the course book. Thirdly, the grouping can act as the basis for giving numerical points for each feature so that a "score" (total number of points) can be given to a course book and thus make comparison of course books easier.

Table 11.2 is a list to choose from. Trying to consider all features could make the process of evaluating and comparing too complicated.

Table 11.3 is a simple evaluation form designed for a beginners' course. The importance of each feature is indicated by its weighting. The evaluator then scores each feature and multiplies the score by the weight given to that feature, to provide an overall score out of 100.

The design of any evaluation form will be determined by the focus of the evaluation. For example, Nitta and Gardner (2005) developed a framework for evaluating grammar tasks, and Reinders and Lewis (2006) proposed a

Table 11.2 A suggested list of features to choose from when evaluating a course book

GOALS, CONTENT AND SEQUENCING	The ideas in the course should help learning in the classroom.
	The ideas in the course should suit the age of the learners and should interest them.
	The content should take account of what learners expect to see in an English course.
	The sequencing of the content should allow for some learners being absent for some classes.
	The language in the course should be able to be modelled and comprehended by the teacher.
	The number of lessons in the course should suit the school term or year.
	The ideas in the course should increase the acceptability and usefulness of the course outside the classroom.
	The content should suit the proficiency level of the learners.
	The content should take account of what learners want.
	The content should be what learners need.
FORMAT AND PRESENTATION	The layout of the content should attract the learners.
	The learners should have the skills to do the activities.
	The activities could be used for self-study.
	The activities should take account of whether the learners share the same first language.
	The activities should be suitable for a range of levels of proficiency in a class.
	The activities should suit the size of the class.
	The activities should fit the learning styles of the learners.
	The activities should be able to be presented and managed by the teacher [e.g. the teacher should be able to organise group work].
	The course book should be easy to carry.
	The material in the course or the course book should not be too expensive.
	The amount of material in a lesson should suit the length of a class.
	The activities should suit the physical features of the classroom [e.g. move desks for group work; sound proof for oral work].
	The learners should be able to successfully complete the activities.
	The activities should take account of what the learners expect to do in a language-learning course.
	The kinds of activities should be useful to the learners in their future use or future learning of the language [e.g. knowing how to rank; knowing how to negotiate].
MONITORING AND ASSESSMENT	The course should show the learners that they are learning to do what they want to do.

Table 11.3 An example evaluation form for a beginners' course book

Features	Weight	Score out of 5	Score × Weight
Interesting content	3		
Useful language items	3		
Avoidance of interference	1		
Interesting and useful activities	2		
Illustrations support activities	1		
Coverage and balance of the four strands	3		
Attractive layout	1		
Reasonable cost	1		
Opportunities for self-study	1		
Number of lessons and length of each lesson suit the time available	2		
Suitable for the teacher's skills	2		
		Total	

checklist for evaluating self-access materials. Occasionally an evaluation may be concerned with wider social concerns in addition to language learning features. There may, for example, be a desire to avoid a sexist or racist depiction of the world through the course book.

Evaluating the Evaluation Forms

A comparison of the evaluation forms designed by Tucker (1968), Sheldon (1988) and Ur (1996) shows how current theories of second-language learning influence course book evaluation. An evaluation form that seemed adequate twenty or forty years ago now seems inappropriate. When examining the adequacy of an evaluation form we can use the same criteria as we use for evaluating a test:

- Is the form reliable? Would different people using the same form on the same course book reach similar conclusions?
- Is the form valid? Does the form cover the important features of a course book? Is the choice of features to examine in agreement with our current knowledge of curriculum design and second language learning?
- Is the form practical? Is it easy to understand? Is it easy to use? Can it be used to evaluate a course book in a reasonably short time? Are the results of the evaluation understandable and usable?

Presenting the Results

A course book evaluation form is a tool. A completed form is not always the best way of presenting the results of an evaluation if others are to use the results or be convinced by the results. Excellent models for presenting results of evaluations can be found in reviews and survey reviews in professional journals, such as *ELT Journal*, and also in consumer magazines where the results of evaluating items like hairdryers, toothpastes and washing machines are presented. These typically combine tables and written text, the written text serving to explain, justify, emphasise, and sum up what is presented in the tables.

For many teachers the evaluation of course books is more important than designing courses because their teaching situation determines that they should work from a course book. It should be clear from this chapter that evaluating and adapting a course book draw on the same knowledge and procedures that are used when designing a course. Evaluating a course book is a small but important exercise in curriculum design.

Summary of the Steps

1 Evaluate the course book.
2 Decide how the course book will be used.
3 Adapt the course book.

In the next chapter, we look at something which is related to choosing a new course book – getting others to accept change.

Tasks

Task 1 Designing a course book evaluation form

1 Look at the statements in Table 11.2. Look also at the list of principles in Chapter 4. Make a list of no more than 12 of these features to use for evaluating a course book.

2 Where necessary, add detail to the statements to suit your particular teaching situation. For example,

The material in the course or the course book should not be too expensive can be rewritten as

The course book should not cost more than ¥3,000.

3 Decide on the essential criteria and put them in one group. Weight your remaining criteria. For example, important but not essential criteria should have three stars, two stars or one star. When you have evaluated a course book you can add up the number of stars.

4 Carefully design the layout of your form.

Task 2 Evaluating a course book

You foolishly told a colleague that you followed a course on curriculum design. Now that colleague has come to you with an English course book that she wants to recommend for use in her school. She wants your informed opinion on the course book before she goes any further. Do this task with one or two course books.

1   List the questions that you will ask your colleague before you look at the book.

_____

_____

_____

_____

_____

What systematic approach did you use to guide your choice of questions?

_____

2   Use the course book evaluation form from Task 1, or the one in Table 11.3, or one taken from Williams (1983), Sheldon (1988) or Ur (1996) to evaluate the course book.

3   List the headings that you will use to organise your response to your colleague's question. How will you organise your report? (Summary first then details; Table with ticks or stars; Use curriculum design diagram headings . . .)

_____

_____

4   If your colleague decides to adopt the course (no matter what you tell her!), what improvements should she make?

_____

_____

_____

_____

Task 3 Course book evaluation schedules

1   Look at the course book evaluation schedules developed by Tucker (1968), Williams (1983), Jones (1993), Sheldon (1988) and Chambers (1997). What is included in their schedules that you did not include in your statements in Task 1?

2   Which form do you like the best? Why?

3   Prepare a brief critical review of one of the published schedules or one that your classmates have made.

Task 4 Using a course book

1   Choose a teaching situation that you know well and complete column three of Table 11.1 to show who performs which role in that situation.
2   Be ready to make a brief oral statement about how you use and adapt your course book.

Case Studies

1   Look at reviews of textbooks, particularly survey reviews in *ELT Journal* Volume 36 onwards, to see the criteria that are used to evaluate courses. What criticisms could you make of the criteria and their application?
2   See the Book Notices section in *TESOL Quarterly* for short evaluative reviews of textbooks. How useful are these? How could their usefulness be increased?

Chapter 12

Introducing Change

The aim of this part of the curriculum design process is to get teachers and learners to accept a new course or changes to an existing course.

Curriculum design usually involves change, especially when a new course replaces an existing course. This change or innovation (White, 1993) needs consideration so that the work that goes into planning and designing is rewarded by the acceptance and appropriate use of the course. As we shall see, an effective way of doing this is to involve the users of the course as closely as possible in its design and development.

There are many kinds of change that can occur in an educational system. Here is a list of some changes that could have a direct effect on what happens in the classroom:

- Introducing a new course book
- Changing to a new approach to teaching
- Introducing new teaching techniques
- Changing the National English test for entering university
- Changing part of the country's school system to English-medium
- Introducing computer-assisted language learning
- Moving to standards-based assessment.

Attempts to introduce change are not always successful, of course. One reason for this is that the change may be viewed as culturally inappropriate, perhaps imposed by an outsider. Adamson and Davison (2008) describe how a curriculum introduced in Hong Kong was seen as a Western import and was reinterpreted by teachers to accommodate to the local culture. Another reason why attempts to introduce change may not succeed is that the process of introducing the change to teachers is flawed. The cascade model of diffusion, with a small number of teachers attending train-the-trainer workshops in preparation to train other teachers, is often used but does not always succeed, as Goh and Yin (2008) found in Singapore.

There are two important, related aspects to any major curriculum change – the change that occurs in the curriculum, and the change that needs to occur in the minds of the various people affected by the curriculum.

If a teacher is only making changes within their own course, changes in attitude (both of the teacher and the learners) are still very important.

If the teacher has not taken a fresh viewpoint on the course, the change may really be no change at all. If all the changes to the course are significant, the learners may find it difficult to cope with something that is too far outside their experience and expectations. Thus an important issue related to curriculum design involves the management of change. This area of study and research is sometimes called "innovation theory" and is relevant not just to curriculum change but to the many different kinds of change that occur in human experience – restructuring businesses, changing the laws of the country, and bringing about changes in social behaviour such as reducing smoking or drink-driving.

Let us look first at the steps that could be followed when introducing change. Attention to these steps will increase the likelihood of a change being successfully introduced.

Steps in Introducing Change

1   Make sure that the change is really needed:

    Are enough people dissatisfied with the present situation?
    What is the real reason for the change?

2   Plan the type of change so that it is not too great and not too small (Stoller, 1994):

    Is the change too simple or too complex?
    Is the change too insignificant or too visible?
    Is the change too similar or too different from existing practices?

3   Make sure that enough people see that the kind of change is possible:

    Will the change involve more gains than losses?
    Are there practical obstacles to the change, such as a lack of resources?

4   Use a wide range of change strategies:

    Does the change have official support?
    Do people understand the value of the change?
    Are the users involved in the change?
    Is there frequent and good communication between all involved?

5   Be prepared for the change to take a long time:

    Is there enough time and money for the change?
    Is there long-term support for the change?

We will now look at each of these steps in more detail.

Seeing the Need for Change

Change occurs most easily if people are dissatisfied with the present situation. If a language course is not achieving the results that it should, or if the nature of the course causes dissatisfaction for the teachers or learners, then one of the first prerequisites for change is present. If the whole range of people affected by the change see the need for change, the conditions are ideal. Often however not everyone sees the need and those who are dissatisfied may have to convince those who are not. This often occurs when change in the classroom becomes necessary because our understanding of effective language-learning practices change.

Deciding on the Size of the Change

Research by Stoller (1994) suggests that the size of the change should not be too great or too small. If it is too great, people feel threatened or awed by the change. If it is too small, then it is not seen as being a real change and it is thus not worth putting effort into. Stoller suggests six scales for describing the size of the change, the best size being in the middle area of each scale. The scales are explicitness, visibility, originality, compatibility with past practices, difficulty/complexity and flexibility. Change is most favoured if it is obvious, different, challenging and requiring adjustment, but not too obvious, different, challenging and requiring adjustment. If the proposed curriculum change is too small, it may not win much support from others who do not see it as a real innovation, and thus not worth a lot of effort. If the change is too large, then those affected will see many obstacles to its implementation and may be reluctant to put in the considerable effort needed to support it. Stoller (1994) calls this need for the size of the change to be of a medium size, the "Goldilocks syndrome" (from the children's story *Goldilocks and the Three Bears*) – not too big, not too small, but just right.

The size of the change should be a matter for planning, adjustment and negotiation.

Let us look at the Book Flood experiment (Elley and Mangubhai, 1981) as an example. The change that they wanted to introduce was spending three-quarters of the four hours of class time on extensive reading. This is quite a big change from the normal teacher-fronted course. However, one-quarter of the class time remained the same. In addition only a little training was needed to get teachers ready to handle extensive reading. Attractive resources were available in the form of 200 books. The teachers were expected to read quietly when the learners were reading quietly, so it was a reduction of work for the teachers. Overall then we can see that the change was a significant one, but did not involve extra work or substantial retraining of the teachers.

Interestingly, one teacher in the experimental group could not accept the change and continued to teach his class in the old way. This was not discovered until the experiment was over. The achievement of his class was at a similar low level to the control group, without the high gains of the experimental group.

Realistic Change

Change may start from dissatisfaction with the present situation. If it does, it must also be obvious to those involved that the proposed change is possible and will be an improvement. That is, that it will involve more gains than losses. It is useful to look at the change from several viewpoints: (1) the resources to support the change, (2) the people involved in the change, and (3) the people who will receive the ultimate benefit of the change.

1   We have already looked at the size of the change itself, seeing that the change must be in a medium "zone of innovation" (Stoller, 1994) rather than at the extremes of too little or too much. The change must also be feasible given the resources that are available, the amount of time, and the number of people affected by the change. Consideration should also be given to the resources and support that classroom teachers will need during the change process, which may be on-going for a number of years (Wedell, 2003).

2   The people involved in the implementation of the change need to see that there will be benefits from the change, that it can be achieved, and that eventually it will not make them more over-worked than they are at present. If their involvement in curriculum change can be shown to add to their professional development through publication, official recognition, and gains in status for them or their institution, then this favours change (Kennedy, 1987).

3   The people who will receive the ultimate benefit of the change, usually the learners, are often not negotiators in the change process. At the very least, it must be clear to those involved that the learners will benefit from the change and be more satisfied as a result of it. Most curriculum change has the aim of producing better learning, and teachers will usually get involved in innovation which results in considerable work for them, if they see that there are substantial benefits for the learners. Learners may also be directly involved in curriculum change. The ideas behind the negotiated syllabus stress the benefits of learner involvement in such change.

A change to a communicative approach to language teaching can involve the learners in suggesting and endorsing, or rejecting certain types of activities.

Although they might not be involved in the decision to go to a communicative approach, they could be involved in how the approach is applied.

Holliday (1994) warns that when making change we must be very careful when trying to transfer teaching methodologies from one context to another. Holliday points out the likely mismatch of methodologies from Britain, Australasia and North America, when transferred to state tertiary, secondary and primary education in other parts of the world. Holliday's message however is much wider than this, suggesting that we need to suit teaching methodologies to the wider culture of the teachers and learners. This wider culture includes classroom culture, institutional norms, societal norms, and the role of education in society.

Teacher Beliefs

We have already noted that for change to be realistic it needs to be looked at from several viewpoints, including that of the people involved in the change. A core group of people involved is the teachers, who will usually be the main group responsible for implementing the change.

What teachers do in the classroom is to some extent going to be determined by what they believe. The importance of examining the role that teacher beliefs play in deciding what happens in the classroom has been increasingly recognised in language education research. The old-fashioned notion that a teacher's role is to transmit knowledge from the curriculum to the learners has been replaced by recognition that teachers have complex mental lives that determine what and how teachers teach (Freeman, 2002; Borg, 2006). These complex mental lives – often called teacher cognition – are "the hidden side of teaching" (Freeman 2002: 1) and multiple factors, which could loosely be described as teachers' knowledge, beliefs and personal histories, contribute to them.

Introducing change to teachers, then, means addressing teacher beliefs because what teachers believe affects how they teach (Garton, 2008). At the same time, however, it is important to remember that teacher beliefs and teacher behaviour in the classroom are not necessarily the same. Contextual factors can either facilitate or constrain teaching practice based on teacher beliefs. For example, language teachers are likely to believe that extensive reading has beneficial effects on language learning and yet extensive reading is often absent from the teaching programme. This absence may reflect factors in the teaching–learning context, such as assessment requirements or a lack of suitable reading resources.

One of the factors that can contribute to teacher cognition is professional development, and it is through professional development opportunities that change is often introduced to teachers. As teacher cognition is not static, changing beliefs is possible. Both pre-service and in-service training are intended to introduce change. It is important, therefore, to recognise that participants arrive at both forms of training with pre-existing beliefs. Trainee teachers who enter a pre-service course already have well-developed ideas about teaching based on their experiences as learners. Practising teachers who attend an in-service course (the focus of the next chapter) arrive with well-developed ideas based on their experiences as teachers and their understanding developed through their own pre-service training, as well as beliefs based on experiences as learners.

When introducing change to teachers, therefore, it is useful to gain some idea of their existing beliefs. Needs analysis tools can provide information about lacks (e.g. questionnaires and free interviews can tell us what participants believe now) and necessities (e.g. analysis of curriculum documents). Understanding what teachers already believe can help in the process of introducing change.

Using a Variety of Change Strategies

So far we have looked at the requirements for change, but how can this change be done? Kennedy (1987), drawing on Chin and Benne (1970), describes three major approaches to change, (1) power–coercive, where change is achieved through authority, rules and top-down pressure, (2) rational–empirical, where change is achieved through explaining, justifying and showing the reasons why the change is good and necessary, and (3) normative–re-educative, where change is achieved through discussion, involvement and negotiation. In the short term, power–coercive involves less time than rational–empirical which involves less time than normative–re-educative. Each approach to change is typically associated with a particular model of change and style of leadership (Markee, 1997). The power–coercive approach is typical of a centre–periphery model, such as the educational innovations promoted by an international aid agency from a "developed" nation, the rational–empirical approach is typical of a research, development and diffusion model (favoured by academics who do the research), and the normative–re-educative approach is typical of a problem-solving model that is driven by bottom-up pressure.

These three approaches should be seen as supporting each other rather than as alternatives to choose from, however. Change is more likely to occur if people see that it has the support of authority such as government, the education department and school administration (power–coercive), if they see that there are good reasons for the change (rational–empirical), and if they feel that they are participating in the change, that they are a powerful, valuable and useful part of the change, and that they "own" the change (normative–re-educative). A nice parallel can be seen in the civil rights movement in the United States. Racial equality was supported by legislation (power–coercive), the aims of the movement were publicised and explained (rational–empirical), and people became actively involved in the struggle for equality (normative–re-educative). Similarly, we can look at the attempt to get people to change their habit of smoking, that is to get them to give up smoking. Law-based strategies include making smoking illegal in buildings and on school premises, raising the tax on cigarettes, and making the advertising of cigarettes illegal. Reason-based strategies include educating people about the dangers of smoking, advertising the dangers of smoking on cigarette packets and in television advertisements. Involvement-based strategies involve quit-line phone services, support groups and local non-smoking initiatives.

An essential factor in all change is that there is good communication between all involved (White, 1987). A major strength of the normative–re-educative approach is that the cooperative work that is involved in such an approach makes communication easier. Teachers who are not well-informed will not take responsibility for the innovation. Good communication encourages greater responsibility. Kouraogo (1987) points out that a normative–re-educative approach to change will probably mean that the kind of change first proposed will be altered and renegotiated if there is true shared involvement.

Table 12.1 lists a variety of factors related to each of the three strategies for change. Short names for the strategies could be *Law, Reason* and *Involvement*. These are indicated in brackets in the means of change row in Table 12.1.

Table 12.1 Strategies for change and their characteristics

Type of change	Power–coercive	Rational–empirical	Normative–re-educative
Means of change	Force: laws, rules, directives (Law)	Reason and explanation: changes in understanding and knowledge (Reason)	Collaborative negotiation: ownership of change and personal change (Involvement)
Conditions encouraging the use of a particular strategy	Reluctance to change	Good communication channels, well-educated teachers	Time available and willingness to be involved
Examples in ELT	National syllabus, prescribed texts	Seminars, in-service courses, information sheets	Problem-solving workshops
Benefits	Official support, stresses necessity of change	Encourages understanding and keeping informed	Involves teachers' professional development, provides a personal stake in the results

Each strategy is favoured by certain conditions as indicated in the third row of the table, but these do not have to be there at the beginning if they can be developed during the change. As can be seen in the row giving ELT examples, movement towards change of some sort or other is almost always happening in well-organised systems, even if on a very small scale. The row describing benefits refers to the benefits of the change process rather than the outcome of the change.

Innovation, Management and Long-Term Support

A curriculum change usually has more effects than were first planned for. It may involve the retraining of teachers through in-service course work, and the adjustment of a curriculum to changes that are caused by the change.

In addition there is a need to evaluate the innovation to ensure that it is in effect a real improvement over past practices. The results of this evaluation may suggest that further changes are necessary.

White (1987) sees innovation as involving the management of the following stages:

1   Defining aims.
2   Defining end results. This should make clear what the particular benefits of the innovation will be.
3   Gathering information – what we already know and what we need to know.
4   Defining what has to be done. This involves allocating particular jobs, setting time limits, setting up procedures and preparing alternative plans.
5   Action – making the changes.
6   Reviewing and evaluating.

These stages show the need for careful and detailed planning plus follow up to check on the change. Innovation can involve many people and considerable time, and it is important that this is allowed for when the financial support and commitment to an innovation is sought. Defining the end results is a good way of checking if change is really needed or wanted. This involves getting those involved to describe what the ideal outcome will be. This clearly will sharpen views of at least the goals of the curriculum design.

Markee (1997) suggests a very useful list of principles to guide curricular innovation. These principles provide a nice summary of some of the ideas covered in this chapter.

1   Curricular innovation is a complex phenomenon. This means that it is affected by a large number of factors and by many features of the environment in which it takes place. This often makes its implementation and effect unpredictable.

2   The principal job of change agents is to effect the desired changes. This principle stresses that the person primarily responsible for the change needs to bring practical skill and energy to what they are doing.

3   Good communication among project participants is a key to successful curricular innovation.

4   The successful implementation of educational innovations is based on a strategic approach to managing change. This principle underlines the idea that innovation involves short-term, medium-term, and long-term strategies. It also involves different approaches to change, such as power–coercive, rational–empirical, and normative–re-educative approaches. At different times in the change process different strategies are likely to be appropriate.

5   Innovation is an inherently messy, unpredictable business.

6   It always takes longer to effect change than originally anticipated.

7   There is a high likelihood that change agents' proposals will be misunderstood.

8   It is important for implementers to have a stake in the innovations they are expected to implement.

9   It is important for change agents to work through opinion leaders, who can influence their peers.

Summary of the Steps

1   Make sure the change is needed.
2   Plan or examine the size of the change.
3   Use a range of strategies to get people to support the change.

Let us conclude this chapter by looking at ways of resisting change. You may recognise many of these subversive strategies from your own observation of working in teachers' groups and of political debates.

- Agree to everything but do nothing.
- Accuse the change proposer of seeking personal gains. Argue that although the ideas may be good, they will not work in the local conditions.
- Question the credentials of the change proposers. Find examples of unsuccessful change in other places or at other times.

More positively, each of these ways of resisting change can be countered by taking account of the particular steps in the change process outlined at the beginning of this chapter.

   In the next chapter we will look at one way in which change can occur, through in-service courses.

Tasks

Task 1 Change that failed

1 Think of a situation where an attempt to introduce change failed. Briefly list the reasons why the attempt failed.

_____

_____

_____

2 Match the reasons you just listed with conditions listed in the steps at the beginning of this chapter.

_____

_____

_____

3 For each of those conditions that caused the attempt to fail, suggest ways of making the attempt successful.

_____

_____

_____

Task 2 Change in a school's programme

You are planning to introduce some changes in the way English is taught in your school. These changes might be getting rid of the old textbook and using a new one, beginning the development of a negotiated syllabus, changing the way English is tested to include much more oral work, introducing regular in-service training for teachers, or moving to a communicative approach to language teaching.

1 Choose one of these changes (or think of another one) and briefly note the situation – what country, how many teachers, what support outside the school . . .

_____

_____

_____

2 List the two most important conditions which favour the change.

_____

_____

_____

3   List the three most important conditions that do not favour the change. For each condition describe the means you will use to deal with it.

Task 3 Investigating teacher beliefs

The focus on student-centred learning in communicative language teaching has brought changes in the role of the teacher. A recent survey found that many classrooms in your area are still very teacher-centred despite the adoption of a communicative curriculum some years ago. You have been asked to run a series of workshops to make teachers re-think their behaviour in the classroom following the changes to the curriculum.

1   Design a short questionnaire (about ten items) that you could ask teachers to complete in advance of the workshops. The aim is to find out teachers' current beliefs about their role/s.
2   How will you use the information from the questionnaires to plan the workshops?
3   How will you know whether the teachers have changed their beliefs about their role/s?

Case Studies

1   Look at the implementation of the Book Flood experiment (Elley and Mangubhai, 1981) and decide what conditions favoured its implementation and what did not. Note that one or two teachers in the study did not go along with the change. What suggestions would you have to ensure the successful implementation of a book flood in your school system?
2   "Our younger teachers attend courses on new methods of language teaching and come back to our institution. They are very keen on introducing changes in their courses and start to do so. But after a while they drift back to the old ways and soon there is almost no change from what they did before they attended the course."
    What could be the reasons for this?
    What could be done to help support and maintain some of the changes?

Chapter 13

Planning an In-Service Course

After working through this chapter you should be able to plan an in-service course for teachers.

In-service courses involve teacher development after initial teacher training and after the teachers have had some teaching experience. In-service courses may be long-term courses leading to Diplomas, Masters degrees or Doctoral degrees. They may be short term, lasting only a few hours or a day or two. In this chapter we look at short-term courses, and the planning that is needed for their success. The planning of short-term in-service courses is included in this book for two main reasons. First, short in-service courses represent a small-scale exercise in curriculum design. That is, planning a short in-service course involves very similar decisions to planning a language course, and the model of curriculum design used in this book is relevant. Second, in-service courses are a major way of bringing about innovative curriculum change. Curriculum change involves teachers, and teachers need to be informed and involved in the planning, development, implementation and evaluation of change. In-service courses are an important means for doing this. In this discussion, the term "workshop" will be used to refer to short-term in-service courses. The term "participants" will be used to refer to the teachers coming to the workshop for in-service development, plus the organiser and visiting speakers. Most attention will be given in this chapter to the inner circle in the curriculum design model – goals, content, presentation, and assessment and evaluation.

Features of an Effective Workshop

An effective workshop has clear goals, and involves new content, and its presentation encourages the involvement of the participants.

Goals

In general, workshops can have one or more of the following five goals – understanding and remembering new ideas, experiencing and evaluating exercises, producing material or exercises, planning units of work, and problem solving. When deciding on the particular goals of a workshop, it is important to decide which of these five general goals are most appropriate. For example, if a teacher is running a workshop for other teachers on the information transfer activity (Palmer, 1982), then it is important to decide:

1 Is it a goal for the participants to know what an information transfer activity is, what principles of learning it draws on, what it can be used for, and what material it can be based on?
2 Is it a goal to experience what it is like to be a learner doing an information transfer activity, what it is like to teach using an information transfer activity, and is it a goal to judge whether a particular information transfer activity is a good one or not?
3 Is it a goal for the participants to learn how to make their own information transfer activities?
4 Is it a goal to integrate information transfer activities into larger units of work?
5 Is it a goal for the participants to use information transfer activities to solve problems, such as learners' lack of motivation, the need to develop note-taking skills, or strategies for planning writing?

Goals will be looked at later in this chapter.

Content

Workshops need to involve the input of new information, otherwise there is a danger that they will result in unproductive discussion. When planning a workshop it is important to plan where this new information will come from. Here are some possible sources:

1 Pre-reading of articles and notes distributed several days before the workshop.
2 Prepared talks by the workshop organiser, an invited speaker or selected participants.
3 Prepared model activities either on video, demonstrated live or in written form.
4 Spontaneous discussion involving informed participants.
5 Feedback by an informed participant.

Presentation

For a workshop to be successful, participants need to be interested and active. Ideally a workshop should provide a learning experience that could not be gained by working alone. Involvement can be encouraged if there is a clear task to do with a clear, well-described outcome which the participants see as important and valuable for them. Group work can be effective, but often participants are more interested in gaining input from a visiting speaker than in gaining input from their colleagues. If a visiting speaker is the main source of input, it is possible to do small amounts of group work with feedback during the presentation.

It may be necessary for the visiting speaker or workshop organiser to develop some credibility with the participants by initially presenting a short informative talk to present some new content and to show that there are useful things to be learned by participating.

The participants in workshops are usually teachers who already have a demanding full-time job. A workshop which lasts even half a day can be tiring. Making arrangements to have tea and coffee and something to eat during the workshop is almost obligatory. It is also useful to plan the activities in the workshop so that there is a variety of activity and several changes of pace. In general, over a two-hour period there should be about four changes. This prevents activities from becoming boring because they go on too long, and allows some movement. The types of changes can include:

1   Changing the type of activity, for example, from observing to sharing evaluations of the observation, from brainstorming to ranking.
2   Changing group size, for example, from whole group to individual to pair.
3   Changing the focus of attention, for example by a change of main speaker or from main speaker presentation to individual learners.
4   Changing the medium, for example, from listening to speaking to writing.

For example, in a workshop on assessment, the workshop might begin with a short talk. There is then a change to looking at examples and getting participants to comment on them. The next change may be back to the speaker again, and from there to pair work.

Procedures and Activities for Reaching the Goals

Ellis (1986) distinguishes between experiential practices for teacher training and awareness-raising practices for teacher training. Experiential practices involve actual teaching, either real or simulated. Awareness-raising practices involve conscious understanding of principles, techniques and issues.

The goals of gaining teaching experience and developing a conscious awareness of teaching options can be achieved in the same teacher training activity.

Awareness-raising practices involve choosing from each of three ranges of options:

1   The input data that participants can work on. Ellis (1986) suggests video or audio recordings of lessons, transcripts of lessons, teaching – classroom, peer, or micro-teaching – readings particularly journal articles, ELT textbooks and materials, lesson plans, case studies, samples of students' written work.

2   The tasks or operations that the participants perform on the data. Ellis's list includes tasks like *comparing* ("Look at the two lesson plans provided and decide which one you prefer and why"), and *preparing* ("Prepare a marking scheme that you could use to correct the attached samples of students' written work"). Tasks will be looked at more fully in the following discussion of each of the five goals.

3   The workshop procedures that are used to get the participants performing the tasks on the input data. Ellis's list includes lectures, group/pair discussion, individual work, demonstrations, class discussions and materials making activity.

We will now look at each of the five types of workshop goals – understanding and remembering new ideas, problem solving, producing material or exercises, planning, and experiencing and evaluating exercises.

Understanding and Remembering Ideas

This goal differs from the other four goals in that it does not directly resemble a skill that a teacher makes use of. Teachers have to present material (represented by the goal of experiencing), make teaching material (the making goal), plan units of work (the planning goal), and deal with course and classroom problems (the problem-solving goal). Understanding and remembering ideas enables these other four goals, but the immediate result of the understanding goal is a better-informed teacher rather than a better-performing teacher. For this reason, the understanding goal is often the goal of the first part of a workshop. Understanding can lead to better-informed experiencing, making, planning or problem solving. Experiencing, making, planning and problem solving can also lead to understanding, usually with the aim of better understanding leading to better future presenting, making, planning and problem solving.

Understanding is listed as a separate goal for workshops because in some workshops it is the only immediate goal. If this is the case, the workshop organiser may wish to consider if adding another goal would add to the likelihood of the understanding being later applied to teaching, or if the participants will make that application themselves after the workshop.

Lamb (1995), reporting on a follow-up evaluation of a workshop one year after the workshop, points out the weaknesses of workshops that do not take account of the participants' own teaching and how they see their own teaching. Lamb found the following range of effects on the participants a year after the workshop:

1   No uptake – most of the information was not remembered.
2   Confusion – information incompletely and inadequately remembered.
3   Mislabelling – a term introduced during the workshop was used to incorrectly label their usual practice.
4   Appropriation – an idea from the course was used to justify a change that was not anticipated by the course tutors.
5   Assimilation – techniques were incorporated into the participants' teaching without really understanding the rationale for them. These were usually just "a slight elaboration of [an] existing routine" (p. 76).
6   Adaptation and rejection – suggestions were tried but rejected because the suggestions did not solve the problems the participants were most concerned with. The problems that the participants wanted to solve were different from those envisaged by the workshop tutors.
7   Engagement – participants "engage with new ideas and gradually accommodate them within their own belief structures by making adjustments in their own thinking" (p. 77).

Lamb's (1995) main point is that the main focus of short in-service workshops should be the teachers' beliefs themselves. Once these are understood both by the tutors and participants, then the participants will be more likely to accommodate the new ideas encountered in the workshop.

Lamb's study can be interpreted in several complementary ways. First, workshops should not just focus on understanding material but need to involve other goals, particularly problem solving and experiencing, to get participants to engage more realistically with the material. Second, understanding is not immediate and there needs to be some written record that participants can later consult to help recall ideas, resolve misunderstandings and deepen their understanding. Third, workshops should set modest and realistic aims. A few good ideas well worked through are more valuable than a lot of ideas poorly understood.

The input data (the content) of the understanding component of a workshop can come in several forms:

1   Talks and lectures
2   Set reading
3   Discussions.

Part of the aim of the workshop may be to help participants develop strategies of notetaking or questioning that help the understanding of information, and strategies that help in the evaluation of ideas.

Experiencing and Evaluating

Often short workshops involve participants being introduced to new techniques and activities. This is also what participants most often expect and want to get. An important way of making a technique part of teaching is to experience the technique in use, both as a learner and as a teacher, and to reflect on this experience. The outcome of this component of a workshop is to get the participants to feel capable of presenting an activity effectively and to be able to judge the qualities of a good presentation of the particular activity.

Several things can be done to reduce the threat of such practice presentations during the workshop. Firstly, working with the activity can be termed "experimental" teaching to stress its newness and therefore tolerance of initial problems. At this point a teacher-training principle can be applied, namely, if you want teachers to use the activities you demonstrate for them, you should do a poor demonstration. If you demonstrate the activity well, the participants' response will be, "I couldn't do it that well". If you demonstrate it poorly, they will think "I can do better than that" and then, will do it. Secondly, practice can be done in small groups first without the workshop organiser being too closely involved. Edge (1984) suggests that evaluation at the small-group level is also "face saving".

Video may be a useful form of demonstration, particularly where workshop conditions are far removed from classroom conditions.

The evaluation aspect of experiencing can be an opportunity for information provided in the understanding component of a workshop to be put to use. The workshop organiser can provide short evaluation checklists, or the participants can design their own and thus deepen their understanding of the activity they observe.

Table 13.1 is an example of a checklist based on the idea of learning from comprehensible input. It can be used to evaluate a participant's presentation of a listening to pictures activity (McComish, 1982), where learners look at a complex picture and listen to the teacher's description of it, occasionally having to answer true/false questions based on the picture.

After using a checklist on one or more presentations of an activity, participants may wish to revise the checklist to make it more valid and more practical.

Making Material

Often using new activities or procedures will require the teacher to produce material for the activity. This may be because such material at the

Table 13.1 Evaluating a listening input activity

Points to notice	Notes
Was there a large amount of listening?	
Would learners be able to understand the language they listened to? Why?	
Did the teacher check that the learners were keeping up? How?	
Was the activity friendly and non-threatening? Why?	
Were there new language items in the listening? How would they be understood?	

appropriate level is not commercially available, but also because making material can develop a deeper understanding of an activity. Participants struggling with making activities may also provide feedback to the workshop organiser about where further input and discussion is needed on the focus of the workshop.

When making material, participants should always keep their own learners in mind. This will ensure that the material is appropriate and consistent. At the least, the material which is made is something from the workshop which can be used in class, and at the best a prototype for similar activities.

There are two major approaches to making. One is perfection through gradual approximation, and the other is perfection through preparation. In perfection through gradual approximation the participants see a model activity and then quickly try to make their own, knowing that it is just the first of several attempts and will need to be improved. They receive feedback from other participants and the workshop organiser and then revise what they made or make another similar activity. The advantages of this approach to making is that (1) there are several opportunities for making, (2) feedback and input is more meaningful once participants have experience with making the activity, (3) speed at making is an aim, helped by repeated practice. The disadvantage of this approach is that the first attempt may not be so good.

The perfection through preparation approach involves looking at a model, analysing it, studying the steps involved in making the activity, planning the making, and then making the activity. The advantages of this approach are that (1) the first attempt is likely to be reasonably good and usable, and (2) theory and practice are more closely related. The disadvantage of this approach is that the preparation input reduces the time available for the actual making.

A few participants may find that workshop conditions are not favourable to materials production and they may feel that they can do it more efficiently in their own time and with better access to resources such as a photocopier, a computer, magazines to cut up and other source materials.

The outcome of this component of a workshop is actual materials, and the skill to quickly make a suitable activity. The making goal is a time-consuming one in a workshop and its relevance may be questioned if participants are using a prescribed text in class. It may be that adapting material is more relevant. However, being able to make good material quickly is a very valuable skill and can be a striking demonstration of understanding of what lies behind an activity.

Planning Lessons and Units of Work

Workshops can focus on planning. This involves fitting activities together, so that principles of selection and sequencing are effectively applied. This goal for a workshop is particularly useful when participants have been introduced to a new activity and now have to decide how it can be used in their own teaching.

Harmer (1984) describes an interesting activity that can be used to encourage discussion through choosing and sequencing activities in a plan of work. The learners are given a blank timetable and a collection of small cards containing the name of an activity and the time needed to fill the slots on the timetable. The participants work in small groups to fill the timetable. There may be a list of principles that must be followed. Each group has to explain and justify their timetable to others.

Input to this component of a workshop may be sample lessons from a course book, participants' descriptions of their own lessons and units of work, and content and sequencing principles.

The outcome should be participants who are able to choose activities to meet a particular learning goal, who are able to decide what techniques will be the ones they will use most often in their teaching, and who are able to plan an integrated sequence of work.

Problem Solving

The problem-solving goal of workshops aims to apply the ideas gained in a workshop, or to use the support of others in a workshop, to solve common classroom problems. These can include problems like the following:

- In communication activities my learners often speak their first language instead of English.
- My learners are not motivated to learn English.
- My learners are not good at reading.

- My classes are very big.
- We have to make our lessons more communicative.
- I want my learners to speak more in class but they are shy.

Problem-solving activities in a workshop can be conducted at a general level but they will be more effective if they are related to a particular teaching situation. This then helps participants to relate the ideas in the workshop to the reality of their own classrooms.

There are several kinds of input to problem-solving activities:

1   The problems can come from the workshop organiser or from the other participants.
2   The problems can be in the form of simple case studies, either spoken or written, that detail the circumstances surrounding the problem.
3   Problems can be role played.
4   Solutions as well as problems can be examined and the solutions evaluated and expanded.
5   The presentation of the data can involve lesson transcripts, interview transcripts, recordings, videos.

The type of activity in the workshop can include brainstorming, ranking solutions, using set steps for problem solving, and dividing the participants into attackers and defenders of solutions. Often a problem is best solved if there is a systematic approach to finding solutions to it. This systematic approach could involve some kind of guiding framework. Here (Table 13.2) is a list of possible frameworks drawing on some of the ideas covered in this book on language curriculum design.

Problem solving should encourage participants to reflect on their experience and to examine it with the help of others. The outcome of the problem-solving component of workshops can be a range of solutions to a particular problem, but it can also be teachers who are better at reflecting on their problems and using systematic ways to find solutions to them.

Sequencing the Components of a Workshop

Earlier in this chapter it was suggested that workshops should involve several changes in the focus of attention in order to keep participants involved and interested. The kinds and order of the component goals in a workshop should also relate to the way knowledge and understanding can develop.

In a study of innovation, Palmer (1993) found that experiencing, problem solving and making activities were more likely to lead to the adoption of ideas than understanding. Palmer describes a workshop where the most effective sequencing of goals involved participants first experiencing the innovation, second reflecting upon the impact of the innovation on their

Table 13.2 Frameworks for problem solving

The following frameworks are ways of finding a range of solutions in a systematic way to particular problems like large classes, unmotivated students, or students unwilling to do homework. The goal of using a framework is to make sure that a wide range of possible solutions are being considered and to work out a rationale for solutions. Different frameworks suit different problems. Sometimes any one of several frameworks could be used. Sometimes only one framework makes sense for a particular problem.

1 Opportunities for learning: The four strands

The four strands are meaning-focused input, meaning-focused output, language-focused learning and fluency development. For example, if learners are unmotivated are there meaning-focused input solutions to lack of motivation, such as encouraging enjoyable extensive reading with only a small report on reading being required? Are there meaning-focused output solutions, and so on?

2 Learning goals: LIST

LIST stands for Language, Ideas, Skills, Text. This framework can be used as a framework to solve problems like a wide range of proficiency in a classroom, or a lack of classroom materials.

3 Experience, Shared, Guided, Independent

Sometimes solutions to a problem fit nicely under the classification of learning tasks that we looked at on Chapter 6 on format and presentation.

4 Cognitive, Affective and Situational

See Nation (1997) for an example of applying this framework to learners who use L1 in the classroom.

5 Group size: class, group, individual

This framework works well with the problem of handling large classes and has many other applications.

6 Change strategies: law, reason, involvement

Chapter 12 describes this framework. It can be applied to a wide range of problems where change is involved.

7 A curriculum design model

The curriculum design model used in this book is a useful framework for problem solving. Some problems, like making English teaching more communicative, are best approached from a curriculum design perspective and so this model or one like it can be a useful framework.

8 A principles framework

Principles are a part of the curriculum design model. However looking at principles alone can provide a useful framework for suggestions for solving a problem. For example, the problem of dealing with writing and large classes could examine how the following principles for designing a writing course could be implemented – (1) providing plenty of opportunity to write, (2) providing feedback on writing, (3) making learners aware of the parts of the writing process and giving them help with those parts, and (4) providing a purpose for writing.

own teaching (planning), third adapting the innovation to their own circumstances (making), and finally evaluating the innovation in the light of actual experience.

A major sequencing decision involves deciding whether input by a speaker should come at the beginning of the workshop or after participants have had a chance to explore their own needs and teaching environment. There is no one correct answer to this. Speaker input can provide a structure and information that may make participants' examination of their experience more revealing. Examining experience and needs first may allow the participants to make more focused and effective use of a visiting speaker and ensure that their needs are met.

Evaluating Workshops

Once a workshop has been planned, and again after it has ended, it is worth reflecting on its planning to see if improvements are possible. The list of questions in Table 13.3, focusing on goals, content and presentation, can guide this evaluation.

Workshops may also be assessed by using the parts of the curriculum design diagram by looking at needs and whether they were met, whether environmental constraints were considered, whether sensible principles were followed, and so on.

Table 13.3 Questions for evaluating a workshop

Goals

Which goals did the workshop have? How clearly were these communicated to the participants?
Were the goals achieved?
Was there a feeling of achievement or successful completion at the end of the workshop?

Input

What was the new information in the workshop? Where did it come from?
Was there enough input?
Was the input presented in the most suitable way?

Presentation

Were the learners really involved in this workshop?
What was the reason for the involvement?
Did the workshop remain interesting from the beginning to the end?
How many changes occurred during the workshop?
Were they effective and well spaced?

Summary of the Steps
1 Decide on the goals of the workshop.
2 Decide on the types and sources of input.
3 Decide on activities and ways of getting participants involved.
4 Plan the evaluation of the workshop.

In the next and final chapter we will survey what has been covered in this book by underlining how the parts of the curriculum design process apply to the daily work of teachers.

Tasks

Task 1 Principles for in-service courses

List five principles that are the most important for short in-service courses. You will have to think of most of these principles yourself. You might find it easier to do this by completing this sentence five times – "An in-service course will be successful if . . .". Rank the principles if you can.

1 _____
2 _____
3 _____
4 _____
5 _____

Task 2 Designing an in-service course

You are going to run an in-service course for teachers. There are some others to help you run it, but you have to design the course.

1 Decide:
   (a) the subject of the in-service course

   _____

   (b) the length of the course

   _____

   (c) the number of participants.

   _____

2 How will you do a needs analysis?

   _____

   _____

What will your goals be?

_____

_____

3 Do an environment analysis. Rank the three most important constraints
   and their effects.
   (a) _____
   (b) _____
   (c) _____

4 Design the format of the course in the form of a timetable.

Task 3 The conference workshop

One form of in-service training is the workshop offered at a conference. The
conference workshop shares some features with the more traditional in-
service training workshop discussed in this chapter, and is another way of
introducing teachers to new ideas and activities, with the aim of contributing
to improved teaching practice. Yet it also has some important differences
including:

- the exact number and background of participants are unknown
- time is restricted by the conference programme
- the workshop will be just one of several sessions participants will be
  attending over the course of the conference.

You have been invited to present a workshop on fluency development at a
conference in Cambodia.

1 You have asked the conference organisers what to expect. They have
   told you that many of the teachers at the conference will be from rural
   schools, but there will also be some expatriate teachers from schools in
   Phnom Penh, the capital city. They have also said that teachers typically
   teach from the textbook, and that there is little opportunity for teachers
   or students to use English outside the classroom.
   What effect will these constraints have on your workshop?
2 The workshop is scheduled for a 90-minute session. What will your
   goal/s be?
3 Identify the core content for your workshop, and then decide on the
   sequencing. Relate the content and sequencing to the goal/s, and reflect
   on the principles that underly the decisions you have made.
4 One week before the conference begins, the organisers email you again
   and ask if you could reduce the time from 90 to 45 minutes. How will
   you respond?

Case Studies

1   Choose an account of a short in-service course and analyse it carefully using the framework of goals, input and involvement described in this chapter. Present a short description and evaluation of the course. If you were observing the course, what would you look for? For accounts of short in-service courses see Knight (1992), Taylor (1992), Nolasco and Arthur (1986), Lopriore (1998), Waters and Vilches (2005).

2   Survey the topics of published in-service courses to see the sorts of issues addressed in in-service courses. The journal *English Teaching Forum* (1987) surveyed its readers to see what they were interested in reading in the journal ("What our readers told us about themselves" *English Teaching Forum* 25, 2: 30–33). Here is their list which is ranked from most wanted to least wanted.

Specific techniques
Methodology
Games and songs
Listening comprehension
Language analysis
Literature
EST
Broad philosophical articles.

Chapter 14

Teaching and Curriculum Design

After working through this chapter you should be able to help teachers and learners get the best out of a course.

Throughout this book the emphasis has been on seeing curriculum design as a process with a variety of starting points and with continual opportunity to return to parts of the curriculum design model to revise, reconsider and re-evaluate. It has also been shown that curriculum design does not need to be a large-scale operation. The whole curriculum design process can be applied to something as small as an activity in a lesson. Alternatively, attention can be focused on just one part of the curriculum design process.

It should be clear from this that curriculum design is not the exclusive possession of full-time curriculum designers. Teachers need to make decisions relating to curriculum design in every lesson:

- Is this item worth spending time on?
- How will I present this material?
- What should I test?

These questions require curriculum design decisions and teachers need to develop an awareness of the parts of the curriculum design process, the range of options that are available, and the principles that can guide the application of the process and the choice of options.

As a way of reviewing the model of curriculum design described in this book, we will look at how the parts of the curriculum design model apply to the daily work of teachers in language classes. The reason for doing this is to show that even decisions which just relate to part of a lesson could be improved by an understanding of the wider curriculum design process.

Environment Analysis

Every day teachers have to consider questions like the following:

- Will this activity be interesting enough for my learners?
- Do I have enough time to do this activity?

- Will this activity be too noisy?
- Do the learners know how to do this kind of activity or will I have to explain it to them?
- Will this activity create a lot of marking for me to do?

All of these questions relate to environment analysis. They look at the practicality of doing such an activity in the situation in which the teacher is working. The purpose of environment analysis is to make sure that what happens is likely to be successful because it takes account of the local situation. An experienced teacher does not have to think very deeply about most environment analysis decisions, because such a teacher knows what has worked in the past and is aware of what the difficulties may be. One danger, however, of relying solely on experience is that the teacher may be reluctant to try new things or may not consider trying new things. Research on vocabulary knowledge suggests that teachers tend to underestimate their learners' vocabulary size, and if we extend this research to other areas of knowledge, it could be that teachers tend to have conservative views of what their learners are capable of doing. This means that it is probably worthwhile for a teacher to occasionally be a little adventurous in trying something which will stretch the learners in their language use. The results might be surprising.

It is important to remember when doing environment analysis, that it is done to see its effect on the language course. Teachers can either work within an environmental constraint, or they can try to overcome the constraint. If an activity is not likely to be interesting for the learners, then that activity could be avoided. On the other hand, the teacher could ask: How can I make this activity interesting? What do I need to change in the activity to involve the learners? Most problems like this do have solutions.

Needs Analysis

One of the most common problems in teaching is suiting the activities and material in lessons to a class with a wide range of proficiency. Every day teachers have to consider questions like the following:

- Is this material too difficult for my learners?
- Is there something new for my learners to learn in this activity?
- Will everyone in the class be able to cope with this activity?

All of these questions relate to needs analysis. Needs analysis involves looking at what the learners know now, what they need to know by the end of the course, and what they want to know. It has been suggested several times in this book that doing needs analysis is like doing research or assessment. Because of this, good needs analysis is reliable, valid and practical. Teachers themselves are very good sources of needs analysis information because they typically know their learners well, have seen them perform various tasks and have seen the results of those tasks. Teachers' intuitions can be reliable, valid and practical. It is always good in research and in needs analysis however to draw on more than one source of information.

There are now many web-based tools that can be used in needs analysis. It is now possible to run texts through a vocabulary-level checker to see what the vocabulary load is going to be. A very good example of this can be found on Tom Cobb's website (www.lextutor.ca); on the same website there are various tests that can be used to measure where learners are in their vocabulary knowledge.

It is important that teachers keep checking their own intuitions of learners' language knowledge against the results of tests and careful observation of the learners using language.

Principles

Every day teachers have to consider questions like the following:

- Will this be a good activity for my learners?
- Are my learners doing enough reading?
- Is it good to get learners to memorise words and phrases?
- Should I do the same activity again?
- Should my learners be doing homework?

All of these questions can be answered by looking at principles of teaching and learning. Information about teaching and learning can come from research, but such information can also come from teachers' experience and observation of teaching and learning. It is always good to check these two sources against each other. On some occasions, what seems to be good teaching practice may actually have a negative effect on learning. The research on interference (Nation, 2000) is a good example of this. Teaching a group of closely related words together actually makes learning 50 per cent to 100 per cent more difficult, even though intuitively we feel that is a good idea to bring similar items together. On the other hand, teachers' intuitions about the importance of repetition and meaningful input are well supported by research.

Part of the professional development of teachers involves keeping up with current research findings. It is thus useful for teachers to attend conferences, take part in workshops, and be familiar with at least one professional journal. There are now several very good professional journals that are available free on the web. You can find links on this web site: http://iteslj.org/links/TESL/Journals_on_the_Web/.

A good goal to have when reading articles from such journals is to ask the question, what principles of teaching can I draw from this article? The next question is, of course, how can I apply this principle in my teaching?

A very pleasing development in the field of applied linguistics over the last 10 to 20 years has been the reduction in the advocacy of "*methods*" of language teaching. This is clearly a sign of maturity in the field. There is no one right answer to how languages should be taught or learnt. Different environments require different approaches, and different teachers and learners are comfortable with different approaches. Rather than looking for the magic method, it is better to work at the level of principle, seeing how the same principles can apply in different situations. If research or experience shows that a principle is no longer valid, then this does not require the abandonment of the whole way of teaching, but simply requires some adjustments to what is being done.

Environment analysis, needs analysis and principles make up the three outer circles of the curriculum design diagram. These three parts of the curriculum design process provide data and guidance for the parts of the inner circle of the diagram. Without the information from the outer circles, setting goals, deciding on the content and sequencing of items in the course, deciding what activities and lesson formats to use, and monitoring and assessing, learners' progress would be uninformed, ad hoc processes.

Goals

Not all teachers set language learning goals for the activities they use in class. Beginner teachers are primarily concerned with making sure that the learners have something to do and that they are happy while doing it. It is a brave teacher who asks, is this activity resulting in any useful learning? Technique analysis and the detailed investigation of particular techniques are largely neglected research areas. It is likely however that these areas will gain more attention as interest in task-based syllabuses grows. The setting of performance objectives was also a move in the direction of technique analysis, but was largely concerned with the product rather than the process which achieved that product.

Technique analysis draws strongly on the application of principles of teaching and learning. One possible model of technique analysis involves looking at the learning goals of a particular technique and activity, the mental conditions which are needed to achieve these goals (this is where principles of learning and teaching most apply), the observable signs that these mental conditions might be occurring, and the design features of the technique which set up these mental conditions (Nation, 2001: Chapter 3).

Here is a brief technique analysis of the very common technique of getting learners to answer comprehension questions after they have read a text. The analysis has been put in the form of a table (Table 14.1) because this

Table 14.1 A technique analysis of the activity of answering comprehension questions

Goals	Conditions (signs)	Features
Comprehension of the text	Understanding of the text (Correct answers to the questions) (Providing the answers to the questions quickly) (Answering without having to consult others)	Questions which involve the required degree of comprehension of the text If the questions are in the same order as the information in the text, answering them will be easier
Learning language items	Understanding of the text and the questions (Correct answers to the questions) (Providing the answers to the questions quickly) (Answering without having to consult others) Retrieval of the language items needed to understand the questions or to answer them (The target language items occur in the questions or answers) (The learners answer the questions without looking back at the text) Generative use of the language items in the questions or in the answers (The questions or the answers contain the target language used in ways different from which they are used in the text) (The learners discuss the questions and the answers with each other and this discussion involves use of the target language items)	The questions include the target items The answers require use of the target items The learners are told not to look back at the text when they answer the questions The questions contain the target items used in ways which are different from those in the text The questions require the learners to process the text in a new way, such as relating it to other experience

makes it easier to keep track of the parts of the analysis. Note that column 2 includes both conditions and signs of learning. The signs of learning are given in brackets after each of the conditions that they relate to.

The activity is seen as having two learning goals. In technique analysis, each goal should be analysed separately, and this is done by providing a separate row for each goal in the table. The first goal and the conditions for reaching that goal are the same. Comprehension is a mental condition. Not all questions are good comprehension questions, and so to reach the goal of good comprehension the questions should ask for the kind of knowledge which can reasonably be expected from the reading of a text. The degree to which the questions match the text in terms of order and the language involved in the questions and answers will affect the difficulty of the questions.

Comprehension questions may also have the goal of helping learners learn language items which were previously unknown or only partly known. This can occur through learning from comprehensible input, or through having to produce the items in the answers. If the questions require the learners to think about the information in the text in relation to other information, then this could encourage productive generative use of the language items in the answers to the questions. If the questions contain the target items and the questions are not an exact copy of the wording in the text, then this provides receptive generative use of the target items for the learners.

It is important in doing such technique analysis, that each goal is related to its own conditions and signs, and these conditions are related to the design features of the technique. This is because features, conditions and goals are in a causative sequence. That is, the design of the technique sets up certain conditions which encourage the learners to reach certain learning goals.

Goals are represented in the small inner circle of the curriculum design diagram. This is because the whole purpose of the language course is centred around what the learners need to learn. Goals are central to any curriculum design.

Content and Sequencing

Every day teachers have to consider questions like the following:

- What reading passage will I use?
- What vocabulary will I get the learners to focus on in this activity?
- Which items shall I use for the blanks in the blank-filling activity I'm making?
- How can I repeat the language items which were used in the previous lessons?
- What topics should I get the learners to talk about in my discussion activities?

All of these questions relate to content and sequencing because they focus on what will be in the course and the order in which it will occur. The choice of a reading passage involves two kinds of content – the topic of the passage and the language items which occur in the passage. These two kinds of content are related, but one of the big problems teachers face in any lesson is to give attention to language features which are important beyond that lesson. The immediate attraction in a particular reading passage is the vocabulary which is very closely related to the topic. This vocabulary, however, tends to be vocabulary that is not very useful beyond that topic or closely related topics. A very useful question that the teacher can ask when deciding what language features to focus on in a reading text is: Will these language features help the reading of tomorrow's reading passage? If the answer is no, then the teacher should be focusing on more generally useful items.

The choice of the ideas content of a course can involve the application of several principles. The idea behind content-based instruction is that a course which focuses on a content subject like mathematics, technology, literature or tourism can also be a very useful means of language development. There are two major dangers to be aware of in such courses. Firstly, a focus on the content matter is necessarily a message-focused approach to language learning. The focus is on the content matter of the material. It is important in such courses that language-focused learning is not neglected. That is, there should be some deliberate focus on language features in such courses (Langman, 2003). Language-focused learning has a very important role to play in any language course. Secondly, a focus on a particular subject area can mean that more generally useful language items might not be met often in the course. Content-based instruction, however, can be a very effective way of improving content matter knowledge and language proficiency.

Some courses follow themes as a way of dealing with the ideas content of the course. The positive feature of themes is that a continuing theme can provide opportunities for the same language features to be recycled and thus better learnt.

Some courses jump from one topic to another with no particular connection between them, except perhaps the desire to capture the interest of the learners. Keeping the learners interested is a very important principle in language teaching. However, using a wide variety of topics inevitably results in a very large amount of different vocabulary occurring, often with little repetition. Teachers, however, can deal with this issue if they are aware of it.

As indicated above, it is no longer difficult for teachers to keep track of important vocabulary in lessons. Vocabulary profile checkers such as those on Tom Cobb's website make this task very straightforward.

Format and Presentation

Format and presentation decisions are among the most common ones made by a teacher. Every day teachers have to consider questions like the following:

- What activities will I get the learners to do today?
- Shall I get the learners to do this activity individually or in pairs or groups?

- Should I pre-teach these items before the learners meet them in the reading passage?
- Shall I write this on the blackboard?
- Should I have a pre-reading discussion or should I get the learners to talk about the text after the reading?
- Have I got a good balance of activities in this lesson?

All of these questions relate to format and presentation, because they involve what the learners do in the lesson and the order in which they do these things in the lesson. It is not too difficult to see how format and presentation decisions are influenced by principles, needs analysis and environment analysis.

The choice of a particular technique or activity can bring certain learning principles into play. Does the technique provide an opportunity for retrieval? Does the technique avoid interference between the items in the activity? Does the technique provide an opportunity for fluency development or meaning-focused input?

The choice of an activity also depends on environment analysis factors. Does the physical arrangement of the classroom make it easy to do group work? Is there enough time to complete the activity? Are the learners well-behaved enough to be able to work quietly and independently? Have the learners done this activity before or will they need to be taught how to do the activity properly? Most teachers will make these decisions intuitively. However, if the technique or activity is unsuccessful, it is always worthwhile looking at the environment factors to see if changes can be made so that the activity will work well. For example, group work might not be successful simply because the learners are not sitting in a good group work arrangement. Changing the seating arrangement could make the activity successful. Similarly, pair work may be unsuccessful because learners are not working with an appropriate partner. Changing the way the learners form pairs could make the activity successful. Some activities may be seen by the learners to be too much like a game and not serious enough to be considered as opportunities for learning.

The choice of an activity also depends on needs analysis factors. Some activities may be asking the learners to do things they are not yet able to do. Some activities may be too easy. Fluency development activities should involve easy material that the learners are already familiar with. This means of course that learners either have to be aware of why they are doing the activity, or there is some other challenge to the activity such as an increase in speed which adds an element of difficulty to it. For each of the four strands of meaning-focused input, meaning-focused output, language-focused learning and fluency development, there is a proficiency condition which must be met in order for that strand to truly exist. Meeting this proficiency condition involves decisions which relate to needs analysis.

Monitoring and Assessment

Every day teachers have to consider questions like the following:

- Is this activity going well?
- Are all the learners participating in the activity?
- Are some learners doing more work than others?
- Have the learners learnt anything from this activity?
- Should I give the learners a test to encourage them to keep on learning?

All of these questions relate to monitoring and assessment, because they involve the teacher looking carefully at what learners are actually doing and they may involve the teacher in some kind of testing or measurement.

Monitoring probably plays a much bigger role in most courses than assessment does. Monitoring occurs whenever the teacher observes what the learners are doing or what they have done in order to see if things are going as they should. This happens many times in any lesson and can take many forms. Most monitoring is informal and does not involve testing. Teachers often develop a feel for what is going well. It is always good to check this with some guided or focused observation. This guidance can occur in the form of a question, for example, "Is each learner taking a turn in the activity? How many times were the target words repeated by the learners in the activity? Are all the learners completing the activity?"

Teachers need to remember that assessment can be done for many different purposes. It can be used to encourage learning, to find areas of difficulty, to place the learners in the right group or class, to measure learning from the course, or to measure how much their language proficiency has improved.

Evaluation

Every day teachers have to consider questions like the following:

- Is the course going well?
- Are the learners happy with the course?
- Am I happy with the course?
- Would other teachers think that my course is a good course?
- Can I see ways in which I can improve the course?
- Did today's lesson go well?
- Will I get through the course book by the end of the course?

All of these questions relate to evaluation because they involve making a judgement on whether the course or some aspect of it is good or not. In the curriculum design diagram, evaluation is a large circle which includes all of the parts of the curriculum design process. This is because evaluation is very wide-ranging and can focus on any aspect of curriculum design.

Like needs analysis, evaluation is a kind of research. Typically it involves asking a question about the course, and then deciding what will be the most valid and reliable way of answering this question. Practicality can come into this decision, but reliability and validity must be given prominence in deciding the means of evaluation. If we are not really answering the question (validity), or are answering it in ways which would give us a different result tomorrow from what it does today (reliability), we are wasting our time.

By far, most evaluation of courses is done by the teacher and by the learners, often independently of each other. Learners have opinions about the courses they follow, and teachers similarly have opinions. These opinions are important because they involve people closely related to the course. However, it is always useful to check these opinions against more independent measures. Very enjoyable courses may be achieving very little in terms of language development. Courses that students complain about with heavy workloads and demanding tasks may be achieving a lot. Or they may not. When a teacher says that a course is going well, this is useful, but not very convincing, evidence for outsiders. Having some measurable form of evaluation may be more convincing. It is always useful for teachers to keep records of learners' performance, and where possible to include some formal evaluation at various times in their courses. This evaluation can consist of brief questionnaires, examples of students' work, records of improvement such as speed-reading graphs or writing graphs, and the amount of work completed such as the amount of extensive reading that the students have done.

It is a useful professional development exercise for teachers to evaluate their language course using some principles of language teaching. That is, for each principle, the teacher describes how it is being implemented in their course. For example, "Is the course providing a balance of opportunities for learning across the four strands? Is the teacher providing opportunities for repetition? Is the learners' progress being monitored? Are the learners being helped to become independent learners?"

The study of curriculum design requires the integration of knowledge from a number of fields. First, curriculum design for language teaching is part of the wider field of curriculum design in education. Much of the research and theory drawn on in this book has its roots in this larger field. Second, curriculum design inevitably involves assessment and evaluation and these are both part of a wider field, and represent rapidly growing areas of knowledge in second-language teaching. Third, curriculum design involves the consideration of learning and teaching and the principles that guide those activities. Fourth, curriculum design involves teacher training, innovation and the continuing development of teachers.

Curriculum Design and Learner Autonomy

Language courses typically involve learners in activities that are set up by the course book and teacher and that often involve working with other learners. Crabbe (1993) points out that these "public domain" activities usually do not prepare learners for "private domain" learning, that is the learners studying alone or taking responsibility for their own learning. Crabbe suggests two major ways in which learners can be encouraged to take this responsibility – through classroom discussion about learning tasks (their goals, why they are done in certain ways, signs of learning, necessary conditions for learning, etc.), and through the use of tasks that model the sorts of things that learners could usefully do alone or without the need for teacher guidance (Cotterall, 1995). Such tasks could include fluency development repetition activities like 4/3/2 (Maurice, 1983; Nation, 1989b), and ask and answer (Simcock, 1993), that learners can use alone or with a friend and where progress is easily observable; reading for pleasure; self-directed vocabulary learning using cards (Nation, 2001); and notetaking from written and spoken text.

If course books are truly to help learners they need to show the learner how to use the book to its best advantage and how to continue to learn beyond the book. Encouraging learner autonomy is thus an important goal in curriculum design.

We have now reached the end of our description of language curriculum design. As a result of reading this book you should now be familiar with an easily remembered model of curriculum design, and should be aware of the ways that the parts of the curriculum design process can affect common classroom issues.

Because of the size of the field of curriculum design, and because of the very practical aims of this book, it has been possible to only touch on most of the important aspects of curriculum design. The knowledge of the curriculum design process that has been gained from this text should allow teachers to read more widely in the field with an informed and critical eye.

Tasks

1   List the arguments for and against following a set method of language teaching like the grammar-translation approach or the communicative approach.
2   Consider if the curriculum design model used in this book could be applied to non-language courses, such as a driving course or a mathematics course.
3   Without looking back at this chapter, systematically go through the curriculum design model recalling or creating curriculum design questions that teachers might have to answer when teaching a lesson.

Appendix

A Verb-Form Frequency Count, based on George (1963a)

Occurrences per 1,000 verb-form occurrences

stem+ed, Simple Past Narrative (for telling stories)	156.4
stem/stem+s, Simple Present Actual (referring to now)	120.4
stem+ed, Simple Past Actual (referring to the past)	83.1
stem/stem+s, Simple Present Neutral (with no time reference)	69.7
stem+ed, past participle of occurrence	58.9
stem+ed, past participle of state	32.6
verb + *to* + stem	27.5
stem+ing = adjective in noun groups	24.6
stem+ed = adjective in noun groups	23.3
imperative *don't* + stem	16.9
stem+ed, past participle + prepositional object	15.1
stem+ed, Simple Past Neutral	15.1
narrative *had* + stem+ed	14.9
stem+ing in free adjuncts	14.9
stem+ed, Simple Past Habitual (referring to repeated actions)	14.3
noun + *to* + stem	13.3
stem/stem+s, Simple Present Iterative (referring to repeated actions)	11.4
verb + *to* + stem (dominant)	10.1
verb + noun/pronoun + *to* + stem	10.0
stem+ing = noun	9.8
stem, Imperative	9.5
noun + preposition + stem+ing	8.7
verb + noun/pronoun/possessive adjective + stem+ing	8.6
verb + stem+ing (dominant)	6.2
has/have + stem+ed, Perfect Present	6.1
has/have + stem+ed, Resultative Present Perfect	6.0
am/is/are + stem+ing, Present Progressive "now"	5.8
stem+ed, participle + *to* + stem	5.7

stem+ed, Simple Past Irrealis (subjunctive use, *If I were . . .*)	5.3
'll + stem	5.1
verb (dominant) + stem+ing	4.7
was/were stem+ing, Past Progressive "at the moment"	4.7
to have + *to* + stem (obligation)	4.7
could + stem (reported *can* characteristically able)	4.6
could + stem (reported *can* immediately able)	4.6
feel etc. + noun/pronoun + stem	4.3
verb + preposition + stem+ing	4.3
can (immediately able) + stem	4.2
may (possibility and uncertainty) + stem	4.2
would (reported *will*, future) + stem	4.0
stem/stem+s, Simple present, "Future" in main clause	4.0
can (characteristically able) + stem	3.8
must (necessity due to circumstances) + stem	3.7
adjective + *to* + stem	3.7
had + stem+ed (from Perfect Present)	3.7
after *would* (indicating probability of assumption)+ stem	3.5
to + stem = noun	3.4
do/did interrogative (expressing astonishment, etc.) + stem	3.4
has/have + stem+ed, Continuative Present Perfect	3.4
will (future) + stem	3.2
was/were + stem+ing, Past Progressive Habitual	3.1
can't (improbability due to circumstances) + stem	3.1
vicarious *do/did*	3.0

References

In the following list of references, the number in square brackets [ ] at the end of each reference refers to the chapter number of this book. So, the Allwright (1981) article relates to Chapter 6, Format and Presentation, and also Chapter 11, Adopting and Adapting an Existing Course Book. The number [20] indicates that the article describes a case study.

Adamson, B. and Davison, C. 2008. English language teaching in Hong Kong primary schools: Innovation and resistance. In D.E. Murray (ed), *Planning Change, Changing Plans: Innovations in Second Language Teaching*. Ann Arbor, MI: University of Michigan Press. [12]

Adaskou, K., Britten, D. and Fahsi, B. 1990. Design decisions on the cultural content of a secondary English course for Morocco. *ELT Journal* 44, 1: 3–1. [5]

Alderson, C. 1990. Testing reading comprehension skills (Part two). *Reading in a Foreign Language* 7, 1: 465–503. [5]

Alderson, C. and Hamp-Lyons, E. 1996. TOEFL preparation courses: a study of washback. *Language Testing* 13, 3: 280–297. [7]

Alderson, C. and Wall, D. 1993. Does washback exist? *Applied Linguistics* 14, 2: 115–129. [7]

Allen, V.F. 1970. Toward a thumbnail test of English competence. *English Teaching Forum* 8, 3: 37. [7]

Allen, W. and Spada, N. 1983. Designing a communicative syllabus in the People's Republic of China. In Jordan 1983. [20]

Allwright, R.L. 1981. What do we want teaching materials for? *ELT Journal* 36, 1: 5–18. [6, 11]

Alptekin, C. and Alptekin, M. 1984. EFL teaching in non-English-speaking countries. *ELT Journal* 38, 1: 14–20. [5]

Androsenko, V.P. 1992. A refresher course in communicative teaching. *English Teaching Forum* 30, 2: 2–5, 27. [20]

Arevart, S. and Nation, I.S.P. 1991. Fluency improvement in a second language. *RELC Journal* 22, 1: 84–94. [4]

Asmah, H.O. 1992. *The Linguistic Scenery in Malaysia*. Kuala Lumpur: Dewan Bahasa dan Pustaka, Ministry of Education, Malaysia. [2]

Aziz, Asfah Abdul. 1984. The new Bahasa Malaysia syllabus for primary schools. In Read 1984b. [20]

Baddeley, A. 1990. *Human Memory*. Hillsdale, NJ: Lawrence Erlbaum Associates. [4]

Barnard, H. 1980. *Advanced English Vocabulary*. Rowley, MA: Newbury House. [9]

Bawcom, L. 1995. Designing an advanced speaking course. *English Teaching Forum* 33, 1: 41–43. [20]

Bello, T. 1994. Respecting and serving the needs of ESL senior citizens. *TESOL Journal* 4, 1: 36–39. [20]

Benesch, S. 1996. Needs analysis and curriculum development in EAP: An example of a critical approach. *TESOL Quarterly* 30, 4: 723–738. [3]

Bennett, G.K. 1972. Review of the remote associates test. In O.K. Buros (ed), *The Seventh Mental Measurements Yearbook*. Highland Park, NJ: Gryphon. [7]

Beretta, A. 1986a. Toward a methodology of ESL program evaluation. *TESOL Quarterly* 20, 1: 144–155. [8]

Beretta, A. 1986b. Program-fair language teaching evaluation. *TESOL Quarterly* 20, 3: 431–444. [8]

Beretta, A. and Davies, A. 1985. Evaluation of the Bangalore Project. *ELT Journal* 39, 2: 121–127. [8, 10]

Biber, D. 1990. A typology of English texts. *Linguistics* 27: 3–43. [5]

Biber, D., Johansson, S., Leech, G., Conrad, S. and Finegan, E. 1999. *Longman Grammar of Spoken and Written English*. Harlow: Longman. [1, 5]

Black, M.C. and Kiehnhoff, D.M. 1992. Content-based classes as a bridge from the EFL to the university classroom. *TESOL Journal* 1, 4: 27–28. [20]

Block, D. 1994. A day in the life of a class: Teacher/learner perceptions of task purpose in conflict. *System* 22, 4: 473–486. [6]

Block, D. 1998. Exploring interpretations of questionnaire items. *System* 26: 403–425. [8]

Bloom, B.S. (ed) 1956. *Taxonomy of Educational Objectives. Book 1: Cognitive Domain*. London: Longman. [5]

Boon, A. 2005. Tell me what you want, what you really, really want! *Modern English Teacher* 14, 4: 41–52. [10, 20]

Boon, A. 2007. Mission: Possible. *Modern English Teacher* 16, 2: 40–47. [4]

Borg, S. 2006. *Teacher Cognition and Language Education: Research and Practice*. London: Continuum. [12]

Bosher, S. and Smalkoski, K. 2002. From needs analysis to curriculum development: Designing a course in health-care communication for immigrant students in the USA. *English for Specific Purposes* 21, 1: 59–79. [20]

Bourke, J. 2006. Designing a topic-based syllabus for young learners. *ELT Journal* 60, 3: 279–289. [20]

Brecht, R.D. and Rivers, W.P. 2005. Language needs analysis at the societal level. In Long 2005a. [20]

Breen, M. 1984. Process syllabuses for the language classroom. In Brumfit 1984a: 47–60. [1, 10, 11]

Breen, M. 1987. Contemporary paradigms in syllabus design. *Language Teaching* 20, 2: 81–92 and 157–174. [1, 10]

Breen, M.P. and Littlejohn, A. 2000a. *Classroom Decision-Making*. Cambridge: Cambridge University Press. [10]

Breen, M.P. and Littlejohn, A. 2000b. The practicalities of negotiation. In Breen and Littlejohn 2000a: 272–295. [10]

Breen, M.P., Candlin, C. and Waters, A. 1979. Communicative materials design: Some basic principles. *RELC Journal* 10, 2: 1–13. [4]

Brown, D. 1983. Conversational cloze tests and conversational ability. *ELT Journal* 37, 2: 158–161. [7]

Brown, G. 1978. Understanding spoken language. *TESOL Quarterly* 12, 3: 271–283. [5]

Brown, G., Anderson, A., Shillcock, R. and Yule, G. 1984. *Teaching Talk*. Cambridge: Cambridge University Press. [3]

Brown, H.D. 1993. Requiem for methods. *Journal of Intensive English Studies* 7: 1–12. [4]

Brown, H.D. 2006. *Principles of Language Learning and Teaching* (5th ed.). White Plains, NY: Longman. [5]

Brown, J.D. 1995. *The Elements of Language Curriculum*. New York: Newbury House. [5, 7]

Brumfit, C.J. (ed) 1984a. *General English Syllabus Design*. ELT Documents 118. Oxford: Pergamon Press. [1, 4]

Brumfit, C.J. 1984b. The Bangalore Procedural Syllabus. *ELT Journal* 38, 4: 233–241. [5, 8, 10]

Brumfit, C.J. 1985. Accuracy and fluency: A fundamental distinction for communicative teaching methodology. In C.J. Brumfit, *Language and Literature Teaching: From Practice to Principle*. Oxford: Pergamon.

Bruner, J.S. 1962. *The Process of Education*. Cambridge, MA: Harvard University Press. [5]

Bygate, M., Skehan, P. and Swain, M. 2001. Introduction. In M. Bygate, P. Skehan and M. Swain (eds), *Researching Pedagogic Tasks, Second Language Learning, Teaching and Testing*. Harlow: Longman. [4]

Carroll, J.B., Davies, P. and Richman, B. 1971. *The American Heritage Word Frequency Book*. Boston: Houghton Mifflin. [4]

Chambers, F. 1997. Seeking consensus in course book evaluation. *ELT Journal* 51, 1: 29–35. [11]

Chandler, J. 2003. The efficacy of various kinds of error feedback for improvement in the accuracy and fluency of L2 student writing. *Journal of Second Language Writing* 12, 3: 267–296. [4]

Chikalanga, I. 1992. A suggested taxonomy of inferences for the reading teacher. *Reading in a Foreign Language* 8, 2: 697–709. [5]

Chin, R. and Benne, K. 1970. General strategies for effecting changes in human systems. In W. Bennis, K. Benne and R. Chin (eds), *The Planning of Change*. London: Holt, Rinehart and Winston. [12]

Chung, T.M. and Nation, I.S.P. 2004. Identifying technical vocabulary. *System* 32, 2: 251–263. [3]

Chung, M. and Nation, I.S.P. 2006. The effect of a speed reading course. *English Teaching* 61, 4: 181–204. [6]

Clarke, D.F. 1989. Materials adaptation: Why leave it all to the teacher? *ELT Journal* 43, 2: 133–141. [7, 10, 11]

Clarke, D.F. 1991. The negotiated syllabus: What is it and how is it likely to work? *Applied Linguistics* 12, 1: 13–28. [8, 10, 11]

Clayton, T. 1995. A task-based approach to in-house business programs. *Prospect* 10, 1: 34–40. [20]

Coleman, H. 1989. *Learning and Teaching in Large Classes: A Bibliography*. Project report no. 1, Lancaster-Leeds language learning in large classes research project. [2]

Collier, V.P. 1987. Age and rate of acquisition of second language for academic purposes. *TESOL Quarterly* 21, 4: 617–641. [2]

Collier, V.P. 1989. How long? A synthesis of research on academic achievement in a second language. *TESOL Quarterly* 23, 3: 509–531. [2]

Collier, V.P. 1995. Acquiring a second language for school. *Directions in Language and Education* 1, 4. Available at http://www.ncbe.gwu.edu/ncbepubs/directions/04.htm [2]

Cook, V.J. 1983. What should language teaching be about? *ELT Journal* 37, 3: 229–234. [5]

Cotterall, S. 1995. Developing a course strategy for learner autonomy. *ELT Journal* 49, 3: 219–227. [4, 14]

Cotterall, S. 2000. Promoting learner autonomy through the curriculum: Principles for designing language courses. *ELT Journal* 54, 2: 109–117. [4]

Cotterall, S. and Cohen, R. 2003. Scaffolding for second-language writers: Producing an academic essay. *ELT Journal* 57, 2: 158–166. [4]

Council of Europe. 2001. *Common European Framework of Reference for Languages: Learning, Teaching, Assessment.* Cambridge: Cambridge University Press. [5]

Coxhead, A. 2000. A new academic word list. *TESOL Quarterly* 34, 2: 213–238. [1, 3, 5]

Crabbe, D. 1993. Fostering autonomy from within the classroom: The teacher's responsibility. *System* 21, 4: 443–452. [4, 10, 14]

Craik, F.I.M. and Lockhart, R.S. 1972. Levels of processing: A framework for memory research. *Journal of Verbal Learning and Verbal Behavior* 11: 671–684. [4]

Craik, F.I.M. and Tulving, E. 1975. Depth of processing and the retention of words in episodic memory. *Journal of Experimental Psychology* 104: 268–284. [4]

Davies, A. 2006. What do learners really want from their EFL course? *ELT Journal* 60, 1: 3–12. [8, 10]

Davis, P. with Pearse, E. 2000. *Success in English Teaching.* Oxford: Oxford University Press. [4]

Day, R.R. and Bamford, J. 1998. *Extensive Reading in the Second Language Classroom.* Cambridge: Cambridge University Press. [4]

Day, R.R. and Bamford, J. 2002. Top ten principles for teaching extensive reading. *Reading in a Foreign Language* 14, 2: 136–141. [4]

Day, R.R. and Park, J.-S. 2005. Developing reading comprehension questions. *Reading in a Foreign Language* 17, 1: 60–73. [5]

De Saussure, F. 1983. *Course in General Linguistics.* La Salle, IL: Open Court (trans. Roy Harris). [3]

Dickinson, L. 1987. *Self-instruction in Language Learning.* Cambridge: Cambridge University Press [3].

DiGiovanni, E. and Nagaswami, G. 2001. Online peer review: An alternative to face-to-face? *ELT Journal* 55, 3: 263–272. [11]

Dobson, J. 1979. The notional syllabus: Theory and practice. *English Teaching Forum* 17, 2: 2–10. [5]

Dörnyei, Z. 2001. *Motivational Strategies in the Language Classroom.* Cambridge: Cambridge University Press. [4]

Dowhower, S.L. 1989. Repeated reading: Research into practice. *The Reading Teacher* 42: 502–507. [4]

Dubin, F. and Olshtain, E. 1986. *Curriculum Design.* Cambridge: Cambridge University Press. [1]

Dudley-Evans, T. 1983a. A model for syllabus design for an English-medium technical college in Singapore. In Dudley-Evans 1983d. [20]

Dudley-Evans, T. 1983b. A communicative approach to the teaching of writing. In Dudley-Evans 1983d. [20]

Dudley-Evans, T. 1983c. Designing a course in listening comprehension at Ngee Ann Technical College. In Dudley-Evans 1983d. [20]

Dudley-Evans, T. 1983d. *Papers on Team Teaching and Syllabus Design.* RELC Occasional Papers No.27. Singapore: RELC. [20]

Dušková, L. and Urbanová, V. 1967. A frequency count of English tenses with application to teaching English as a foreign language. *Prague Studies in Mathematical Linguistics* 2: 19–36. [5]

Eckman, F., Bell, L. and Nelson, D. 1988. On the generalization of relative clause instruction in the acquisition of English as a second language. *Applied Linguistics* 9, 1: 1–20. [4]

Edge, J. 1984. Feedback with face. *ELT Journal* 38, 3: 204–206. [13]

Elder, C. and O'Loughlin, K. 2003. Score gains on IELTS after 10–12 weeks of intensive English study. *IELTS Research Report* 4: 62–87. [7]

Elley, W. 1989. Vocabulary acquisition from listening to stories. *Reading Research Quarterly* 24, 2: 174–187. [4]

Elley, W. and Mangubhai, F. 1981. *The Impact of a Book Flood in Fiji Primary Schools.* Wellington: NZCER. [4, 8, 12]

Ellis, R. 1985. *Understanding Second Language Acquisition.* Oxford: Oxford University Press. [4]

Ellis, R. 1986. Activities and procedures for teacher training. *ELT Journal* 40, 2: 91–99. [13]

Ellis, R. 1987. Contextual variability in second language acquisition and the relevancy of language teaching. In R. Ellis (ed), *Second Language Acquisition in Context.* Englewood Cliffs, NJ: Prentice Hall International. [4]

Ellis, R. 1990. *Instructed Second Language Acquisition.* Oxford: Basil Blackwell. [4]

Ellis, R. 1995. Interpretation tasks for grammar teaching. *TESOL Quarterly* 29, 1: 87–105. [4]

Ellis, R. 2003a. Designing a task-based syllabus. *RELC Journal* 41, 1: 64–81. [5]

Ellis, R. 2003b. *Task-based Language Learning and Teaching.* Oxford: Oxford University Press. [5]

Ellis, R. 2005. Principles of instructed language learning. *System* 33: 209–224. [1, 4]

Fedderholdt, K. 2001. An email exchange project between non-native speakers of English. *ELT Journal* 55, 3: 273–280. [11]

Frankel, M.A. 1983. Designing a pre-EAP reading course: Practical problems. In Jordan 1983. [20]

Franken, M. 1987. Self-questioning scales for improving academic writing. *Guidelines* 9, 1: 1–8. [4]

Freeman, D. 2002. The hidden side of the work: Teacher knowledge and learning to teach. A perspective from North American educational research on teacher education in English language teaching. *Language Teaching* 35, 1: 1–13. [12]

Friederichs, J. and Pierson, H.D. 1981. What are science students expected to write? *ELT Journal* 35, 4: 407–410. [3]

Garton, S. 2008. Teacher beliefs and interaction in the language classroom. In S. Garton and K. Richards (eds), *Professional Encounters in TESOL: Discourses of Teachers in Teaching.* Basingstoke, Hampshire: Palgrave Macmillan. [12]

George, H.V. 1962. On teaching and "unteaching". *ELT Journal* 17, 1: 16–20. [3]

George, H.V. 1963a. *Report on a Verb Form Frequency Count.* Monograph of the Central Institute of English, Hyderabad, Volumes 1 and 2. [4, 5]

George, H.V. 1963b. A verb form frequency count. *ELT Journal* 18, 1: 31–37 [4, 5].

George, H.V. 1972. *Common Errors in Language Learning.* Rowley, MA: Newbury House. [1]

Gianelli, M.C. 1991. Thematic units: Creating an environment for learning. *TESOL Journal* 1, 1: 13–15. [20]

Gilabert, R. 2005. Evaluating the use of multiple sources and methods in needs analysis: A case study of journalists in the autonomous Community of Catalonia (Spain). In Long 2005a. [20]

Girginer, H. and Sullivan, P. 2002. The use of discourse analysis to enhance ESP teacher knowledge: An example using aviation English. *English for Specific Purposes* 21, 4: 397–404. [20]

Goh, C.C.M. and Yin, T.M. 2008. Implementing the English Language Syllabus 2001 in Singapore schools: Interpretations and re-interpretations. In D.E. Murray (ed), *Planning Change, Changing Plans: Innovations in Second Language Teaching.* Ann Arbor, MI: University of Michigan Press. [12]

Goldschneider, J.M. and DeKeyser, R.M. 2005. Explaining the natural order of L2 morpheme acquisition in English: A meta-analysis of multiple determinants. *Language Learning* 55, 1: 27–77. [4]

Graves, K. 2000. *Designing Language Courses: A Guide for Teachers.* Boston: Heinle and Heinle. [9]

Hamp-Lyons, E. 1983. Developing a course to teach extensive reading skills to university-bound ESL learners. *System* 11, 3: 303–312. [20]

Harden, T. 2006. Progression in foreign language learning: Subjective experience and objective demands. In Harden *et al.* 2006: 27–44. [5]

Harden, T. and Witte, A. 2006. Introduction. In Harden *et al.* 2006: 11–24. [5]

Harden, T., Witte, A. and Köhler, D. (eds) 2006. *The Concept of Progression in the Teaching and Learning of Foreign Languages.* Oxford: Peter Lang. [5]

Harmer, J. 1984. Balancing activities: A unit planning game. *ELT Journal* 38, 2: 91–97. [13]

Harrison, J. and Menzies, P. 1986. *Orbit.* Oxford: Oxford University Press. [1]

Hess, N. 2001. *Teaching Large Multi-Level Classes.* Cambridge: Cambridge University Press. [2]

Higa, M. 1963. Interference effects of interlist word relationships in verbal learning. *Journal of Verbal Learning and Verbal Behavior* 2: 170–175. [1, 4]

Hill, D.R. 1997. Survey review: Graded readers. *ELT Journal* 51, 1: 57–81. [4]

Hill, D.R. 2001. Graded readers. *ELT Journal* 55, 3: 300–324. [4]

Hill, D.R. 2008. Graded readers in English. *ELT Journal* 62, 2: 184–204. [4]

Hillocks, G. 1984. What works in teaching composition: A meta-analysis of experimental treatment studies. *American Journal of Education* 93, 1: 133–171. [4]

Hindmarsh, R. 1980. *Cambridge English Lexicon.* Cambridge: Cambridge University Press. [1, 4]

Holliday, A. 1994. *Appropriate Methodology and Social Context.* Cambridge: Cambridge University Press. [12]

Holme, R. and Chalauisaeng, B. 2006. The learner as needs analyst: The use of participatory appraisal in the EAP reading classroom. *English for Specific Purposes* 25, 4: 403–419. [8]

Horowitz, D.M. 1986. What professors actually require: Academic tasks for the ESL classroom. *TESOL Quarterly* 20, 3: 445–462. [3]

Hosenfield, C. 1976. Learning about learning: Discovering our students' strategies. *Foreign Language Annals* 9, 2: 117–129. [6]

Hoyt, L. 1992. Language instruction in a refugee camp: Challenges and rewards. *TESOL Journal* 2, 1: 25–29. [20]

Hu, M. and Nation, I.S.P. 2000. Unknown vocabulary density and reading comprehension. *Reading in a Foreign Language* 13, 1: 403–430. [4]

Hutchinson, T. and Waters, A. 1987. *English for Specific Purposes*. Cambridge: Cambridge University Press. [1]

Hyland, K. 2002. Specificity revisited: How far should we go now? *English for Specific Purposes* 21, 4: 385–395 [3]

Iancu, M. 1993. Adapting the adjunct model: A case study. *TESOL Journal* 2, 4: 20–24. [20]

Irujo, S. 2000. A process syllabus in a methodology course: Experience, beliefs, challenges. In Breen and Littlejohn 2000a: 209–222. [10]

Izumi, E. and Isahara, H. 2005. Investigation into language learners' acquisition order based on an error analysis of a learner corpus. In *Proceedings of IWLeL 2004: An interactive workshop on language e-learning*. Tokyo, Japan: 63–71. [4]

Joe, A., Nation, P. and Newton, J. 1996. Vocabulary learning and speaking activities. *English Teaching Forum* 34, 1: 2–7. [1]

Johns, T. and Davies, F. 1983. Text as a vehicle for information: The classroom use of written texts in teaching reading in a foreign language. *Reading in a Foreign Language* 1, 1: 1–19. [4]

Jones, F.R. 1993. Beyond the fringe: A framework for assessing teach-yourself materials for *ab initio* English-speaking learners. *System* 21, 4: 453–469. [1, 11]

Joos, M. 1964. *The English Verb: Form and Meaning*. Madison, WI: University of Wisconsin Press. [5]

Jordan, R. (ed) 1983. *Case Studies in ELT*. London: Collins ELT. [20]

Jordan, R.R. 1990. Pyramid discussions. *ELT Journal* 44, 1: 46–54. [3]

Kachroo, J.N. 1962. Report on an investigation into the teaching of vocabulary in the first year of English. *Bulletin of the Central Institute of English* 2: 67–72. [4]

Kellerman, E., Koonen, H. and van der Haagen, M. 2005. "Feet speak louder than the tongue": A preliminary analysis of language provisions for foreign professional footballers in the Netherlands. In Long 2005a. [20]

Kennedy, C. 1987. Innovating for a change: Teacher development and innovation. *ELT Journal* 41, 3: 163–169. [12]

Kiely, R. and Rea-Dickins, P. 2005. *Program Evaluation in Language Education*. Basingstoke: Palgrave Macmillan. [8]

Knight, B. 1992. Assessing speaking skills: A workshop for teacher development. *ELT Journal* 46, 3: 294–302. [13]

Kouraogo, P. 1987. Curriculum renewal and INSET in difficult circumstances. *ELT Journal* 41, 3: 171–178.

Krahnke, K.J. and Christison, M.A. 1983. Recent language research and some language teaching principles. *TESOL Quarterly* 17, 4: 625–649. [4]

Krashen, S. 1981. The fundamental pedagogical principle in second language teaching. *Studia Linguistica* 35, 1–2: 50–70. [4]

Kraus-Srebic, E., Brakus, L. and Kentric, D. 1981. A six-tier cake: An experiment with self-selected learning tasks. *ELT Journal* 36, 1: 19–23. [5]

Kučera, H. and Francis, W.N. 1967. *A Computational Analysis of Present Day American English*. Providence, RI: Brown University Press. [4]

Lado, R. 1957. *Linguistics across Cultures*. Ann Arbor, MI: University of Michigan Press. [4]

Lamb, M. 1995. The consequence of INSET. *ELT Journal* 49, 1: 72–80. [13]

Langman, J. 2003. The effects of ESL-trained content-area teachers: Reducing middle-school students to incidental language learners. *Prospect* 18, 1: 14–26.

Lett, J.A. 2005. Foreign language needs assessment in the US military. In Long 2005a. [20]

Littlejohn, A.P. 1983. Increasing learner involvement in course management. *TESOL Quarterly* 17, 4: 595–608. [10]

Littlewood, W. 1992. Curriculum design. *Applied Linguistics and ELT* 2, 1: 11–22. [1, 9]

Liu, D., Ahn, G.-S., Baek, K.-S. and Han, N.-O. 2004. South Korean high school English teachers' code switching: Questions and challenges in the drive for maximal use of English in teaching. *TESOL Quarterly* 38, 4: 605–638. [2]

Long, M.H. 1984. Process and product in ESL program evaluation. *TESOL Quarterly* 18, 3: 409–425.

Long, M.H. 1988. Instructed interlanguage development. In L. Beebe (ed), *Issues in Second Language Acquisition*. New York: Newbury House. [4]

Long, M.H. (ed) 2005a. *Second Language Needs Analysis*. Cambridge: Cambridge University Press. [3]

Long, M.H. 2005b. Methodological issues in learner needs analysis. In Long 2005a. [3]

Long, M.H. and Crookes, G. 1992. Three approaches to task-based syllabus design. *TESOL Quarterly* 26, 1: 27–56. [5, 6]

Long, M.H. and Crookes, G. 1993. Units of analysis in syllabus design – the case for task. In G. Crookes and S. Gass (eds), *Tasks in a Pedagogical Context*. Clevedon: Multilingual Matters: 9–54. [5]

Lopez, E.A.L., Santamaria, C.M. and Aponte, R.M.V. 1993. Producing an ecology-based textbook. *English Teaching Forum* 31, 4: 12–15. [20]

Lopriore, L. 1998. A systemic teacher education intervention: The Italian in-service education program for foreign language teachers. *TESOL Quarterly* 32, 3: 510–517. [13]

Macalister, J. 2007. Square pegs and round holes: Getting started in the ESP classroom. *Guidelines* 29, 1: 37–41 [10]

Macalister, J. and Sou, B. 2006. English for science and technology in Cambodia: An exercise in curriculum design. *Guidelines* 28, 2: 9–12. [9]

McComish, J. 1982. Listening to pictures. *Modern English Teacher* 10, 2: 4–8. [4, 13]

Mangilli-Climpson, M. 1995. Tweedledum and Tweedledee: Problems in company curriculum design. *English Teaching Forum* 33, 2: 26–29. [20]

Mariani, L. 1981. The place of modular systems among foreign language teaching materials. *System* 9, 1: 41–49. [6]

Markee, N. 1997. *Managing Curricular Innovation*. Cambridge: Cambridge University Press. [12]

Maurice, K. 1983. The fluency workshop. *TESOL Newsletter* 17, 4: 29. [14]

Meara, P. and Buxton, B. 1987. An alternative to multiple choice vocabulary tests. *Language Testing* 4, 2: 142–151. [7]

Mok, R. 1984. The English secondary syllabus in Singapore – its design and development. In Read 1984a. [20]

Morris, L. and Cobb, T. 2004. Vocabulary profiles as predictors of the academic performance of Teaching English as a Second Language trainees. *System* 32: 75–87. [7]

Mosback, G. 1990. National syllabus and textbook design on communicative principles— "English Every Day". *ELT Journal* 44, 1: 18–24. [10]

Munby, J. 1978. *Communicative Syllabus Design*. Cambridge: Cambridge University Press. [1,3,7]

Murdoch, G.S. 1989. A pragmatic basis for curriculum design. *English Teaching Forum* 27, 1: 15–18. [9]

Naiman, N., Fröhlich, M., Stern, H.H. and Todesco, A. 1996. *The Good Language Learner*. Montreal: Ontario Institute for Studies in Education. [4]

Nation, I.S.P. 1978. What is it? A multipurpose language teaching technique. *English Teaching Forum* 16, 3: 20–23, 32. [4]

Nation, I.S.P. 1979. The curse of the comprehension question: Some alternatives. *Guidelines* 2: 85–103. [4]

Nation, I.S.P. (ed) 1984. *Vocabulary Lists*. E.L.I. Occasional Publication No. 12, University of Wellington, Victoria, Australia. [1]

Nation, I.S.P. 1989a. Improving speaking fluency. *System* 17, 3: 377–384. [4]

Nation, I.S.P. 1989b. Group work and language learning. *English Teaching Forum* 27, 2: 20–24. [6, 14]

Nation, I.S.P. 1990. *Teaching and Learning Vocabulary*. New York: Newbury House. [1, 7]

Nation, I.S.P. 1997. L1 and L2 use in the classroom: A systematic approach. *TESL Reporter* 30, 2: 19–27. [13]

Nation, I.S.P. 2000. Learning vocabulary in lexical sets: Dangers and guidelines. *TESOL Journal* 9, 2: 6–10. [4, 14]

Nation, I.S.P. 2001. *Learning Vocabulary in Another Language*. Cambridge: Cambridge University Press. [7, 14]

Nation, I.S.P. 2006. How large a vocabulary is needed for reading and listening? *Canadian Modern Language Review* 63, 1: 59–82. [3]

Nation, I.S.P. 2007. The four strands. *Innovation in Language Learning and Teaching* 1, 1: 1–12. [6]

Nation, I.S.P. 2009. *Teaching ESL/EFL Reading and Writing*. New York: Routledge. [6]

Nation, I.S.P. and Beglar, D. 2007. A vocabulary size test. *The Language Teacher* 31, 7: 9–13. [3, 7]

Nation, I.S.P. and Hwang, K. 1995. Where would general service vocabulary stop and special purposes vocabulary begin? *System* 23, 1: 35–41. [3]

Nation, I.S.P. and Newton, J. 2009. *Teaching ESL/EFL Listening and Speaking*. New York: Routledge. [1, 4, 6]

Nation, I.S.P. and Wang, K. 1999. Graded readers and vocabulary. *Reading in a Foreign Language* 12, 2: 355–380. [5]

Nation, P. and Crabbe, D. 1991. A survival language learning syllabus for foreign travel. *System* 19, 3: 191–201. [2]

Nitta, R. and Gardner, S. 2005. Consciousness-raising and practice in ELT course books. *ELT Journal* 59, 1: 3–13. [11]

Nixon, U. 1995. Developing appropriate materials: The Vietnam project. *English Teaching Forum* 33, 3: 12–15. [20]

Nolasco, R. and Arthur, L. 1986. You try doing it with a class of forty! *ELT Journal* 40, 2: 100–106. [13]

Nord, J. 1980. Developing listening fluency before speaking: An alternative paradigm. *System* 8, 1: 1–22. [4]

Norris, L. and Spencer, S. 2000. Learners, practitioners and teachers: Diamond spotting and negotiating role boundaries. In Breen and Littlejohn 2000: 195–203. [10]

Nunan, D. 1986. Learner-centred curriculum innovation: A case study. *RELC Journal* 17, 1: 40–51. [20]

Nunan, D. 1989. Toward a collaborative approach to curriculum development: A case study. *TESOL Quarterly* 23, 1: 9–25. [20]

Nuttall, C. 1996. *Teaching Reading Skills in a Foreign Language*. Oxford: Macmillan Heinemann. [7]

Oxford, R.L. 1990. *Language Learning Strategies: What Every Teacher Should Know.* New York: Newbury House. [5]

Palmer, C. 1993. Innovation and the experienced teacher. *ELT Journal* 47, 2: 166–171. [13]

Parkhurst, C. 1990. The composition process of science writers. *English for Specific Purposes* 9, 2: 169–179. [3]

Pascasio, E.M. 1984. An English communicative syllabus in practice: A case study from the Philippines. In Read 1984a. [20]

Pienemann, M. 1998. *Language Processing and Second Language Development: Processability Theory.* Philadelphia, PA: John Benjamins. [4]

Pienemann, M. and Johnston, M. 1987. Factors affecting the development of language proficiency. In D. Nunan (ed), *Applying Second Language Acquisition Research.* AMEP, Sydney: National Curriculum Resource Centre. [4]

Pienemann, M., Johnston, M. and Brindley, G. 1988. Constructing an acquisition-based procedure for second language assessment. *Studies in Second Language Acquisition* 10: 217–243. [4]

Pimsleur, P. 1967. A memory schedule. *Modern Language Journal* 51, 2: 73–75. [4]

Pimsleur, P. 1980. *How to Learn a Foreign Language.* Boston: Heinle and Heinle. [1]

Pongtoncharoen, S. and Wibunsin, D.G. 1984. An activity-oriented syllabus for beginners in a TEFL country: Thailand. In Read 1984b. [20]

Prabhu, N.S. 1987. *Second Language Pedagogy.* Oxford: Oxford University Press. [1]

Prabhu, N.S. 1989. Materials as support: Materials as constraint. *Guidelines* 11, 1: 66–74. [11]

Prodromou, L. 1995. The backwash effect: From testing to teaching. *ELT Journal* 49, 1: 13–25. [7]

Radley, P. and Sharley, A. 1987. *Trio.* London: Heinemann. [1]

Read, J.A.S. (ed) 1984a. *Trends in Language Syllabus Design.* Singapore: Singapore University Press (for RELC). [20]

Read, J.A.S. (ed) 1984b. *Case Studies in Syllabus and Curriculum Design.* RELC Occasional Papers No. 31. Singapore: RELC. [20]

Reinders, H. and Lewis, M. 2006. An evaluative checklist for self-access materials. *ELT Journal* 60, 3: 272–278. [11]

Richards, J.C. 1983. Listening comprehension: Design, approach, procedure. *TESOL Quarterly* 17, 2: 219–240. [7]

Richards, J.C. 1984. Language curriculum development. *RELC Journal* 15, 1: 1–29. [1]

Richards, J.C. 1985. Planning for proficiency. *Prospect* 1, 2: 1–17.

Richards, J.C. 1993. Beyond the textbook: The role of commercial materials in language teaching. *RELC Journal* 24, 1: 1–14. [10, 11]

Richards, J.C. 2001. *Curriculum Development in Language Teaching.* Cambridge: Cambridge University Press. [1, 2, 4]

Richards, J.C. and Rodgers, T. 1986. *Approaches and Methods in Language Teaching: A Description and Analysis.* Cambridge: Cambridge University Press. [4]

Richards, J.C. and Sandy, C. 1998. *Passages: An Upper-level Multi-skills Course.* Cambridge: Cambridge University Press. [1]

Ringbom, H. 1987. *The Role of the First Language in Foreign Language Learning.* Clevedon: Multilingual Matters. [4]

Roemer, A. 2006. *College Oral Communication.* Boston: Houghton Mifflin. [1]

Salaberry, M.R. 2001. The use of technology for second language learning and teaching: A retrospective. *Modern Language Journal* 85, 1: 39–56. [11]

Samah, A.A. 1984. The English language communicational curriculum for upper second-ary schools in Malaysia: Rationale, design and implementation. In Read 1984a. [20]

Saragi, T., Nation, I.S.P. and Meister, G.F. 1978. Vocabulary learning and reading. *System* 6, 2: 72–78. [4]

Savage, W. and Storer, M. 1992. An emergent language program framework: Actively involving learners in needs analysis. *System* 20, 2: 187–199. [5, 10]

Savage, W. and Whisenand, R. 1993. Logbooks and language learning objectives in an intensive ESL workshop. *TESOL Quarterly* 27, 4: 741–746. [7]

Schmitt, N., Schmitt, D. and Clapham, C. 2001. Developing and exploring the behaviour of two new versions of the Vocabulary Levels Test. *Language Testing* 18, 1: 55–88. [7]

Sharkey, J. 1994. Helping students become better learners. *TESOL Journal* 4, 2: 18–23. [20]

Shaw, P. 1991. Science research students' composing processes. *English for Specific Purposes* 10, 3: 189–206. [3]

Sheen, R. 1994. A critical analysis of the advocacy of the task-based syllabus. *TESOL Quarterly* 28, 1: 127–151. [5]

Sheldon, L.E. 1988. Evaluating ELT textbooks and materials. *ELT Journal* 42, 2: 237–246. [11]

Shi, L., Corcos, R. and Storey, A. 2001. Using student performance data to develop an English course for clinical training. *English for Specific Purposes* 20, 3: 267–291 [20]

Simcock, M. 1993. Developing productive vocabulary using the "Ask and answer" technique. *Guidelines* 15: 1–7. [14]

Smith, K. 2000. Negotiating assessment with secondary-school pupils. In Breen and Littlejohn 2000a: 55–62. [10]

Spada, N. 1997. Form-focussed instruction and second language acquisition: A review of classroom and laboratory research. *Language Teaching* 30, 2: 73–87. [4]

Stenhouse, L. 1975. *An Introduction to Curriculum Research and Development*. London: Heinemann. [8]

Stoller, F.L. 1994. The diffusion of innovations in intensive ESL programs. *Applied Linguistics* 15, 3: 300–327. [12]

Sutarsyah, C. 1993. *The Vocabulary of Economics and Academic English*. Unpublished M.A. Thesis, Victoria University of Wellington, New Zealand. [3]

Sutarsyah, C., Nation, P. and Kennedy, G. 1994. How useful is EAP vocabulary for ESP? A corpus based case study. *RELC Journal* 25, 2: 34–50. [3]

Swain, M. 1985. Communicative competence: Some roles of comprehensible input and comprehensible output in its development. In S. Gass and C. Madden (eds), *Input in Second Language Acquisition* (pp. 235–253). Rowley, MA: Newbury House. [4]

Swan, M. and Walter, C. 1985. *The Cambridge English Course*. Cambridge: Cambridge University Press. [6]

Tanaka, H. and Stapleton, P. 2007. Increasing reading input in Japanese high school EFL classrooms: An empirical study exploring the efficacy of extensive reading. *The Reading Matrix* 7, 1: 115–131. [11]

Taylor, R. 1992. The production of training packs in in-service teacher training. *ELT Journal* 46, 4: 356–361. [13]

Teo Hee Lian. 1983. Special problems and special solutions: The administrative officers' course at the Civil Service Institute. In Richards 1983. [20]

Terrell, T. 1982. The natural approach to language teaching: An update. *Modern Language Journal* 66, 2: 121–132. [4]

Tessmer, M. 1990. Environment analysis: A neglected stage of instructional design. *Educational Technology Research and Development* 38, 1: 55–64. [2]

Tessmer, M. and Wedman, J.F. 1990. A layers-of-necessity instructional development model. *Educational Technology Research and Development* 38, 2: 77–85. [10, 11]

Thanachanan, P. 1984. A self-appraising English syllabus in an EFL country. In Read 1984a. [20]

Tinkham, T. 1993. The effect of semantic clustering on the learning of second language vocabulary. *System* 21, 3: 371–380. [1, 4]

Tomlinson, B. 2003. Developing principled frameworks for materials development. In B. Tomlinson (ed), *Developing Materials for Language Teaching*. London/New York: Continuum. [1, 4]

Towell, R. and Tomlinson, P. 1999. Language curriculum development research at university level. *Language Teaching Research* 3, 1:1–32. [5, 20]

Tucker, C. Allen. 1968. Evaluating beginning textbooks. *English Teaching Forum* 6, 5: 8–15. [8, 11]

Tumposky, N.R. 1984. Behavioural objectives, the cult of efficiency, and foreign language learning: Are they compatible? *TESOL Quarterly* 18, 2: 295–310. [7]

Upshur, J.A. and Turner, C.E. 1995. Constructing rating scales for second language tests. *ELT Journal* 49, 1: 3–11. [7]

Ur, P. 1996. *A Course in Language Teaching: Practice and Theory*. Cambridge: Cambridge University Press. [11]

van Ek, J.A. and Alexander, L.G. 1980. *Threshold Level English*. Oxford: Pergamon Press. [1, 5]

Vandermeeren, S. 2005. Foreign language needs of business firms. In Long 2005a. [20]

Wall, D. 1996. Introducing new tests into traditional systems: Insights from general education and from innovation theory. *Language Testing* 13, 3: 334–354. [7]

Waters, A. and Vilches, M.L.C. 2005. Managing innovation in language education: A course for ELT change agents. *RELC Journal* 36: 117–136. [13]

Watanabe, Y. 1996. Does grammar translation come from the entrance examination? Preliminary findings from classroom-based research. *Language Testing* 13, 3: 318–333. [7]

Wedell, M. 2003. Giving TESOL change a chance: Supporting key players in the curriculum change process. *System* 31: 439–456. [12]

Weir, C.J., Hughes, A. and Porter, D. 1990. Reading skills: Hierarchies, implicational relationships and identifiability. *Reading in a Foreign Language* 7, 1: 505–510. [5]

West, M. 1953. *A General Service List of English Words*. London: Longman. [4, 5]

West, M. 1955. *Learning to Read a Foreign Language* (2nd ed.). London: Longman. [4]

West, R. 1994. Needs analysis in language learning. *Language Teaching* 27, 1: 1–19. [3]

White, R.V. 1987. Managing innovation. *ELT Journal* 41, 3: 211–218. [12]

White, R.V. 1988. *The ELT Curriculum: Design, Innovation, and Management*. Oxford: Blackwell. [1]

White, R.V. 1993. Innovation in curriculum planning and program development. *Annual Review of Applied Linguistics* 13: 244–259. [12]

Williams, D. 1983. Developing criteria for textbook evaluation. *ELT Journal* 37, 3: 251–255. [11]

Williams, R. 1986. "Top ten" principles for teaching reading. *ELT Journal* 40, 1: 42–45. [4]

Willis, D. and Willis, J. 2007. *Doing Task-based Teaching*. Oxford: Oxford University Press. [4, 11]

Willis, J. 1996. *A Framework for Task-based Learning*. Harlow: Longman. [6]

Willis, J. and Willis, D. 1989. *Collins' COBUILD English Course*. London: Collins ELT. [5]

Winitz, H. (ed) 1981. *The Comprehension Approach to Foreign Language Instruction*. Rowley, MA: Newbury House. [4]

Witte, A. 2006. Cultural progression in teaching and learning foreign languages. In Harden *et al.* 2006: 205–232. [5]

Wong Fillmore, L. 1982. Instructional language as linguistic input: Second-language learning in classrooms. In L.C. Wilkinson (ed), *Communicating in the Classroom: Language, Thought and Culture*. Advances in the Study of Cognition Series. New York, NY: Academic Press. [4]

Wong Fillmore, L. 1983. The language learner as an individual: Implications of research on individual differences for the ESL teacher. In M.A. Clarke and J. Handscombe (eds), *On TESOL '82*: 157–173. [4]

Woodward, T. and Lindstromberg, S. 1995. *Planning from Lesson to Lesson*. London: Longman. [6]

Yang, S.C. 2001. Integrating computer-mediated tools into the language curriculum. *Journal of Computer Assisted Learning* 17, 1: 85–93. [11]

Index